THE
INCARCERATED
7'S

ISBN: 978-0615831091

ISBN-10: 0615831095

PAPERBACK VERSION

PRINTED IN THE UNITED STATES

FIRST EDITION

PUBLISHED BY: EDUCATED THUG –FAM CARTEL JOINT PUBLICATION

COVER LAY-OUT: AMB Branding and Design

COVER ILLUSTRATED BY: ROBERT GOLDWIRE

DEDICATIONS

From: Professor Born Supreme P.H.D. 7 Allah (also known as BORN)

To my family: Mom, I love you more than words can ever express and I'm going to make sure that you **never** have to work again, right from here, by turning this **Ink into Gold**. Give me some time and I got us! To my daughter Infinity, I'm proud of you for getting accepted into college. Watching you grow into the Woman you've become from a distance was one of the best experiences of my entire Life up to Now. Never forget who your Father is and lay down at night knowing that I'm thinking about you every time that you're thinking about me. I Love you Queen! You're the best parts of me and your mother all poured into someone that is going to do something that impacts the World in a Major way 1day. To My Son Borntiek: It's been a beautiful experience to reconnect with you after all the bullshit that you went thru in my absence. I Love you God and never doubt that no matter how it may seem at times. I didn't have my Father around but you will always have access to yours King. If you need me I'm just a phone call or letter away. Happy 18th B-day too! To THE NATION OF GODS AND EARTHS: Thank you for making this Knowledge available to the Lost ones that Most people have given up on. I know that I wasn't shit before I was taught these teachings and I realize that it's bigger than just me as an individual now. I won't waste what I've been given because I now understand how things can change for the worst in the blink of an eye. Every moment is precious and I would have probably never took the time to stop and look at myself if it wouldn't have been for an Elder God named Lord Malik aka Monty King from Lorain, Ohio, seeing my potential as a knucklehead back in 2003. Wherever you are Malik, Thanks God!! To Manifest Supreme Knowledge God Allah: We've never had the chance to connect in the physical but the jewels you gave and the example of your actions had a big impact on me God. You inspired me to write more which ultimately led to this book. Thanks for just taking the time out to Build with me on the Science of Everything In Life. Congrats on your book too God. Peace MN! To Tuna aka The God BORN SEVEN ALLAH from Springfield, OH: Thanks for the support God. I'll see you at the top because I know you'll be there when I finally get there. I heard the BMW is ill too King. Keep getting it out there. To The God VIRG (Victorious Islam Ruler God Allah): I'm proud of who you've become with what I gave you and we have a lot to do so stay safe and apply the Math out there on them Cleveland, OH, streets King. To The God Divine Intellect (formerly Supreme King Born Allah) aka FOO from 7 ALL in Cleveland, OH: You the smoothest from my family tree but you already know that Right-LOL!!! God, it is a pleasure to know you and to see you Knowledge 120 from VIRG after I taught him was the sign that I needed in order to know that I was doing this correctly. One day all of our seeds will sit at the table and talk about what we are building right Now. To The God Malachi Allah aka Cosmo from Cleveland, OH: I learned so much about how to Enlighten just watching you interact with your fruit in Ross Correctional Institution back in 2005 and 2006. I want a build for my next book since I couldn't catch you in time for this one. To Divine All Wise Allah aka Castro from

Cleveland, OH, by way of NYC: God, we did it and from different Prisons at that. I know you're going to win your case and hit them streets to build that Youth Center sometime in the near future. I can feel it! Just don't get discouraged and keep fighting in them Courts. To Divine Universal aka Drew from Zainesville, OH: I know you thought I would forget to shout you out but you're wrong God-LOL Out of sight isn't out of Mind when 2 people exist as Alikes. Keep studying your Lessons and you will grow to be a very prolific God no doubt. Peace to KNEW GOD ALLAH aka TRES from Lima, Ohio and the A.T.T.A.C.K. from Cleveland, Ohio.

To the Gods in Freeport, N.Y. on LONG ISLAND: I love you and I'll be back sooner than you think. Without you there would be no Professor Born Supreme. My 1st attribute was Positive Born Allah and I was just 14 when the God JUSTICE on Harris Ave, Freeport, N.Y., began to Teach me this knowledge. I didn't understand back then how much of an impact that would have on my life later on. Thank you to ALL the Gods from Harris Ave (Everlasting, Elevation, Infinite was up North when I got sparked but I know who you are). You might remember me as the God who fought the other Justice (Big Justice from Brooklyn) on your block… well, he can't beat me no more HA HA! To The Gods from Hartford, CT: Divine Truth, you were always inspirational to me God because you stayed right and exact among all the negativity that was around you. I didn't forget how you slayed me on the MIC in Shakiems basement at his house in Bloomfield, CT, that 1 time God. I owe you for that. ALLAH SUPREME MATHEMATICS: I used to tease you for writing your beats in that notebook but now I realize that you were just way ahead of your time. I regret not taking advantage of my time around you to learn as much as I could about this culture including how you got the Knowledge of Self from ALLAH SHA SHA. Shakiem Allah: You were the most laid back and smooth of the Elder Gods and I still owe you 70 dollars which I intend to pay you when I see or hear from you again Lord. To the Gods in Medina: Thanks for showing me how to rock this culture and enforcing the rules and regulations whenever you saw a person bullshitting with the culture. The Gods on Long Island needed that back then and I'm sure you're all still doing the same to this day. To my brother from another mother KAPE from Brooklyn: Thanks for the support over the years God. It's crazy because it feels like we always knew each other even though we met out of the state of OHIO. To North from Nostrand Ave, Brooklyn and Hunt: Keep showing the world how to create Businesses from scratch. Your hustle hand is exclusive and I'm taking notes. To Saladin Quanaah: You are the blueprint on how to Gold Brick Build using 120 Lessons as the foundation. I read your BLOG (ASIA) and I've read all your books. I look forward to linking with you and the Gods in ATLANTIS (Niagara Falls, NY) as soon as I liberate myself. To my daughter's Mother Tasha in Hartford CT: You know I love you Right? If not I do! Your attraction powers scare the shit out of me! So, sometimes I have to avoid you! To my son's mother Creshea (The mean baby momma) Thanks for all the help this last year. I won't take our friendship for granted and I know I'm a pain in the ass sometimes. Thanks for being patient with me while I feel my way thru the maze of life. If I forgot anybody, charge it to the head and not the heart. They're rushing me to wrap this up so I'm speeding. Oh yeah, to my sister Cassandra from Freeport, N.Y. and my Grandma (You know I can't forget you Grandma), Thanks for all you do to make me comfortable in here while I'm fighting to get back to you. It's been a long 10 years but I'm a lot more of a Man now than when I began. It feels good to be loved!!! To my cousin Shadina Equality: Good looking out on ALL the help. I Love you Queen and I won't forget. To all the Earths of the Nation, 1 of you belongs in my Universe; you probably just don't know it yet. I seek a righteous Queen to shine on and grow old together with. Get at me if you're on that level mentally. R.I.P. To C-Latiff Allah who was a very wise Mentor to many of us Gods. Respect to Born Logic Allah and the Gods at the Cream City paper in Wisconsin.

Peace
Professor Born Supreme P.H.D. 7 Allah
Aka
BORN

Author's Note

For questions or comments email: incarcerated7s@hotmail.com or contact me at http://TheIncarcerated7sBlog.Blogspot.com. Also, do not photocopy or bootleg this book!!! A portion of this money is going toward financing over brothers and sisters filing civil suits in various prisons to protect our culture. So support the cause by ***purchasing*** as many copies of this book as you can and by telling ALL Gods and Earths on and offline to ***purchase*** this book. Spread this information in rallies, ciphers, parliaments, on Blogs as links, on Facebook and on twitter, etc…

TABLE OF CONTENTS

What We Teach

1. That Black people are the Original People of the planet earth.
2. That Black people are the fathers and mothers of civilization.
3. That the science of Supreme Mathematics is the key to understanding man's relationship to the universe.
4. Islam is a natural way of life, not a religion.
5. That education should be fashioned to enable us to be self- sufficient as a people.
6. That each one should teach one according to their knowledge.
7. That the Blackman is God and his proper name is ALLAH. Arm, Leg, Leg, Arm, Head.
8. That our children are our link to the future and they must be nurtured, respected, loved, protected, and educated.
9. That the unified Black family is the vital building block of the nation.

What We Will Achieve

1. **National Consciousness:** National Consciousness is the consciousness of our origin in this world, which is divine. As a nation of people we are the first in existence and all other peoples derived from us. National Consciousness is the awareness of the unique history and culture of Black people and the unequaled contributions we have made to world civilization, by being the fathers and mothers of civilization. National Consciousness is the awareness that we are all one people regardless to our geographical origins and that we must work and struggle as one if we are to liberate ourselves from the domination of outside forces and bring into

existence a Universal Government of Love, Peace and Happiness for all the people of the planet.

2. **Community Control:** Community Control of the educational, economic, political, media and health institutions on our community. Our demand for Community Control flows naturally out of our science of life, which teaches that we are the Supreme Being in person and the sole controllers of our own destiny; thus we must have same control on the collective level that we strive to attain on the individual level. It is prerequisite to our survival that we take control of the life sustaining goods and services that every community needs in order to maintain and advance itself and advance civilization. Only when we have achieved complete Community Control will we be able to prove to the world the greatness and majesty of our Divine Culture, which is Freedom.

3. **Peace:** Peace is the absence of confusion (chaos) and the absence of confusion is Order. Law and Order is the very foundation upon which our Science of Life rest. Supreme Mathematics is the Law and Order of the Universe; this is the Science of Islam, which is Peace. Peace is Supreme Understanding between people for the benefit of the whole. We will achieve Peace, in ourselves, in our communities, in our nation and in the world. This is our ultimate goal.

PEACE

FOREWORD

PEACE TO MY BELOVED NGE CITIZENS BEHIND THE PRISON WALLS!!!

The time has come to address the complications and obstacles that we presently face and will face in the future striving to live by the Prescribed Laws of Islam. A lot of Gods and/or Earths obtained the Knowledge of Self after they were Incarcerated; so they never have been to A Universal Parliament, the Annual Show and Prove in Mecca or a Rally in the Free Cipher.

Others weren't living right but had righteous names in the Free Cipher. Then they became forced to face and examine our personal Devils, through the mechanism of Universal Justice, in the form of Incarceration, to start taking these teachings that Allah gave us seriously.

Look at who's telling you what to wear, when to eat, when you can see your family, etc… and then ask yourself: Is this the Devil spoken of in the 120 Lessons? The 6th degree in the 1-14th lesson explains that the Devil keeps our people Illiterate, so that he can use them as a tool and also a slave. If Prison is a place that society sends people to correct their behavior, how is it that they have removed most of the funding for the Education programs? Why are there no Legal Classes for Prisoners? You can easily get a Bible but how available are the books that you really need to change your situation through the legal/court system that was used to put you in prison in the first place? Remember, Illiterate means Ignorance, according to the degree. It's important to really pay attention to what is being said and taught in our 120 lessons because the information empowers you to defend yourself, by applying it to real life situations to come out Victorious using wise wisdom (see 22nd degree Supreme Alphabets).

Everything happens for a reason including your present set of obstacles. The Supreme Mathematics isn't just a bunch of words we recite. The principles that each individual degree represents has its own individual vibration. What this means is that applying any 1 or several in combinations, causes an effect every time you do it whether you realize it or not.

1st, lets define it in detail. Supreme means: Most Dominant or Most High. Mathematics is the group of sciences (including but not limited to Arithmetic, Geometry, Algebra, Calculus, Etc…) dealing with quantities, magnitudes and forms and their Relationships, Attributes, Etc… by the use of numbers and symbols.

In essence, Allah and the other 7's that assisted him in formulating the Supreme Math, devised a mechanism to communicate with the Universal energies and each other on a Higher level. We tap into this power through the process of Building within the structure of it individually and collectively. Each Repetition enhances our abilities mentally and activates the dormant energy in the potential Builders that come in contact with the force of its magnetic quality. When the Math is lived out in our everyday interactions, don't ever allow yourself to be convinced that, what you say and do regarding this way of Life, is trivial in any way, shape or form, when you don't see an immediate reaction.

The science behind what we do shows and proves this to be an illusion and so does the evidence of the impact it has had on so many lives up to now. So don't fall victim to what you see on Face Value. Teach by your words, ways and actions. Eventually, the people around you will either attract or repel which is the law of Nature sorting out whose ready to be God or Earth and who's not.

Compiled by: Professor Born Supreme P.H.D. 7 Allah
For questions or comments go to
http://TheIncarcerated7sBlog.Blogspot.com or
Email: incarcerated7s@hotmail.com

THE 1ST TIME I EVER HEARD SOMEONE SAY THAT THE BLACK MAN IS GOD (The Awakening)

PEACE

     I present these words with the sincere intentions of allowing you to travel with me along this path of Enlightenment. The 1st time I heard someone say, "The Black man is GOD" or a person call themselves GOD was in the New York State Division For Youth aka D.F.Y. which is the juvenile justice system. I was incarcerated in that system back in 1993. I was about 11 years old and the culture that came to be the one a lot of my peers adopted was a Gang mentality. The facility I was housed in had Latin Kings, Netas, Zulu Nation, the 5%ers (as the Nation was called back then) and one or two made up clicks of people starting their own thing.

     The 1st GOD I heard say, he was GOD, by the name of Rahsaun. He was 15 years old and when he said, "I am GOD", I was immediately drawn up b.u.t. at that time my mind couldn't comprehend the Knowledge. It really affected me because (1) his personality was of confidence, power, intelligence, etc... (2) He actually believed he was GOD and carried himself in a Supreme manner, (3) the way people responded to him and were drawn to him was also attractive. This initial meeting and interaction planted the seed in the soil of my mind. The seed was continuously watered following that experience by images of Wu – Tang Clan, Mobb Deep, Rakim and others over time. All this led me to search for a deeper Understanding. I was eventually released from D.F.Y. around 1995 and I returned back to Harlem aka Mecca (119th St. and Lenox Ave.). This was the Birthplace of the Nation of Gods and Earths!!!

     When I realized that I was and am GOD, just being that I'm the Black man, was after I went through a long process of searching for answers. I studied religions, such as Christianity and others but I always got stuck because the Christians murdered, Raped and oppressed my people (The Original People) in the name of Christianity. They also used this religion as a tool to enslave the minds of black people and keep them in an inferior position, which they still are doing to this day. To top it all off, GOD aka Jesus in Christianity was taught to be a white man with blue eyes and blond hair!!! That was the exact same description of the slave master, that let the dogs loose on my people, murdered my people and other horrible acts, when we were simply asking for basic human rights, like freedom.

I knew that if this was who and what GOD was I didn't want **any** parts of him or his religion. Eventually, I tried my hand at Sunni and Shite ISLAM b.u.t. I couldn't really grasp the concept of a GOD that Defies rational reasoning (Mystery GOD concept). While I was trying to obtain clarity and understanding, the people I was asking my questions to, constantly redirected me by telling me things like only GOD knows such and such. Then, if I pressed on searching, they would imply that I was committing "Shirk" which is a violation of one of the 5 pillars of that form of ISLAM. It is equal to blasphemy in Christianity.

I began to feel empty. I was being told and taught how to be an Arab and this felt as if I was being stripped of my cultural identity, even more than I had already been. (Who and where I came from) It felt like those Muslims were concerned with everything **except** what really mattered which was answering my deepest questions in a logical way. How could emulating a man from 1400 years ago, help me find "Salvation", when I was faced with obstacles and social ills that were not even around that Muhammad never had to experience? To me, that was like me telling a woman, how to give birth the best way in my eyes!!! The final straw that broke the camel's back was me learning from research that the Arabs were complicit, if not all out responsible for spreading Islam in Africa, by 1st conquering and then enslaving the Africans, which fostered the environment for the Europeans to enslave our people. To me, that made the Arabs as responsible, as the Europeans, for the condition that the Original people are in today, all over the planet Earth.

Learning the history of the world, the sciences, etc… led me along the course to Understanding how I am GOD literally!! Some of the basic things that reinforced this Knowledge are rooted in Anthropology. Most people in this field agree that the oldest man was relative to what is now known as East Africa. We know the climate there and that the people of that region are Dark Complexioned. Biology shows that in Nature a Black man can produce a White man but no evidence shows the opposite to be true backed with science. If the White man were the 1st man on Earth, **how** did the Black man get here? Obviously, the White man is not the Original Man. So where does this leave us?

Study and research has led me to facts. The Black man fits the description of GOD because he is a microcosm (as above, so below). When I say I am GOD, it means that I can create everything in existence. It also means that all of the Gods are ALLAH together which is the ultimate force. That force is manifested in the physical by the ATOM which is an acronym for ALLAH THE ORIGINAL MAN. All things that exist are composed of ATOMS. The 1st ATOM vibrated (moved) and combusted creating a different ATOM. The 2 ATOMS now are in constant Motion (Hydrogen and Helium). They collided with each other creating a new element (Lithium) and this same process continued creating compounds by joining together elements. In chain reactions, an example of this process in the physical body of the Black man is this: A Man shoots sperm into a Woman. This sperm collides with the Egg. These 2 create an Embryo out of the unity of both and continue to multiply until the baby is physically born. This cycle perpetuates itself over and over again as the life cycle.

This is a few of many reasons that I came to logically conclude that the Black man is GOD. For me to believe anything contrary to what the facts have revealed is unintelligent and ignorant. I hope this build will inspire someone to look into the things, I've mentioned – opened my eyes to the realization of who the True and Living GOD is.

PEACE

God in the

Person of:

ALMIGHTY SHABAZZ ALLAH

Harlem, N.Y.C aka MECCA

For questions or comments contact BlackJelani@gmail.com or go to http://TheIncarcerated7sBlog.Blogspot.com

AUTHOR'S NOTE

ALMIGHTY SHABAZZ is currently incarcerated in Massachusetts prison and has his family forwarding his emails to him.

The Biography of Black King Lyfe Allah

My name is Black King Lyfe Allah … The attributes of Allah I manifest is through my self-styled wisdom. **Black** is the original and dominant energy that attracts and absorbs energy. I manifest this actuality with my ability to draw people (alike and unlike) to me. I ingest the best qualities and energies leaving the rest for everyone else. **King** is one who leads by example and is a servant to his people. I strive daily to show and prove that my word is bond through my ways and actions. Basically, I don't just speak of I.S.L.A.M. I also live it out. A true king knows and understands that he doesn't rule his people B.U.T. his is a servant. A king is a representative of his people and to properly represent your people, you must serve their needs, as well as service their dis-eases. Lyfe is the reality consisting of metabolism, reproduction and evolution. I metabolize by turning the knowledge I attain into the necessary energy to do my duty (civilize the uncivilized). I reproduce by sharing the truth with those in triple stage darkness, making like- minded (alike) individuals. Finally, I continuously evolve by constantly elevating into something/someone greater. That is what Lyfe is about… growth! Allah is my family (nation of Gods and Earths) name. Allah is also the all in all … The essence in all existence. I am also the essence within all that exist in my universe. Black + King + Lyfe = Allah!

Now that you know my name, let's get into how it came into reality. Many miles (years/10:40) ago, a very close friend of mine gave me the name "Lyfe". Black King came to me as a pattern for a tattoo. A brother drew it up and thought I best fit the description and gave it to me. Shortly afterwards, that became my attribute of Allah.

I came into the K.O.S. through my righteous brother, Sincere Build Empirical Allah. We met at Licking County jail in the midst of battle for our lives and freedom.

The God and I built on a few subjects and discovered that we see alike. So after an examination, Sincere decided to give ... no ... He decided to "bless" me with my supreme mathematics. Before we could continue on our journey, I rode out to C.R.C. I've known about the Nation for most of my lyfe. I'm from Medina (Brooklyn, N.Y.), born-U-Square (B.U.T.) I was too caught up in the devil's un-civilization to resurrect Jesus within my universe. What gave me the desire to grow (change) was my dissatisfaction with my current culture: slavery (mentally through the devil's systematic trick knowledge to make me "believe" that other original people were actually my enemies, because they're "different", or because we were both being savages in the pursuit of happiness! Also physically, by eating the poison animals and continuously entering their prison (and jail) houses). Suffering (not realizing my fullest potential (I.S.L.A.M.), I allowed others (outside of self) to dictate my way and actions (or lack of). Which many times resulted in my suffering the consequences of another's will and death? (My 3rd eye was completely shut, thus I was mentally dead). Sincere showed me how to use "living" mathematics to attain freedom (free my dome (mind) from the devil's un-civilization), justice (the realization that the energy I give off will be the energy I receive, therefore strive to live righteously) and equality (bring an equilibrium to me Lyfe, ridding of the disarray). The God Sincere, and I, began this journey in Oct. of 2007. We soon separated with me possessing only my mathematics. My first stop was Noble, where nobody in the cipher was qualified to teach. Sincere, being wise to the cipher (O) He (H), asked me, "What are you going to do if you get to a cipher with no structure?" My response was, "Attain my 120 and bring structure." Unfortunately, I did not receive my B.E.T.S. and 120 until I reached Lebanon. This is where my 3 of God, and I being God was born. You see sun/earth God is a title given to the ruler and controller of any given universe. The Black man is God due to his birthright to rule the universe, B.U.T. many of us have relinquished that right, allowing outside energy (real and imagined) to govern our existence; like women, drugs, the mystery gods, urges or lower self, etc… My realization of self being 7 came when I seen how my case (obstruction of justice and kidnapping) stems from my governing of self. Everything that happens to, and around me is a direct (or indirect) result of what I caused and/or allowed to transpire. Basically, everything created in my universe is my doing!!

> Peace,
> Black King Lyfe Allah
> Brooklyn, N.Y. aka Medina

For questions or comments contact
http://TheIncarcerated7sBlog.Blogspot.com or
Email: Incarcerated7s@hotmail.com

TO WHOM IT MAY CONCERN

To whom it may concern,

Proper Education Always Correct Errors. This is the Biography of DIVINE EYE ALLAH'S JOURNEY INTO THE KNOWLEDGE OF SELF.

I've always heard the Gods from the Nation of Gods and Earths say do the Math, b.u.t. before I obtained the proper Knowledge of Self, I never really knew or understood the significance of the term or how relevant it would become to my being!!! My journey began in the Infamous "Lucasville" prison AKA Southern Ohio Correctional Facility in 2008. I was placed in a cell across from a brother who began studying the teachings of the Nation of Gods and Earths that I had grew up with in the streets of Cleveland, Ohio. The God was what we call a Neophyte or a Newborn which means he was still new at building using the 120 lessons. He was the 1st one who ever gave me the Supreme Mathematics and the Supreme Alphabets but some of them were incorrect which I would find out later when I came in time with the God who would become the one who taught me 120 Lessons right and exact. His name was Professor Born Supreme P.H.D. 7 Allah. I met "Born" when I was a porter in the level 4B block. 4B is a higher security in Maximum Security Prison where as 4A is the basic level where one receives all the privileges in Maximum. 4B has to be handcuffed anytime they move and goes in a cage for 1 hour per day s their Recreation.

After I began conversing with "Born" through the bars I kept finding myself going back each time I would work to listen to him speak whether it was to me or someone else? He had a specific way of explaining things that was always very intelligently articulated and logical. In time, the God got out into general population. I hoped he would land in my block but he ended up going to another housing unit. By this time, we were building on different topics in the mail. He dropped a correct set of Mathematics on me via mail but it still wasn't solidified in my mind as anything more than an abstract concept. One day I was at my kitchen job and the newest workers came in. I looked and it was "Born" smiling at me. The God had found a way to get put on my shift at work!!

When I first had the Math, I just memorized them but "Born" showed me that they were principles that could be applied to **any** life situation with examples at work. This was the Wisdom that would lead me to the Understanding of how to use what I learned instead of being a parrot of another man's words. It all just became clearer and clearer and in time these lessons would become the very same ones, that I would go on to teach my own students as a true Master Builder had taught them to me. I eventually left those long hour days and moved to a lower security but I continue to this day to write "Born" at that same prison.

He had always told me to apply myself daily and research everything scientifically because there would come a time where he would not be around to answer my questions. He also said that there would come a time where I would have a seed and have to protect their mind from the Brain washing tactics of the Devils. If I could tell anybody anything that they took from a conversation or reading 1 of my builds, it would be to always do the knowledge, so that you will be able to detect trick knowledge when you encounter it. Though a righteous God would never lead his A-Alike down the wrong path; even those who mean well could be wrong. If you don't study for self, you won't know what is correct from what's incorrect. I'll be leaving Prison after 12 years but of all the lessons this one is the one that changed my life the most during those years locked up.

PEACE
DIVINE EYE ALLAH

AKA

D. Wilson from – Cleveland, Ohio

For questions or comments contact:
incarcerated7s@hotmail.com or go to
http://TheIncarcerated7sBlog.Blogspot.com

THE REALITY OF YOUR NAME

Peace To The Gods and Earths!!!

Today I'm going to Build about the meaning behind my righteous attribute/name using Mathematics. Do you realize that we use Mathematics in our everyday lives constantly? Whether we are conscious of it or not, just getting up in the morning and opening your eyes is your body and brain using Mathematics on a basic level. I want to take a deeper look into this process by building on my name using the Supreme Mathematics, the Supreme Alphabets and the 12 Jewels of Islam from the Nation of Gods and Earths teachings.

My mother and Father gave me the Honorable Name of Marcus D. Baker. As I ventured into the Street Life I became known as Lil Red throughout Cincinnati, Ohio and other places such as Ohio's Juvenile and Adult Prison systems where I was exposed to the life altering teachings of the Nation of Gods and Earths. To signify my rebirth and growth mentally, I chose the righteous name of SOLO RULER ALLAH for myself.

I chose SOLO because in order to love anyone else I had to get to know and fall in love with who I was!! I could only do this by separating myself from everything around me and really looking deeply inside of myself with no distractions. I learned from experience that nobody can save you except you which was something I first encountered when I got up to the 18th degree in the Supreme Alphabets of the NGE teachings.

I chose RULER as a part of my name once I discovered that I have the power to Rule or become a Ruler by obtaining the proper Knowledge of Self. ALLAH was the name that all those who accept the reality of the teachings of the Nation of Gods and Earths unanimously agree represents the Original Black man who has obtained the Knowledge of himself and his proper origin in this world. Its equivalent to the Paternal family name in the NGE, so it's taken on by all male members within their names. The Founder of the Nation of Gods and Earths was a righteous man whom we know by the name of ALLAH and he was the one whom clarified the Lessons taught by the Nation of Islam for the common person outside the temple of grasp the Understanding of on the streets of New York during the 1960's. We carry on this same tradition of mental uplifting and rebirth today which was how I came in contact with the Knowledge.

On a deeper personal level, SOLO represents the Son of Man. The Father and the Son are One unified soul within my D.N.A (Divine Nation of Allah). See, sperm has almost nothing in it except DNA which is the Fathers mind at work. This proves that the Fathers mind is what makes the embryo which is the SOLO soul or the Father/Son. Why? Because I am my Father and your Father and your Father is you!! He creates civilization and shows the son through action how to be God of his Universe and the foundation of his Solar System. (Refer to the 1st Degree in the Supreme Mathematics and the 1st Degree in the Student Enrollment Lesson)

Take a minute to think about it: as long as you live and reproduce, your Father never dies!! His D.N.A. lives on through you, your son, and his son and on and on. The Father and Son are the Solo soul and foundation of everything. Knowledge sets the stage to produce the most beautiful thing which is Wisdom (the Black woman) and both produce Understanding. (Refer to the 1st, 2^{nd,} and 3rd degrees in the Supreme Alphabets and the 1st and 2nd degrees in the 12 Jewels of Islam)

Looking deeper into Ruler or ruler, to Rule is the nature of the Black man for the reason being that to rule means to be the Ruler. The Original man (Black man) wasn't made to be ruled because his knowledge must build unrestricted to make the necessary advancements in civilization at specific times. We are Gods/Kings and thus Rulers by nature and we've made some of the most significant contributions to the advancement of the planet Earth whether people choose to admit it or not. (Refer to 1$^{\text{st Degree}}$ in Lost and Found Muslim Lesson No.1) We also made the Holy Quran and Bible which is a written record of the totality of our experiences. (Refer to 1st Degree in The Lost and Found Muslim Lesson No. 2) We have no beginning, nor do we have an ending and we have no birth record as a Nation. The Original nation is the Nation of Islam. (Refer to the 9th degree in The Student Enrollment Lesson) If anyone doubts that we are the Rightful rulers of the planet Earth they can study Genesis 1:2, 28, 31.

ALLAH is the Supreme Being! Supreme means: Highest in rank. The Black man and Woman are the highest in rank because we were 1st to walk the planet. Everyone came from us!!! Supreme also means: Most knowledgeable. Being means to exist! All these titles fit the Original people. Why? Because the Original people show and prove to be the foundation of all things through objective historical research. The 1st Divine Beings in the physical form. We are Divine because we are naturally righteous. We are beings because we be or exist to the 5 senses. ALLAH is the rightful proper name that the Black man should call himself and be called by all others.

This is the Mathematical Breakdown of my name: **S** – 19 **O** – 15 **L** – 12 **O** – 15   19+15+12+15=61 6+1=7 which is God in the Supreme Alphabet and the Supreme Mathematics   **R** – 18 U – 21 **L** – 12 **E** – 5 **R** – 18   18+21+12+5+18= 74   7+4=11   1+1=2 which is Wisdom in the Supreme Mathematics

A – 1 **L** – 12 **L** – 12 **A** – 1 **H** – 8 1+12+12+1+8=34   3+4=7 or God in the Supreme Mathematics but what does it all mean. Well, 7 + 2 + 7 = 16 or Knowledge Equality in the Mathematics which is all being born to God. 1 + 6 = 7 Translated into plain English it's just saying that I knowledge the reason for my strong Earth (Black man) in my life. She is the Wisdom that I rise to her fullest Equality which is how I show and prove myself to be God. See, the Black woman is vital to our Nations Elevation. She is Secondary but most necessary!! I'd like to give a shout out before I close to the following people whose words inspired me in a book I recently came across called "Knowledge of Self – A Collection of Wisdom on the Science of Everything in Life. Peace to: EBONI JOY ASIATIC, EARTH IZAYAA ALLAT, SCI – HONOR DEVOTION, I – MEDINA PEACEFUL EARTH, MECCA WISE UNDESTANDING, FAATMA BEHEST EARTH, BEAUTIFUL SEEASIA. Thank you all for just being you!! Strong shout outs go to PROFESSOR BORN SUPREME P.H.D. 7 ALLAH (from Freeport, N.Y.) who is my ENLIGHTENER, SHAKING CEHUM ALLAH, AIKUAN ALLAH, DR. SUPREME UNDERSTANDING ALLAH, KNOWLEDGE ALLAH FROM CALI, MANIFEST SUPREME from MN who wrote 5% Neophytes AND DIVINE RULER EQUALITY ALLAH. I Love the builds each of you dropped at various times both published and unpublished. Last but not least, A big shout out to my son AMEIR. Your Father Loves You!!

PEACE
SOLO RULER ALLAH – INTERIOR CIPHER

For questions or comments, go to
http://TheIncarcerated7sBlog.Blogspot.com or
Email: Incarcerated7s@hotmail.com

A JOURNEY TO THE LIGHT
(CULTURE/FREEDOM)

Please Educate Allah's Children Everywhere!!!

My name is DIVINE ALLWISE ALLAH. I was physically birthed on the Asiatic date of Culture – Wisdom Equality in the Build Understanding year (4 – 26 – 1983). I am my Mother's 1st Born Son/Sun, so I was the Foundation of our Solar system. My Biological Father was a Good Man who is Moorish American which by birth made me Moorish American to my Understanding. I was also Born to the righteous Understanding that there is no Mystery God Born U Truth, I had to find Self and Show and Prove.

Culture – As a youth, I would always ask questions about religious people, etc… My Mother and Father gave me the proper Foods and Culture tools to Understand the tricknowledge that was and still is so embedded in the fabric of the Wilderness of North America. Like so many inner city youth, I went to Public Schools system of Education. This made many of us who were at the bottom. There were certain points in those times where I corrected my teachers. For instance, I always found myself correcting them when they spoke about Christopher Columbus "discovering" America!!! It's the part before they attempt to teach after telling us the Indians were already here. It's not really necessary to explain how that usually went.

Moving Forward though, their came a time when my Old Earth and My Dad wasn't seeing Eye to Eye and so they chose to part ways. This was a very awkward and uncomfortable time for all 3 of us. For me, the Sun of Man was no longer shining on me in the capacity that I was used to. It felt like going from Planet Earth to Neptune!!! I mean, He still came through at times throughout my teenage years B.U.T. to his surprise I was changing from his little boy into a "Grown" man or at least striving to act like one.

My father still aided me with the proper foods. He always told me not to eat pork or any meat for that matter. He would say things like "You are God!!! Your past is not even the Colored Man's future. This is when I began to become serious. The Colored Man?? All my life I had been assuming that Blacks and Spanish people were "people of color". My Father began the revolution in my mind when he said NO!! You are **ORIGINAL**. He or they are Colored People. Who is he or they? At this time I was dealing with a White girl, so it really was significant when it became clear who exactly the Colored People were. My Father was not a Citizen of the Nation Of Gods and Earths, though he was a Moor. Some of the science the Moors teach is similar but some isn't.

It feels as if I was given both at once b.u.t. prepped on the Nation of Gods and Earths a little more. This was my Culture (Unit #4 in the Supreme Mathematics). At a young age, I was well versed on World History, the History of the Moors, the Nation of Islam, the KKK, the FBI, the NAZI'S, etc… so my Culture as well as other Cultures was taught early to me.

I began sharing my knowledge with friends. Some listened and some didn't. Some just didn't care at all!!! I learned how to show and prove my Knowledge by my Father not being around all of a sudden because this made me research his every word whenever I got it. This however was not Freedom. Freedom didn't come until years later after I had went savage and fell victim to "The Game". My loss of Freedom became my True Freedom Experience!!!

Freedom – In the year of Cipher Understanding (03), I was convicted of a crime I did not do because I couldn't give any information on who did. As a result, I was placed in what we call "The Belly Of The Beast". I know some will beg to differ but one can find freedom within physically confinement. Of course, I am speaking from a purely mental and Spiritual aspect. By now, we've strayed so far from what I was taught that it didn't matter or so I had thought. I was good at rapping, so I always interacted with different types of people. I was in the County Jail which put me in time to meet a God named Knowledge Born.

From the moment that we met, I knew that he was A-Alike which means one of the same feather. He was also nice on the Microphone which is how we first started kicking it. My brothers are from New York City (The Bronx) so once I heard his name I knew this was a Good person to meet. We became close overtime though we didn't study the lessons at that point. We just talked about his culture which was The Nation of Gods and Earths.

Eventually, we parted ways and ended up at different prisons but in a few years, we ended up linking back up and that when we began to really Build on a more committed level on the Culture. My journey with him was really my first true involvement with studying the Lessons (120). By already being exposed to a very similar set of teachings from my Father, I easily excelled in my learning the 120 Lessons and other teachings that were exclusive to the Nation of Gods and Earths. These Lessons were the keys to my Freedom – The Freedom from Negativity.

Knowledge Born became what the Nation Of Gods and Earths call an "Enlightener" to me. He gave to me the righteous name of DIVINE WISE – DOME ALLAH which in a few years changed to my present attribute/name which is DIVINE ALL WISE ALLAH. The name stuck so I stuck with it. This is the FREEDOM, I mentioned, when this whole build began. The Freedom to look, listen and learn. FREEDOM to FREE the DOME, so you can see that the Black man is indeed God.

To this day KNOWLEDGE BORN has changed his name to SUPREME MAGNETIC. We are **still** the best of friends. Though I credit my Father with giving me the

Knowledge of Self in a most basic sense, SUPREME MAGNETIC, showed me how to Born myself and take my rightful place as a citizen of the NATION OF GODS AND EARTHS. This is how the NATION OF GODS AND EARTHS aided me with the FREEDOM.

PLEASE EDUCATE ALLAH'S CHILDREN EVERYWHERE
MANIFESTED BY: DIVINE ALL WISE ALLAH
AKA
Hon. Demale Rogers from Cleveland, Ohio

For questions or comments, contact these links online:
http://ONESAVIORSCIPHER.BLOGSPOT.COM or
Email: meadowsce@gmail.com,
incarcerated7s@hotmail.com,
http://TheIncarcerated7sBlog.Blogspot.com

THE GODS ON LONG ISLAND AND THE 1980'S

My ability to adapt to and master street and/or prison environments comes from years of watching the best criminals operate as a youth on what's known as "Monks Corner". However, my ability to examine information critically is due to the impact of the teachings of the Nation of Gods and Earth's, which starts with the history of a man known as Allah (The Father). When Allah was killed on that fateful date of June 13, 1969, I wasn't birthed or born yet but what he put in motion was a form of Energy that has not and will not ever die.

Since I've begun to mature and learn the value of researching, I recently went back and investigated the fundamentals of some of the more prominent physicists and scientists of the last few hundred years. According to Sir Isaac Newton's Newtonian physics and Albert Einstein's theory of Relativity, Energy never dies. It changes forms but it never ceases to exist. I looked up Energy in my Webster's Dictionary, and it says that Energy is the property of something that enables it to do work. Thoughts are a form of Energy. A thought that was put into motion in 1964 is still affecting people 48 years later.

Before the first time I ever heard someone say that the Blackman is God, I always felt that the things that I was being taught in Church were inadequate to explain the mechanics of the laws of the Universe.

I can recall the way my questions were redirected unanswered or trivialized by the adults that I asked them to in and out of church. I was a very inquisitive youth and even back then, I had serious doubts about the concept of a Mystery God being responsible for so much of my life and other peoples.

It just felt like there had to be more to it that I wasn't being told. I began to go to the Freeport Public Library (Freeport, N.Y., which is on Long Island) and just peruse through various books with no real destination in mind back in 1988. This was where I came across books presented alternative explanations to the teachings of religion in regard to how we (men and women) were created, as well as how the Universe came to be.

I read Almanacs that chronicled The Big Bang theory in vivid detail and also came across books by H.P. Blavatsky, Annie Besant and other prominent authors of Theosophy. It was around that time that I heard Rakim Allah rap about the same topics in "Follow The Leader", which was a song off of an album with the same title. I purchased the tape and in the comfort of my grandparents' basement, I began to put the pieces together by dissecting every line of the album.

The seeds were planted and I began to see myself as one of the Gods. I told my grandma that I was cool on the bacon and BBQ spareribs. That summer I met a God named Justice, who I convinced to give me the knowledge of self by coming around him and repeatedly bugging him. You have to remember that I was a lot younger than the other Gods in the 1st Cipher I was sparked in. There was a God named Elevation God Allah whom I had known as Roger, who woke up around the same time. He was a few years older than me, which really mattered back then. I would go to Harris Avenue in Freeport and build with the God Justice, Elevation, and a wise older God named Everlasting. Back then I had no understanding of our family tree and how we all should be able to trace our history to the Father Allah, and the first 9 born through our Enlightener, so I didn't actively seek that information back then.

I was so happy to be around people who thought like me, and seeing the way all the females worshipped the ground that the God's walked on was an added incentive for me to learn as much as I could from them.

I was never taught about the Father or the Nation History by the Gods I was around back then. I did my 3 day fast, and was given a Righteous attribute by Justice which was (Positive Born Allah) and then the Supreme Mathematics.

After I showed and proved that I could recite the breakdowns of both my attribute and then the Supreme Mathematics, I was given the Supreme Alphabet 3 degrees at a time.

I mastered what I was given and shortly before I was to receive the next science, I ended up stealing my grandfather's starter pistol out of his drawer and hitting someone in the head with it at a party as I was in the midst of being jumped (or about to be). That situation would land me in New York's Juvenile Corrections system Upstate. The 1st stop was a place that served as reception in Westbury, New York. There were a few cats who had the knowledge of Self in there, but we were all so young that most of us thought that all we needed to do was memorize the degrees and that quoting them was the goal. I didn't have any understanding of the application of the lessons back then, so by the time I got to the Student Enrollment I was a simple parrot just going through the motions with no Wisdom of the Knowledge.

This was also my introduction to resistance from the powers that were our handlers concerning the validity of my culture. I would spend hours striving to explain that our culture wasn't a Posse (back in the 80's word) and why we weren't black supremacists to the staff who usually had their minds made up already. It was as if they just didn't want to understand us and wanted to take any or everything that we found that we could relate to away from us. This only pushed me towards the Lessons as an act of civil disobedience.

I spent about 14 months in the juvenile systems that time and in the course of going to different facilities and group homes I met Gods that I picked up different jewels format various stages. The God's from Medina (Brooklyn) were the 1st Gods that I saw really representing this way of life with strength and holding people accountable under the penalty of corporal punishment. They would fuck you up over the lessons and everyone knew it! We would have ciphers and people would get punched in they shit and/or stomped out for playing with the culture, violating the dietary laws or just doing weak shit period. I didn't know 120 back then, but I made sure that I knew what I claimed to know, which was up to the Student Enrollment 10th degree. Back then, we tried to spark others into this way of life, and before we knew it we had 120 because we didn't know any better. So a God who didn't know 120at all might have 3 people that were calling him their Enlightener. I now know that this wasn't right or exact, but back then we did it. I got out of juvenile when I was almost 16 and I went to Medina's Fort Greene Rallies and saw a few Gods that I had met in juvenile. I also went to Harlem, a.k.a. Mecca just to see what the parliament was all about and how it ran.

I bumped into Everlasting at Harriet Tubman High School in the late 90's, which was the last time I saw the Elder God. I didn't realize until after I knowledged and wisdomed 120 to begin the process of understanding 120 how important the God Everlasting was to my history as a person. See, the God was the reason that my Enlightener and a lot of the other Gods in the 1st cipher I was in as a youth even had access to this knowledge in that area in the first place.

If I knew then what I know now, I would have taken full advantage of the opportunity to learn more about the application of the culture from him instead of casually rubbing elbows with the God on my way to places or people that couldn't teach me what he could have.

Now we fast-forward to 2012. I am currently incarcerated in Ohio where I have been for the last 10 years of a 20 year sentence. I knowledged 120 in 2003 and began teaching people the science of Everything in Life after earning my Universal Flag from an Elder God from Ohio that I came in time with named Lord Malik King. I went back and amassed a library of cultural books, newspapers, and internet material from the Allah Schools of The Nation to make the information on how to live out this way of life right and exact available to anybody sincerely seeking to know in this environment.

Over the last 8 years I've dedicated myself to the academic study, as well as living application of the Nation of Gods and Earth 8 Point Curriculum. The positive results are obvious to anyone who knew me before I began this swim and saw me again after I swam 9000 miles mentally 120 times. I started an organization called the Incarcerated 7's which is a loose knit group of Gods in various prisons throughout the United States, state and Fed).

It was just an idea based on my inability to get answers to questions about various degrees in the lessons. I began writing incarcerated Gods in The Five Percenter Newspaper to build, and it quickly began to spread. Through the Gods I met, I began writing the God STRO a.k.a. Divine All Wise Allah and Asiatic Prince from Cleveland, Ohio.

These brothers were instrumental in spreading the culture in Ohio's prisons. Asiatic went home and created a group called One Cipher-20 on-line, which we used to build with the On-line Nation members and exchange ideas to this day.

In 2011, I began compiling my first book, which is called the Incarcerated 7's Anthology, Volume #1. It contains writings, essays, short stories, poetry, and things like that from Gods that are on lock as well as a few friends that aren't in the Nation that I found worthy of being in the book. It makes me feel good to know that I am having a positive impact on so many lives despite the attempts of the wicked to smother me out and take a large chunk of my life.

I plan on destroying these various policies that restrict the Nation members from living out the tenets of the culture behind these prison walls, to show forth my power and then after I'm done doing that I am going to liberate myself and walk out of prison a free man with no strings attached. I'll be back in New York with the Universal family shining with my Greatest and only Universal Flag Tattoo exposed for the whole world to see long before my projected release date.

Until then, I'm here via the Incarcerated 7's Blog where I will be visibly building constantly on relevant topics concerning the Nation behind these walls to keep the Gods in here connected. I'm not going away quietly, and I won't be mentally broken or driven to dysfunction anytime soon. I plan on using this time to multiply our numbers behind these walls the same way that the Father Allah multiplied our numbers while he was in Mattewan State Hospital.

Peace to the Gods and Earths like my cousin Shadina Equality who support me out there. I'm looking for a sincere Earth of my own that is willing to take this journey with me and face these obstacles with this King while reflecting my light. If that sounds like you, contact me on our Blog at http://TheIncarcerated7sBlog.Blogspot.com, on Facebook at Robert Born Goldwire, on Twitter or by Email at Incarcerated7s@hotmail.com.

These are serious times that call for a serious approach and the strength of a 5% woman. I leave you how I came, which is in a state of peace. Until the book hits the stores and internet for sale, be on the lookout for it and the excerpts that I'll be posting on the Blog in the near future from the book.

PEACE
PROFESSOR BORN SUPREME P.H.D. 7 ALLAH
AKA
BORN FROM FREEMONT, N.Y.

http://TheIncarcerated7sBlog.Blogspot.com
Email at Incarcerated7s@hotmail.com.

THE SWIM TO UNDERSTANDING 120 LESSONS

In the Name Allah, the Beneficent, the Merciful, whom all praise and gratitude is due, the sole controller of the boundless Universe. The creator! The Originator who is none other than the True and Living God, the Original Man, the Asiatic Black man. The Maker, the owner, the cream of the planet Earth, Father of Civilization, God Almighty of the Universe; Peace to Allah and Justice for teaching and building this Nation of Gods and Earths. I Greet U all with our Universal Greeting of PEACE!!!

My righteous Attribute is Victorious Islam Ruler God Allah. Victorious represents the Victory I maintain over the Devils civilization and his attempts to keep our people illiterate by teaching our people the Truth. Islam represents that Truth being taught as, I Self Lord and Master or I Sincerely Love Allah's Mathematics. Islam is the True way of life for the Original human family of the planet earth but Islam the science, not the religion called Islam, that's taught by the 10% who deal in deceit to keep 85% of the total population stuck in the triple stages of darkness (Blindness, Deafness and Dumbness) as they continue to get filthy rich off their labor due to their ignorance.

We, the Nation of Gods and Earths, show and prove our Divine natural way of life (Islam) via the Supreme Mathematics because Math never lies!! Ruler represents the tool (3rd Eye/Divine Living Mind) I use to simply measure out the whole of my cipher (any, person, place or thing) in order to become the Ruler of my cipher. God is who I am by nature of my birthright. The Black man possesses the power to build and destroy by way of using his 7 ½ ounces of Original brain (Supreme thought power). Allah is the manifestation of self no longer living in the Triple stages of darkness (Blind, Deaf and Dumbness) which is the devils civilization and realm of Equality. Allah is the Supreme

Being Black man from Asia. The sole controller of and ruler of his Universe! Allah is the educated Black man who has the Knowledge of himself. To know self is to know all things in existence for Allah is all things and all things were made manifest from Allah, b.u.t. he is not unseen. Allah is seen and heard everywhere for he is the All Eye Seeing, the Arm, Leg, Leg, Arm Supreme Head, and the most High to exist. (Supreme Being) Lord of all Worlds. Allah is Victorious Islam Ruler God Allah and Victorious Islam Ruler God Allah is Allah!!! With that knowledge made born, my physical degree is wisdom, God. The purpose of this build is to build, in hopes of birthing an Understanding of my Understanding, of my understanding of having knowledge of self. Also to share my personal journey of the first time, I heard that the Black man is God, as well as my coming in time, with the Teachings of Life (120 Lessons). Okay, what is Knowledge of Self? My understanding of Knowledge of self can be explained first, by dissecting each word at a time. This is so my Understanding of knowledge is to possess the know how to do whatever at hand and beyond. It is to know a person, place or thing for certain by way of learning from looking, listening and observing respectfully. From it, one can then accumulate a body of facts of a person, place or thing (to know the truth of a whole). Knowledge is also, to know the ledge of a person, place or thing, so that one doesn't over do or fall into the edge of hardship, errors, mistakes, problems, hell, etc…

Self is just that! A person, man or woman, living being! One who lives!! Without Knowledge of Self, that being is mentally dead or living in the triple Stages of darkness. Blind to the light (truth) of the true and living God, Deaf to the wisdom (wise words) or the true and living God, Dumb (Illiterate/Ignorant) to the knowledge of the true and living God (Black man) so to have knowledge of self would be to exist in the light of truth that the original Asiatic Black man is most high to exist (Supreme Being/Allah/God). He was 1st and will be last for all things must return from where they came. This is why he/self is the Father of Civilization. Without the Black man number 1, no other man or woman could exist. Having knowledge of self, also enables one to build (add on and elevate) with facts destroying the lies, falsehoods, trick knowledge of religion, superstition etc… of the devils civilization. Knowledge of self, also is knowing the history of whole, of our people, (original Asiatic Black Family) as well as righteousness, freedom, Justice, equality, love, peace and happiness, along with the science of everything in life; for this is not only the duty of God, but its gods nature along with civilizing the uncivilized people who are savage. I know about these people all too well because I was once a person, who had lost all knowledge of self and I was living a beast way of life (savage).   However, although in the triple stages of darkness, hearing that the Black man is God from someone was the shining light that I followed out of the dark and it led me into my true way of life (Islam) though not overnight. Everything has a process and an order in life and anything in life worth having will never come easy. Knowledge - 120 Lesson sure was not easy but with the 36 keys (Supreme Mathematics and Alphabets) it was interesting unlocking the lessons which are Infinite in Knowledge, wisdom and Understanding. This is needed in order to live out our Divine Culture with a freedom to exercise my power which has to remain refined for the best results in life. This is so, that my equality as God will always show and prove my ability to build up a righteous nation, while destroying the devils uncivilization, borning Gods and Earths of the truth of our cipher.

So, after the 9 steps or stages, I was born in truth of Allah's Supreme Mathematics and went on to the 120 Lessons which is the Nation of Gods and Earth curriculum that is mandatory for every true active citizen to memorize word for word, which to me was a big challenge. Shortly after I accomplished that task, I discovered that the next and true challenge was applying the knowledge, living out the knowledge of God (wisdom) in order to get the best part from it which was the understanding of it. Only then are the Lessons made manifest as Living Mathematics examples, which is the language spoken by the Universe. The Lessons aren't outdated as many think. I suggest instead of trying to decipher them literally, you should apply what you learn, in order to achieve an understanding of them. Knowledge without wisdom is senseless but wisdom without an understanding is useless!! This is the most important, "Lesson", I learned in my journey to Understanding that the biggest lesson isn't even on the paper!! 1st you Knowledge 120 Lessons, then U Wisdom 120 Lessons and if your fortunate enough and patient, finally you'll swim 9000 miles, mentally 120 times and begin to Understand 120 Lessons. Then and only then can you apply, the best part to make a difference in your life, as well as the lives of others! Peace to all the Gods, Earths and 85ers looking to learn about themselves by obtaining the proper Knowledge of Self. It's truly a journey that is worth travelling.

PEACE
VICTORIOUS ISLAM RULER GOD ALLAH
AKA
V.I.R.G. OR V
from Cleveland, Ohio

AUTHOR'S NOTE

V.I.R.G. returned to Cleveland, Ohio after 8years of incarceration in 10-2-2011. He currently has a job and is maintaining and enjoying his freedom.

The Science Behind My Forearm Tattoo

Recently a few Earths have asked me for the Science on one of my most visible and controversial tattoos. As a true and living attribute in Allah World Manifest I-Self-Lord-And-Master felt compelled to draw the knowledge behind it up into a fine mist and distill it back down on the Earth and other readers of this blog.

For those unaware the tattoo is in a sleeve form on my right forearm. It depicts a beautiful black woman still in an 85% state of mind, dressed in panties and bra, standing backwards to show off her apple-bottom while looking over her shoulder. She's also standing in stacks of money. To the left is a connecting wall of bricks that reads BUILD-N-DESTROY with the bricks beginning to crumble under the word DESTROY. To the left of that is the final depiction that connects the three. It's a true and living Queen covered in 3/4th by a nice dress. She's rocking her natural hair and is kneeling down while holding the planet Earth atop her shoulders.

Now, what does this symbolize and how is it righteous? Well, it shows-n-proves my growth and development as God. How? Cause only God has the knowledge of His power and realizes He must deal in equality. My attracting powers have always had women gravitate towards me and with the majority of them being Blind, Deaf and Dumb to their true self, they chose to dress sexually explicit, or chase money recklessly. Knowing this eye teach them the knowledge of Self and Build positively with them while destroying their savage ways. This leads her to the understanding of her culture, dressing in 3/4th, and to use her 6 ounces mentally instead of her 6 sex-tillion tons physically.

Atop of all, this eye placed our "Universal Flag of Islam" because it's only then the knowledge of God am eye able to Build-n-Destroy all within my circumference. Some say "You God so you shouldn't have a half-naked woman on your arm". Those are the ones still accepting things on face value and not doing the knowledge. As long as one's heart is divine, his ways and actions will always destroy negativity.

With that explained those who acknowledge my wisdom will understand my plight to deal in equality with my culture. Peace to the Earth "Queen Wisdom Born AKA Modesty Blaise", eye support what you're doing with the Blaise Infitness video. Peace to Eboni Joy Asiatic and the rest of Earths at the 14th degree. Peace to I Medina, Sci-Honor Devotion, Beautiful See Asia, Mecca Wise Understanding, Faatma Behesht Earth, and Earth Izayaa Allot for all the builds that you've added on. There's no woman like a 5% woman.

Peace
Hon. ADONTE "TUNA" CHERRY AKA BORN SEVEN ALLAH
Springfield, Ohio

Contact info: Facebook/Adonte Born Seven Cherry
http://Adonte'CherryBlog.Blogspot.com

AUTHOR'S NOTE
Tuna aka Born Seven authored a new novel titled-STREET ROYALTY 937 that is making a lot of noise online and in the Springfield/Dayton, Ohio streets. It's available at www.educatedthug2publishing.com

ENLIGHTENMENT

This is a story about a conversation between me and a flower. I know how this may sound but I assure you that the Flower never said a word. Before I start this story, I have to tell you a few things, so that you can understand the storyline.

The first thing that I have to explain is the knowledge of Buddhism and the second thing that I have to elaborate on is the conversation that took place (prior to the Flower situation) between me and my Girlfriend. I will start with Buddhism.

Buddhism is an Asiatic Religion/way of Life that teaches Self- Denial. Gautame Buddha is the Patriarch of this Religion. The Religion is named after him because his followers, like Christians, profess his principles Religiously. However, don't misunderstand me; Buddhism is nothing like Christianity.

I learned about Buddhism over 10 years ago. What I learned about Buddha was learned in bits and pieces but I never forgot what I learned. I learned that Buddha achieved all 7 Levels of Consciousness through Self Denial. Buddhists believe that you can achieve absolute Peace by giving up everything that makes life comfortable. Buddha was a Prince who gave up his Royal life style after he learned that everyone didn't live like him.

I was told a story about Buddha that I thought was so awesome that I never forgot the story. They say that after years of meditation, Buddha achieved all 7 Levels of Consciousness, which is known as True Enlightenment. Enlightenment is a conscious awareness. By being truly Enlightened, he had the ability to talk to animals, plants and insects. Inanimate means: things that is not alive, such as rocks, dirt and water.

I always thought that the story of Buddha was awesome but that it had to be something similar to Jesus coming back to life after 3 days, until ... 1 day it hit me, when me and my Girlfriend were talking about my ways and actions. She asked me, "Why are you so sarcastic?" I responded by explaining to her that I believe that every question is Self-Explanatory, even though they say, there is no such thing as a stupid question. I personally believe, that if you give a question that you ask someone else enough thought, you can answer you own question.

Now that all this has been said, I feel that we are ready for me to tell the story. That same day, I was walking the track on the Recreation Yard of the Prison, that I am currently housed in daydreaming when I saw this Blue Flower. The Blue Flower was actually a part of a weed. The thing about this Flower, is that I saw a lot of them on the other side of the Prisons gate. I picked the flower but I didn't have any intentions of doing anything with it. I continued to walk the track daydreaming about getting out of Prison. As time went by, I was eventually stopped by this dude who asked me what I was doing with the Flower. It was at that moment that I recalled the story about Buddha and how he was able to talk to different objects. I thought to myself about how sweet it would be if the flower could talk. What would it say and what would its voice sound like?

At that moment I had an Epiphany. I figured out how Buddha was able to conversate with different objects. The conversation between me and my Girlfriend gave me the answer to the question Buddhist probably spent most of their lives looking for. It's the ability to be aware and understand your existence. I told my Girlfriend that if you were smart enough, you could answer any question you can think of. So my logic was that all I had to do was think of a profound question to hear the Flower speak.

I really put a lot of thought into what I was going to ask the Flower. As I continued to walk the track, I noticed all the Flowers on the other side of the gate again. I began to think to myself: Can a Flower get lonely? If it does get lonely, does it look sad or sick? I heard people who practice horticulture say that plants need love to grow.

The more thought I put into it, the more questions came into my mind. So, I told myself that I could only ask the Flower 1 Question. I made it harder on me. See, if I could ask more than 1 question, the questions wouldn't mean as much as just 1 question would. I smiled to myself because I knew the question was going to be truly profound.

For 2 days, the Flower sat on my windowsill and I noticed that it had begun to wilt. I knew that whatever the Flower said would be its dying words. I had to make my question worth asking out of respect for the life that the flower represented so I sat down and wrote out all of the things that I wanted to ask the Flower. These are some of the questions that I wrote down: When I picked you up, did you feel any pain? What is the life of a flower truly like? What do you think of Humans? What do you think about the relationship between plants and humans?

There were so many questions that I wanted to ask. The thing that I did not want to ask was what I would call a stupid question. I felt that all my questions were good but I knew that there was still a better question to be asked. How do you come up with a better question to ask a Flower? Then it hit me!!! Stop thinking of the Flower, as a plant and start thinking of the Flower as an Equal.

By doing this I opened up my mind to so many things and options. This put me in the State of Mind that I needed to be in to hear what the Flower had to say. I wrote the Question down to see what 2 days of work looked like.

I wrote: Why would you choose to grow on this side of the Gate with so much misery, when you could have grown on the other side with more of your kind? This was the most profound question that I could think of. You may be thinking that this question is simple compared to all the other questions that I thought of, so I say to you: Do not let the complexity of the question escape you because of its simplicity. I Incorporated many of the questions that I wanted to ask into this 1 Question.

You have to remember that the Flower will have my level of Intelligence and my ability to read between the lines. The manner in which you ask a question betrays your limits. Those answers you will accept and those that you will reject or confuse with misunderstanding. Knowing this, I knew at that moment I had saw the Flower that it was no longer a weed but my true equal. That was when it spoke to me. It said: You asked me why would I grow on this side of the gate with so much misery when I could have grown on the other side of the gate with my kind?

I say to you: Why not grow on this side of the gate? I was given water unobstructed view of the Sun, so that my body could grow green and healthy. I was given water and good soil, so that my roots could grow strong and embrace life itself. I am lucky that I didn't grow on the other side of the gate with my own kind because if I would have I would have had to compete, for all the things I just told you that I am thankful for. Taurean, you know better than anyone that the grass is not always greener on the other side.
Remember this: The best of your todays can always be the worst of your tomorrows.

ALL that I could say to that was
………………………………….DAMN!!!!!!!!!!!!!!!!!!!!!!!

TAUREAN SMITH AKA T.WAVES
Toledo, Ohio

COMMUNICATION IS THE KEY

P.E.A.C.E. God's And Earth's

What is communication? That's a good question and I think there's an array of answers. My 3rd eye (mind) took a look at this question and born this perception.

Every discipline has its language: every skill has its language, and if we don't speak the language of our discipline, or our skill well, we are not successful in communication. Every time, every era has a language that is peculiar to that time. If you don't speak the language of the time, then you are not communicating properly, and you will not be successful. Every culture has a language that is peculiar to that culture. If you don't speak the language of that culture then you are not communicating properly, and you will not be successful. This theology can be applied to everything in life. Think about it . . . language basically is not spoken well, when you speak and don't use grammatical correctness.

Remember in school, in English class, and the teacher was trying to teach us about proper grammar. They talked about how there must be subject and verb agreement: If the subject is in the present, then the verb, or the action, must be in the present, otherwise you don't have subject and verb agreement. Therefore, you're not speaking grammatically correct, and it impairs your communication.

As you use language to communicate your ideas, communicate your thoughts. You must speak in a way that your words, your thoughts and your ideas are clearly perceived by the one, or ones, to whom you are speaking. The less possibility there is for misunderstanding, what you're trying to communicate, the better it is that people will understand us.

Think about this … Slavery was supposed to be over once the "Emancipation Proclamation" was established. Yet black people today, in 2012, still have a slave mentality, looking for the white man (devil) to provide the necessities of life. (food, clothing, shelter, employment, and education) That action is of the past, to an era that is long gone by.

We are in the present, where we have the ability to do what the fuck we want to do and that's subject and verb agreement. With that slave mentality, you're communicating well with the white man (devil), but we are not communicating well with one another because you are not speaking well; get it!!!

Communication is thought transference, exchange of talk or ideas, to make one aware. With that being said, if we as black people can't properly communicate amongst each other (with grammatical correctness) then we will never be able to take back what's rightfully ours – "This World", because we aren't all speaking the same language.

P.E.A.C.E.
Intelligent Knowledge of Self Allah

(Intell)

Interior Cipher

Toledo, Ohio

NOW, NATION, END

In the Name of Allah, I greet my Alikes and whomever these written words have found with the Universal Greeting of Peace!!! I was taught by some very wise Men that Peace is the absence of confusion but through research, I've grown into the Understanding of what confusion really is.

The etymology of the Word CONFUSION shows that this word is derived from the Latin Word CONFUSIO which is defined as; (1) A state of disorder, (2) Bewilderment, (3) Embarrassment, (4) A failure to distinguish between things according to Webster's New World Dictionary (2nd Edition).

In these particular days and times, there is a lot of confusion going on everywhere and most of it is intentionally manufactured to distract a segment of the population or to pre-occupy them while those who manufacture the confusion grow rich from the confused people. One method of causing confusion that affects large groups of people at the same time is to cause confusion through the programming on the Televisions. Each time we turn on our Television we have opened our Mind to someone else and allowed them to decide what will be thought about if we are not choosing the actual material or creating the programs that our people are watching.

Most of the programs on Television Stations throughout the Americas are controlled by people who don't have the best interests of the viewers in Mind at all. The Agenda of the Television is either to plant a suggestion through creative, yet insidious marketing to the viewer or to reinforce a specific idea that society conforms to through emotional manipulation. It's very important as a first step to obtaining the Knowledge of Self that people be taught the seriousness of allowing our subconscious Minds to be tampered with by people who don't care what happens to us.

This information may seem unrealistic in scope but regardless of whether the majority of people agree with it or not it has to be expressed in order to be considered. This is the 1st step in a series of steps that are designed to Free the domes of the blind, deaf and dumb into a state of awareness. Once a person has this Knowledge, it's up to them to test the validity of it and those who do will begin to awaken themselves going through the process of critically examining the facts as they are presented to them.

Knowledge empowers a person to make a decision to seize a specific moment in time and to alter its course through the application of his willpower. A person gains this ability simply by realizing that change is possible in that moment through his choice to exercise his power. Once the Black man makes the choice to take responsibility of creating his own reality and marries this idea, he is instantly rewarded with an altered state of mind. Inwardly, he sees the reward outwardly expressed in his exterior environment, in some way as a wedding gift, from the Universe for his being in accord with his Nature once again.

To obtain this result, one wise man in 1964 came up with 2 mechanisms to instigate a change in the psyche of the Black minds in the wilderness of North America known as the THE SUPREME MATHEMATICS and THE SUPREME ALPHABET. These 2 vehicles would be used to transport the masses of lost minds back to the Knowledge of themselves (Self Identity) which could then Empower them to assist others to the same place through the same process of gradual Enlightenment.

The SUPREME MATHEMATICS are 10 principles that correspond to the numbers in the Hindu-Arabic Numeral Systems (0,1,2,3,4,5,6,7,8,9). THE SUPREME ALPHABET consists of 26 principles that correspond to

the Alphabet of the English/American system
(A,B,C,D,E,F,G,H,I,J,K,L,M,N,O,P,Q,R,S,T,U,V,W,X,Y,Z
). The Founder of the Nation Of Gods and Earths crafted
the usage of these systems as a method to unlock the minds
of the Black youth in 1964 by teaching them to form
profound relationships with themselves and the things
around them using these tools of change.

Applying the science of Supreme Mathematics to
today; today's Math manifests as Knowledge (1)
Culture/Freedom (4) all being born to Power/ Refinement
which is the 5th degree in the Supreme Math (1+4=5).
Within the SUPREME ALPHABET, the 14th degree is
NOW, NATION, END. This degree is one of 26 principles
in the Supreme Alphabet that were designed to be
Mathematically applied by Black people to lost Black
people, to assist the lost in finding their way back to their
Original state of Mind and their Culture. On an individual
level, the application of each degree brings a person back to
self – identity through a gradual process and the application
of each principle in one's life reveals deeper insight into the
ways of the world and the sociology of people.

In essence, NOW, NATION, END is a pragmatic
person solution. It advocates the Unification of Black
resources for one common cause (THE NATION) and lays
out the timeline, to initiate things in order for the
application, of the said degree to achieve its maximum
positive impact (NOW or IMMEDIATELY). It's the
walking and talking expression of the Universal Flag that
was designed by the Universal Shamguaad Allah in 1966.
The 14th degree drawn up proposes the use of the
Knowledge (1) of the ones Culture (4) to free his or her
dome which is all being born to the Power (5) to Refine
Self and eventually ones surroundings through the
Advancement of Living Science in those environments that
a practitioner is exposed to.

As more people begin to multiply the effort, it will have a ripple effect on other communities until it reaches all 4 corners of the planet Earth. Properly applied, the 14th degree of the Supreme Alphabet has the potential to solve a lot of the social problems that Black people experience from the lack of our own cohesion regarding matters that affect us all. Let's take a minute and break down the meaning of NOW, NATION, END. NOW is: This present moment in time as in Right NOW!! A NATION is: A stable, historically developed community of people with a territory, economic Life, distinctive culture and language in Common. An END is: An outcome or consequence (as in "a means to an END").

Building a righteous Nation of our own is the only way that Black people will ever be able to control their own lives, communities and sit themselves in heaven. NOW is the time to build a righteous NATION and put an END to the devils un-civilization. We can start that process right NOW by finding a way as individuals to do our part in the struggle. Simply extend a hand to a God that's already doing something to advance the NATION in some way. Wishing a God well while he is performing his duty **is not** adding on!! If you are serious about living out this and all the other degrees you will have to roll up your sleeves and get involved like the others who are truly doing something that matters. Find a thing that you think should be happening to advance the cause and just do it.

PEACE
PROFESSOR BORN SUPREME P.H.D. 7 Allah

UNDERSTANDING CIPHER

Today's Mathematics is Understanding Cipher all being born to Understanding (3+0=3). Sight is related to Understanding and Cipher relates to one's environment. Can you see completion around you or within yourself? To See with your 3rd eye (mind) is to Understand. Could you recognize Gumar Oz Dubar (Wisdom, Strength and Beauty) if you encountered these attributes within as 85%er who did not yet realize that he is God or within yourself?

If not, you may not have a sure Knowledge of self yet. There is a difference between basic knowledge of self and knowing and Understanding how to put the knowledge into action or use to bring about a specific result. For instance, One can have a recipe for a great dish but if one can't operate a stove what's the point!!? The Original man (The Blackman) whom is Asiatic is both the Knowledge Born and the Understanding seen and heard. A person may talk the talk, as if they are science up but without tangible results that can be shown and proven it's simply lip profession. To be God, One has to be able to understand (See) the Cipher and do the Knowledge in a Mathematical way to the Cipher to do Justice to the environment. If one is not building they are automatically destroying. Dr. Martin Luther King Jr. sacrificed his physical life for the sake of the whole which was a cipher.

Though he may have speak a different language and saw God as a Mystery on some level his sacrifice proved that not only do great minds have great thoughts, those with powerful visions and ideas often make enormous sacrifices to realize those goals. Martin was God whether he knew it or not. Gods Build civilizations, mentally as well as physically, by actualizing their ideas! The truth is the light that will lead our people out of the darkness, so that they can see that the Black man is and has always been God on this plane of existence. Take time to Understand the Cipher of yourself. Know God to see God and elevate your mind to become Allah. The proper name for God is Allah which is an acronym for Arm, Leg, Leg, Arm, Supreme Head within the Nation of Gods and Earths.

POSITIVE ENLIGHTENMENT ATTAINS CONSCIOUS ELEVATION

KNEW GOD ALLAH
INTERIOR CIPHER, OHIO

AUTHOR'S NOTE

Knew God Allah earned his universal flag from Professor Born Supreme in the infamous Lucasville prison in 2011. He is originally from Lima, Ohio and was known as "Trez" in the streets of Lima before he borned his righteous attribute/name.

WORD IS BOND!!!

I came in the divine attribute of "God Born Justice Allah," and as I enter your mist I would like to greet all the True & Livings Gods and Earth with the universal greeting that is "Peace"!

Those who are in tune with the 11th degree in the "Last and Found Muslim Lesson #1" should know the science or the weight of your word. The degree states: Have you not heard that your word shall be bond regardless to whom or what? Answer: Yes, my word is bond and bond is life. I shall give my life before my word shall fail. If you do the Math you will find that bond borns build destroy (35; 3+5=8). We as Supreme beings and fathers and mothers of civilization must do the duties of civilized people, which is to add on our culture (That I Love Sincerely) by building.

After gaining a Supreme understanding of the 11-degree, we as Gods and Earths need to be very aware, that when we say things our words are to be divine as our culture. Bear in mind that the Nation of Gods and Earths is all wise and does everything right and exact … (Do the Math) "Word" borns equality (60; 6+0=6) and equality borns wisdom (110; 1+1+0=2) so, in turn wisdom is your word and your wisdom is also yours ways and actions which has to be equal in strength. So, before you speak evaluate what you say, for the cause, the words you speak just may cost you your life!!! Indeed that is an extreme price to pay for wisdom because you did not gain the knowledge 1st to what you manifested.

Apply the 11th Degree in a supreme fashion (The only way) and you have taken on the responsibility to be held accountable for your words and deeds. Remember "I shall give my life before my word shall fail".

Daily, I hear things that are said and followed by "Word is Bond". If your square is as Devine as it should be than there is no need to even state that, for the cause, your wisdom is your word.

This degree is not to dictate your manifestation, B.U.T. to all those aware that your words are not to be spoken frivolously. For the cause, they will not be taken lightly, for the cause; they reflect the very essence of yourself and your state of mind. Before I exit, leave you with this question: Have you not heard that your WORD SHALL BE BOND, regardless to whom or what?? "Peace" to all true and living Gods and Earths, living according to the laws of Islam.

True and Living and God Born Justice Allah
Rahway, NJ07065
(New Jerusalem)

In The Name of   Focused (**F**)
Energy (**E**) Brings (**B**)
The Vital Building   A Wisdom (**2**)
To God (**7**) and Helps Him Free (**4**)
Block To Our Nation,   Those Living
Destructively (**8**)
The Unified Black Family.

How To Eat The Right Foods

Peace and Blessings,

What's the science Brothers and Sisters? I trust you all are striving for improvement and empowerment. And only through **unity** will achieve these goals. And that is one of the many purposes of the book you're reading. The God, Professor Born, asked I King (7) to put together a build concerning the obstacle of observing our dietary laws within the confines of the injustice system. So let us travel the universe and add on to our nation and destroy the devil's un-civilization.

The 2nd lesson of our 120 lessons, the English lesson C · 1, shows us how to move beyond this obstacle, and why it's so important. This lesson is expressed mathematically as Master (**13**) Equality (**6**). Despite your situation, you're supposed to know (**1**) and understand (**3**) your surroundings (**6**). The first step to getting beyond this obstacle is knowledge of self... 1∘: my name is W. F. Muhammad. The foundation to mastering your equality, is knowing self. Example: 1∘: my name is Black King (**7**). I know I like to eat; so, the wise thing to do is figure out a way to substitute the swine (and beef, for self) that they serve with something I do eat. 10∘: the devil taught him how to eat the wrong foods; this degree shows us why we shouldn't eat of the swine (and beef) because it alters our mind to produce mis · understandings (poor · under-standings). The 7∘ - 10∘ shows how poor food, produces poor understandings. **7**∘ why does he like the devil? **8**∘ because the devil put fear in him, when he was a little boy. **9**∘ why does he fear the devil now that he is a big man? **10**∘ because the devil taught him to eat the wrong foods! Cee Suns and Moons, fear is a result of a poor understanding, or a lack of understanding. Someone may fear dogs, B.U.T. this is due to their lack of understanding, or their poor understanding of dogs. Once they do the knowledge to, become wise to, and understand dogs, their fear will no longer exist.

Back to the purpose of this build ... So how does one cope in this situation of incarceration, and observance of our dietary law? Through the reality of today's mathematics (pure coincidence Pro. **9**): Be a wise (**2**) God (**7**) and Born (**9**) create an avenue of alter natives. (For our sisters: Be the wisdom (**2**) of God (**7**) and Born (**9**) an avenue of alternates). In other words my beloved people ... **Hustle** does not mean be a savage in the pursuit in happiness. No... Hustle means to make something out of nothing, (Create) and who is the ultimate Hustler? G.O.D!!! That is why K.O.S is so relative to overcoming the reality of limited options in our current situations of injustice. Without knowing self, how can you be wise enough to successfully hustle? What kind of hustle? Use your God point power sun, or your excellence Moon (7 ½ or 6oz of **original** Brain).

PROBLEMS EXTIRPATE AFTER CONSCIOUS
EFFORT

Your Brother in Mind and Struggle
Black King Lyfe Allah
Interior Cipher, Ohio

THE FOUNDATION OF SUCCESS

Everybody wants success, but everybody doesn't know the systematic fundamentals of obtaining success. I'm like a lot of other young black men that at a time in my life thought success strictly consisted of getting rich and being wealthy. I have discovered that true success starts within self. I have learned that in order to obtain success within self, a set of virtues must be applied to your life. Virtues are a kind of moral excellence. The virtues that must be applied are: Integrity; which is the ability to be honest with self and others, having adherence to a strict moral or ethical code. Discipline, which is having self-control or a state of order is based on submission to a set of virtues. Discipline is training that's expected to produce a specific character or pattern of behavior. Self- Awareness, which is the knowledge of self, is your true culture, and identity. The importance of self-awareness is that it will give you a synopsis of your true character and the origin of your pattern of behavior. This is so that you can then reform and refine yourself.

Reformation and refinement are important components in the foundation of success. Reformation is improvement for the better. Reformation is the process of correcting all the mis-information that was pushed on your mind as an adolescent. Refinement is finishing of the reformation process by finding a new way to live, taking on a new culture that's more righteous and subtle.

The true essence of success is surmounting or overcoming any difficulty or obstacle within your life, but you have to realize that the first obstacle is yourself. Success has nothing to do with monetary or material gain. That's just a façade that a lot of young Black men have fallen victim to. This foundation of success is a basic blueprint to real success, which is the knowledge of self and the application of that knowledge to bring about profound results in all aspects of your life.

Intelligent Knowledge of Self Allah

(Intell)

Interior Cipher, Ohio

For questions or comments email: Incarcerated7s@hotmail.com or go to http://TheIncarcerated7sBlog.Blogspot.com

AUTHOR'S NOTE

Intell was known on the Toledo, Ohio, streets as LiL Rahbie from the notorious "X Block" before he started reading books and became conscious. He is currently learning the Supreme Alphabet and how to apply what he has learned to situations in prison.

A SCIENTIFIC EXAMINATION OF THEOLOGICAL BELIEF SYSTEMS

AND THEIR ORIGINS

In the name of the Mighty Nation of Gods and Earths, I greet everyone in our universal greeting, which is Peace. Within our supreme mathematics!

Today's living reality/mathematics is knowledge (1) Cipher (0) all being born back to knowledge. (1+0=1). A lot of people don't realize it, but, doing the knowledge to a person, place, or thing could actually save your life! A lot of people that claim to be NGE think 120 Lessons are just a bunch of empty words on paper, or some abstract theory, or hypothetical concept. In actuality, the 120 Lessons are a set of lock picks that allow certain minds to access different dimensions of the universe. A Dimension is just a degree, or quality, of existence.

In the context of this essay, the universe is a mutually agreed upon reality created by the Power of the Original Black Mind. My understanding is that the first mother was also created by this Supreme controlling force. The Mother Element was sparked from the Father Element, and the process is now infinitely replicated in the formation of the first two elements.

Presently, hydrogen is the lightest of all the elements, and was the first ever. Helium is the second lightest, and is referred to as the Mother Element by most scientists. These same facts are taught in most school textbooks throughout the world, but what is seldom spoken on is the actual science of how hydrogen came to exist without any other element existing before it.

When most people hear that the Nation of Gods and Earths teachings are that the Black man is G.O.D., people think that it's an absurd idea to even analyze scientifically. People who come across these teaching ask things like, "If you are God, who made you, and how did you get here?" I think that these are legitimate questions. So, I direct these types of peoples' attention to the Sun, because the Sun is also an Independent Source of Life and Matter, like me.

Research shows that our present Sun, that sustains earthly life in this solar system, is the first thing known to have exhibited activity in this solar system. Our Sun presently regulates its own temperature, internally, 24 hours-a-day/7 days-a-week. This Sun never deviates or makes mistakes! If the Sun's temperature were to suddenly increase by just a few degrees, hotter or colder, the Earth would not be able to sustain LIFE as we know it. If it were to suddenly heat itself hotter, the earth's form would change from solids to liquids to all gases. All the solids and liquids would evaporate.

The logical conclusion that one could draw is that, for some reason, the earth hasn't changed forms significantly in over, at least, one million years. This would have to mean that the sun is aware of the earth on some level, and that the sun is interacting with the earth to calculate and maintain the temperature necessary to sustain its existence. I really don't understand why skeptics won't just question this observable fact; there is at least some type of bond, or active communication between the sun and our planet. It's very obvious that it exists.

In the same way that you can observe the interaction between the earth and the sun, there is also observable proof that Black people's melanin goes through physical changes from being subjected to sunlight. This is verification of the sacred bond between the solar system's physical form and the mind of the Black man. The sun is the material center of this solar system reflecting the will of our highest consciousness. The same faculty of hour higher selves, governing the sun's activity, regulates the breaths we take, blinking, and other activity that we seldom acknowledge.

Why is it taboo or absurd to a lot of people to consider that the ever-expanding universe may be the effect, caused by the energy of our minds as they distribute information amongst the collective consciousness of the universe as the consciousness is consistently calculating and applying the mathematical algorithms to solve different problems?

The universe may be expanding to accommodate birth and growth of new ideas and thoughts. Seeing the way the planets submit to the sun's attracting powers is nature's way of silently acknowledging our supremacy. It's as if the universe is winking at us Black men and women, and assuring us that our plight is a temporary condition that can be eradicated at any point in time, as it soothes us with its celestial rhythms.

I recently began the process of reviewing and renewing my knowledge, wisdom and understanding of every degree in the Nation of Gods and Earths' body of information that is collectively known as 120 Lessons, 120 Degrees, etc. 120 Lessons contain a lesson named the Lost-Found Muslim Lesson No.2.

In the NGE, we do not consider ourselves Muslims, but we do study Muslim lessons that are a series of in depth conversations between Wallace Fard Muhammad and the Honorable Elijah Muhammed of the Nation of Islam.

Within the Lost-Found Muslim Lesson No. 2, there is a degree(the 10th degree) that has Wallace Fard Muhammad asking Elijah Muhammed the question, "Who is that mystery God?" In response, Elijah Muhammad, of the Nation of Islam, explains that there is no mystery God, and that the only God is the Sun of Man, whom we learn, as we progress in our studies, is the Black man.

This is just one of many titles given to the Black man within this body of lesson, but the gist of the degrees is that there is no mystery God in the sky. The Black man has searched for trillion of years for that mystery God, but was unable to find that so-called mystery God, and collectively agreed that there is no mystery God controlling their lives. We learn that this conclusion was reached a trillion or more years after the billions of minds searched for evidence of this mysterious unseen being.

I want to point out the fact that I realize that a lot of people have never heard what I'm saying in this essay, and know nothing about the existence, or teachings of the Nation of Gods and Earths, aka, the Five Percenters. My goal is to provoke analysis and thought with my writings. I am not interested in coercing anyone to accept what Elijah Muhammed said, or what I am saying as a fact, automatically, which is a very different approach than what most writers probably use. I would like you take a few minutes to think about what I've said up to now first. After you have wrapped your brain around the points I've brought to the table, I would like you to stop reading this and write down five sources of evidence that are independent of what anyone else has taught you, or told you, that irrefutably support the idea of the existence of a mysterious unseen being that is seen and heard everywhere. I want you to reach inside of yourself (not the Bible, or any other source), for the answers. Don't ask anybody else what they think about it. This is all about you!

When did you come to the conclusion that a mysterious unseen force controls everything in this world by it will? What percentage of your life do you estimate that you control, and how are you doing your math? I want you to walk through it slow, and write down the specific method you're using. Can you pin-point the exact place that you were when you independently used science to research this topic, and what exact evidence brought you to be convinced that an Omnipotent Unseen Force is invisibly doing covert surveillance on the entire universe from a stationary position somewhere?

I'm willing to bet money that you won't be able to recall any memory of doing any in depth research. Have you asked yourself this question before? Write down the date. The average person out there, you've probably never even asked yourself these types of questions before. To accurately critique your belief system, you would need to not only have asked yourself why you are convinced that a mystery God exists, to be confident from the evidence; but you also need to know how to really did deep to put any doubts of it to rest with serious evidence that can stand without belief of faith. I personally only recently began to use this process to evaluate the facts, and separate them form a lot of beliefs that I had been conditioned to accept in my childhood by other people. If you're grown, you should not want to still be making important life decisions using someone else's outdated belief system, or some inferior method, or any type of system that's not working.

It may be time to question why you believe a lot of things and where you got your beliefs from. If any of this information applies to you, I think that one of the counter-productive ideas that a person can utilize is to blindly accept a belief in a mystery God as a fact without investigating its origin. How does the world's history document this idea's origin and what is the historically supported evidence, or lack of evidence that you have found on this topic? Your first question should be, "When did any ancient society document the idea of God being an unseen being, outside of themselves?" Do you already know the answer? What is the first date where you can find evidence of this idea ever recorded by anyone?

People simply assume that this was always the way it was, but that's not a fact. This may be your first opportunity to break the cycle of blindly accepting whatever is presented to you as a fact without doing any research to verify what is presented. Look on the internet, or in a public library for a book called, "A History Of God" by Karen Armstrong. Karen gives a convincing account of the origin and evolution of man's belief in a God outside of himself, and she supports her findings with a lot of convincing evidence.

The Holy Bible also speaks of "Gods" in a plural form in quite a few passages, such as John 10:34, Psalms 82:1 & 6. Why do the author, or authors, of the Bible acknowledge that man accepted the existence of multiple Gods in this book? You should research this question yourself and see what you can find, because a lot of things, in other areas of our lives are affected by our acceptance or refutation of the mystery God idea, individually and collectively.

Some people believe that they have no control over any aspect of their lives because the Mysterious Unseen Force decides their fate, regardless of any of their decision. To a large amount of people, you can see how this small belief could sabotage a person's goal-setting ability, or sap their motivational power and confidence in their own abilities before their goals ever get put into motion.

If a person is introduced to a system of beliefs very early in their childhood, how much of what they believe could actually not be decided by them? Most of us are deprogramming ourselves from the beliefs of others just to find out our own likes and dislikes. Why do you tie your shoes the way that you do? It's because the first person that ever taught you how to tie your shoes, tied their shoes that way.

Beliefs work the same way, until we consciously evaluate them and reset our thoughts to assess what we want to keep and what has become a liability to us. This is the correct and only way to come to know self. One has to strip away the bullshit to expose what is real and then one can see what they are truly working with and decide what to build and what to destroy.

This process has to be done independent of any preconceived ideas and beliefs, or the process of beginning the scientific exploration of self, will be impossible without the trauma of feeling like a traitor, or insincere adherent to one's previous and present beliefs or ideas.

The biggest distinction between the 5, 10 and 85 percent, is that the 5 percenters are trained to become aware of the effects of action, as well as inaction. The 10 percenters are trained to take advantage of inactivity to further their agendas. The Nation of Gods and Earths is unique in the sense that it is not religious by nature. Member of the NGE do not pray in the tradition of most organized religions. Also, it is not obligatory or required by members of NGE. My personal observation has made me realize that people who pray are telling the world, through action, that they subscribe to the idea of something or someone higher than themselves being responsible for their success or failure, directly or indirectly, whether they think that way or not.

This is one reason that a person who prays can't be an example of the teachings of the NGE without contradicting themselves through his ways and actions once they bend and bow their head asking for salvation from something outside of themselves. There's only a small segment of the population of America who sympathize with some of the NGE teachings or the 120 lesson, but their actions over time are the true evidence of what's in their minds and hearts.

So called Nation members, who pray with no understanding, fail to put forth the effort to memorize and incorporate 120 LESSONS into their daily lives or indulge in fruitless endeavors, displaying their lack of confidence in the information that Father ALLAH (the man who founded the NGE) left in 1969, when he returned to the essence. I am a product of what he put in motion in 1964; and this makes me see myself as the verification of a determined idea, that he put in motion from his mental.

Simply put I'm one of the Father Allah's ideas that live on through another being. The Supreme Mathematics, are my family's exclusive intellectual property that he gifted to us along with our Supreme Alphabet. We use these 36 platinum keys to unlock the 120 Lessons in a way that no one outside of our family can.

The 10th degree in the Lost-Found Muslim Lesson No. 2 is more than just words on paper to us, just like all of the lessons that we're taught. Our elders picked these specific jewels for reasons, and they are the wisest scientists on the planet. In the Supreme Alphabet of the NGE, the 10th degree is justice. This makes the 10th degree, in the Lost-Found Muslim Lesson No.2 the justice degree being applied to the science of unlocking that degree with the Supreme Alphabet.

Justice is one's reward or penalty for their actions or deeds. According to the degree, the original man wasted trillions of years as a consequence of his ignorance, failing to look inside of himself, instead of outside of himself. The wisest men of that time (our forefathers) had to agree that there was no mystery God to begin to move forward again, advance civilization as a whole by mastering time again, ceasing to waste their collective energy and their resources searching for something that has never existed.

A mystery God doesn't have to be religiously related. It can be symbolic. For example, if you're a crack-head, your God is crack. If your life revolves around sex, that may be your mystery God that you're wasting your time and energy worshipping, when you could be doing more constructive things with your time and resources.

In closing, the use of the Supreme Mathematics and Supreme Alphabet to unlock the 120 Lessons is a technique that was developed by the founder of the Nation of Gods and Earths. It is impossible for a person to know and use the information in 120 Lessons without these tools to unlock these lessons. Simply reading them or casually skimming through the information will not get you to the same place as a person who has been properly taught by someone who is qualified as actively living out this way of life (culture). People, who aren't willing to change how they think or live will never, see any lasting benefits; no matter how many lessons they read or memorize. One has to become responsible for everything in their life and stop blaming things on forces or people outside of themselves. Don't focus on what you don't think you can affect. Start by focusing on what you know you that you can affect immediately, which is your belief system. Just sit down and think for five minutes about every question in this essay.

P.E.A.C.E.
Professor Born Supreme P.H.D. 7 ALLAH
Interior Cipher, Ohio
For Questions or Comments
Email: incarcerated7s@hotmail.com
or go to http://TheIncarcerated7sBlog.Blogspot.com

RECOMMENDED READING

1. *A History of God*, by Karen Armstrong
2. *Knowledge of Self - A Collection of Wisdom on the Science of Everything in Life,*
   By Dr. Supreme Understanding Allah, C'BS Alife Allah, Sunez Allah & Lord Jamar
3. *The Pedagogy of the Five Percent – A Doctoral Dissertation,* submitted to the Doctorate panel of Argosy University by Sujan Kumar Dass in 2006.

4. *2012 World Almanac,* for Information on the Planets, Solar System Elements and the Sun.
5. *The Nation of Gods and Earths 120 Lessons, Supreme Math and Supreme Alphabet.*

ZIG ZAG ZIG

TO ALL THE TRUE AND LIVING:

First, let me say that my Mind gravitates to the Knowledge, Wisdom and Understanding of the Real or True facts of this Universal galaxy. I greet you with the strongest, most powerful Universal word on the planet earth ... PEACE!!!

To my A-Alikes across the globe, this is your brother DIVINE SUPREME ZIG ZAG ZIG ALLAH. ALLAH is the Lord of all Worlds. ALLAH is one. He is the energy that pushes forward or pulls backward (Builds or Destroys). For example, when one is reading a book, the Energy force that moves you on to the next word, sentence or page is the power of ALLAH. In the same instance, he is the energy force that pulls you backward, if you choose to stop reading after the 1st chapter. I state this because some may say, "Now Cipher, the Devil made you stop out of Laziness b.u.t. one may have stopped after the 1st chapter to evaluate and/or analyze the material they just took in which is the power of ALLAH in travelling... PEACE!!

There are 3 Dimensions or Vision spheres. The 1st is: Understanding which is a form of identifying every person, place or thing. The second is Innstanding which gives the observer after observation his direction or guides him toward which way he will see. Third is Overstanding; this one is very important, powerful and potent. Sometimes it can be misread or mistaken for any of the 1st two b.u.t. its manifestation or simply drawing a thing up to its finest mist.

With this in Mind, I know the task will be difficult b.u.t. the journey will be blissful. Every step must be a calculated one!! Every conversation, look, statement or action by every person, place or thing must be critically evaluated. ALLAH is the ALL knowing. ALL EYE SEEING, so our duty is to evaluate all ways and actions in the lens of our refined 3rd Eye to utilize clear vision. This is the only way we will be able to see that object for what it is and not what is appears to be. Eye am blessed to be bestowed with the vision of Allah.

In the Book of Mathew in Bible, Chapter 27, Verse 16, it states: "Many will be called but only a few will be chosen". The "many who will be called" is the Original Asiatic Blackmen that travel successfully through the physical triple stages of darkness (womb) and show and prove that they are Allah by Nature. Those few that are chosen are the True and Living gods that take on the criticism, ridicule and difficulty in the journey to manifest our Divine way of life. This is ALLAH'S original plan!!!

Since we are speaking on the righteous way of life… Eye also sees the need to surface a strong and great concern to my A-Alikes that are manifesting Unlike ways and actions. Father Allah stated it best: "Keep it simple" so stop hiding behind the lessons!!! Stop coming in the Name of Allah and dealing dope or Gang Banging and definitely immediately cease claiming you are God having sex with those Homosexuals (boys)!!! If you come in the Name of Allah, just show that you are sincere period!! The Knowledge degree in the student enrollment Lesson states: Q) Who is the Original Man? The Answer is; The Original man is the Asiatic Blackman, the maker, the owner, the cream of the planet Earth, Father of Civilization, God of the Universe.

We as True and Living gods must uphold these 7 characteristics and manifest these Attributes fully. Let the content of our character radiate, as we travel through whatever land we plant our feet on. Before U move on, U have to ask yourself, what is My purpose for coming in the Name Allah? Some may say, "to become righteous" or "to cut the misery out of my life" which I can see as aright and exact; b.u.t. a lot of the so-called A-Alikes I've encountered, are not living out 120 Lessons or they feel that knowing that the Original man is God gives them the authority to do whatever they feel with their lives.

It seems as if they don't fully understand their responsibilities. For those of you reading this: Take this Culture as serious as life itself!! The wisdom Knowledge degree in the English C-Lesson No.1 (1-36) states, "Do you mean to tell me that some of the 17 million do not know that they are Muslims?" 1+7=8 so travel to the Build/Destroy degree in the same lesson. It says, "Because the Devil put fear in him when he was a little boy". This fear that's being spoken of will disappear once True Knowledge of self and the devil is obtained because one will Knowledge (1) God (7) Build or Destroy (8) depending upon if he is righteous or savage. Putting Wisdom before Knowledge is like the Woman being the Head of the Household – Emphatically Now Cipher!!! The True and Living does not Travel "21 Ciphers".

I was watching Television the other day and I saw the toxic effects of a medication being exposed indirectly. The medication was called "Avandia". Now, keep in Mind that this medication is supposedly for the treatment of diabetes in patients. What I saw in it however was that a substantial amount of people were having heart attacks on it. It was only after 57 people were documented as having died as a direct result of Avandia. Over a period of approximately 7 years that the FDA, felt that it might be "time" to take it off the shelves and re-evaluate the safety of this drug, Huh!!

The whole experience brought me to the Wisdom Build/Destroy Degree in the Lost and Found Muslim Lesson No.2. These are Yakubs people. They are all about population control, capital gain and putting fear in the people to make them believe a Mystery God. One of the biggest errors that the masses in society make is falling victim to misdirection. The common distractions that are taking place, such as having to work a job, pay bills, etc… are misguiding, misdirecting and misleading them from the truly valuable things in life like Family. There's an old saying that says that "People would rather believe a dressed up lie than the Naked Truth"!!!

What is "the Naked" truth? Who made "Avandia" anyways? The answer is: the Scientists!! The same scientists that Yakub controls who continue to teach trick-knowledge! If people actually believe in the Holy word like they claim, why is there so much chaos? Why are there people working jobs and hustling, if they feel or believe that a Mystery God will Bring them food, clothing and shelter? A lot of inconsistencies are right in plain sight but people would just rather not respect the truth.

This is why we as A-Alikes have to help each other move through this time, land and world to uplift our people with the Knowledge of themselves. Help me lead my people that are tormented, torn, down, defeated and misguided. With the proper guidance and Knowledge, we can evaluate, grow, blossom, reach, strengthen, travel, develop and advance into the most influential society civilization has ever experienced. It amazes me that after seeing evidence of the systematic slaughter of our brothers and sisters, the assassination of our leaders, (for being righteous) and the present use of the agents of Law enforcement to attack the Original people. There are actually some Black people that still think we can afford to waste any more time. I don't! Father Allah said to "Keep things simple as possible, so that everyone can understand it". So put away the elaborate tricks and free your mind from mental slavery. Once you do this, you will Understand that everything is a part of Arm, Leg, Leg, Arm, Head. Everything in the Universe exists with and within our bodies. It's real easy to say something or someone came from you but can you show and prove it?

As a people, Nation and culture, we must share one knowledge and bring our resources together. This is how we can begin to open doors for those in the future that will come behind us striving to move ahead. To all my comrades who wish to walk the path that this way of life puts you on right and exact; I ask you to teach with knowledge, love and energy that you have obtained. Also, Bless the Generation behind you … Each one teach one.

SINCERELY YOU'RE A-ALIKE

DIVINE SUPREME ZIG ZAG ZIG ALLAH
INTERIOR CIPHER, OHIO
Contact Info:
http://TheIncarcerated7sBlog.Blogspot.com
Email: Incarcerated7s@hotmail.com

AUTHOR'S NOTE

Divine Supreme was known on the streets of Cincinnati by the name "Drugs" prior to joining the Nation of Gods and Earths and borning a name that personifies his current level of awareness after he received the knowledge of Self in prison.

THE REFLECTION (WISDOM)

Reflection: 1. To throw back (heat, light or sound), 2.To mirror, 3. To think seriously, 4.To bring blame or reproach, esp. as a result of one's actions (Webster).

Wisdom is the necessary component that allows self to show who you Be (2) & what you're building with. What type of knowledge your building with shows & proves self to be truth (20). Wisdom is the reflection of the knowledge; it is also the application of what you know (Knowledge). Wisdom is also to "show", to make Knowledge Born (Known) at the speed of sound, which is 1,120 ft. per sec (which Borns Culture-Freedom). Through your Wisdom you show what culture you are representing. The culture of righteousness (Power Nation/God Culture) or the culture of devilment (Devils culture).

If self is building with righteous knowledge & a higher elevation of Knowledge, you won't have to shout it because your Wisdom (ways & actions) will shout it for you. The same goes for the blind, deaf and dumb (mentally dead). If your ways & actions be weak & wicked, then it shows & proves that you're dealing with a low degree of knowledge, or no knowledge at all. Wisdom is also the science of your word being bond regardless to whom or what. Zig-Zag-Zigging & looking back in antiquity (past), I have never heard of one God not keeping his word bond. Father Allah-As Allah had told them, "If they ever needed him all they had to do was come together". This is an example of Allah keeping his word to our nation. In the present time I Cee (3) God keeping His Word by holding fast to what he prescribes to others. Gods Wisdom is His Equality, it equality because it shows the connection between knowledge (1) & understanding (3). You must show & proves what you know & understand, if you don't or can't show & prove, this makes you a lip professor. And if you know & are not showing & proving, then you must be one of those in whose mind is a disease (Disease).

Note – Qu'ran Sura 2 Iyat 8:20 Speaks of the (Lip Professor). "The Gods who wrote this history elaborates on how the lip professor seeks to deceive Allah & the people. They seek to use the people, so they use weak Wisdom. Similarly, Sura 2 Iyat 10 (In their hearts is a disease, so Allah increased their disease & for them is a painful chastisement because they lie).

The Original Man who wrote that Qu'ran (His-story) is referring to those who use weak or low Wisdom in an attempt to come amongst the Gods for their heir own selfish reasons. Those reasons are & have been documented. (i.e. theft, of land, resources, physical labor, knowledge & to cause death mentally & physically). This is still happening today when the Lip Professors come amongst this nation (Power Percent) thinking they can get what they want & or take what they want in pretense to cure their dis ease that comes from their conditioning in devilment & the grafting of the Original Mind. Born-U-Truth, they don't come undetected by God, who can sense their dis ease by taking them through the hell which is a chastisement. God can sense their dis ease (i.e. ways & actions, wisdom, motivation, deceit) God can detect the lie (Low-Wisdom). This is the Justice of Allah only deals in truth & the truth come from right & exact knowledge (1), which proves & produces right & exact Wisdom (2).

Allah's Wisdom is not a profession from the lips, but rather a profession of who He be. Allah's Wisdom is to build an understanding for His knowledge to show & prove he be the King. W-I-S-D-O-M= 23-9-19-4-15-13=9=83=11= (2) Wisdom, the Ways & actions of I Self who is Divine in this Cipher standing as a Master.

MANIFESTED BY
SINCERE BUILD EMPIRICAL ALLAH
INTERIOR CIPHER, OHIO

AUTHOR'S NOTE

Sincere was known on the streets of Newark, Ohio, as IKE. He is currently working on authoring his 1st book from prison while fighting for his freedom in both state and federal courts from the prison's law library.

Contact Info: http://TheIncarcerated7sBlog.Blogspot.com

Email: Incarcerated7s@hotmail.com

10-15-2010

PEACE TO THE GODS!!!

I come in the name of Allah. Through a live air seed particle to a blood clot, I became the true and living as well as the actualized manifestation of the Supreme Mathematics. Knew God Allah borned himself as Arm, Leg, Leg, Arm, supreme Head!!! In this Celestial aspect I come as a representation of a world to come. Let's continue to Build a Righteous Nation Kings and Queens!!!

Today's Math is Knowledge Understanding all Being Born to Culture/Freedom. As Righteous teachers, One must know and Understand everything within their circumference. Circumference pertains to one's Community, family as well as one's self. The Blackmans Knowledge of himself qualifies him to civilize 85s with Great Orderly Direction and the benefits he acquires through the application of Knowledge and Understanding. Each one teaches one. When one know better they can then do better. When you know for a fact, who you are, (the 5% culture is the only culture that makes it obligatory that one be able to show and prove anything they profess) you become duty-bound and responsible to be who you are.

What this means is that if a man with children comes into the Understanding of who he is that will automatically cause him to realize that he is now the Father of small Nation (family/universe) that he has to civilize. To do so, his ways and actions must change to accommodate the change within his mental circumference. If he is unable or unwilling to perform his duties as a Father the Universal Laws of cause and effect will create a situation that will bring about desired or undesired change based on his ways and actions.

We can apply this same logic to individual Gods that know and understand their duty to teach our culture. If they are unable or unwilling to perform this duty they will be <u>forced</u> to choose their allegiances by a situation or circumstances!!! That's Universal Law at work and it always is. If every God were to cease doing their duty there would be no Allah Schools built in the Name of Allah because the whole foundation of Allah's World Manifest is the Education of the Babies. Teach, Leadership, Responsibility, Accountability, Manhood, Womanhood, purpose, discipline. These are just a few words that a poor righteous teacher has to acquaint themselves with. As for all the "Real" Enlighteners, Recognize the fact that a person has to do much more than recite 120 Lessons to earn the right to wear the Greatest and only Universal Flag of Islam!!! Without the Understanding of why we teach what we teach, those who can simply recite 120 Lessons will neglect key aspects of the Enlightenment process when they teach others and cause undesirable effects within the Nation Of Gods and Earths. A God should spark a revolution in the mind of those he speaks to or teaches <u>not</u> create parrots for personal vanity issues. We can't be victorious if we don't teach our Natural way of life properly. How can one build right and exact with improper blueprints and measurements? Take more time to study what's being done with the jewels that you give people. Make sure that the whole cipher knows and understands how to apply what they are learning and if they don't slow down until they can prove their intent and Understanding is sufficient to the wiser Gods.

For the newborns, defend the decisions and positions of the Enlighteners!! Why would you choose someone to teach you, if you're not going to trust their choices? You're getting taught something new that you don't know or Understand. If you did have all the answers, you wouldn't need Knowledge of Self. Stop wasting your time and everyone else's. If you don't want to listen and learn just leave the cipher instead of interfering with everyone else's elevation with foreign theories that you can't prove are correct in life situations. 9 times out of 10, you are seeking because you haven't borned the correct results up to now in your life. So open your mind and quit trying to sabotage those who are investing time into striving to Build Allah's Nation up with Bullshit. If any newborn sees another doing this you should be the one checking that person for your Enlightener so that he can spend his time doing his job instead of dealing with distraction. Love this Nation and go through Hell to make it Right!!!

                                    PEACE
                          KNEW GOD ALLAH
                    INTERIOR CIPHER, OHIO

For questions or comments – Email: Incarcerated7s@hotmail.com or go to http://TheIncarcerated7sBlog.Blogspot.com

GOD ESSAY PART 2

Compiled By:

Manifest Supreme Knowledge God Allah

INDEX

Introduction Page

"Who is the Original Man?"

Regardless of how learned we are in African history, how many kings can we name? Or contributions to civilizations we can cite, until we can correctly answer the question "who is God?" Then we will never cross the threshold of true knowledge of self.

To be concise – the Original Blackman is God. My last essay, I demonstrated to you different reasons pertaining to why the Original Man is God. This essay I am going to show and prove through scientific facts, Albert Einstein's $E = MC2$ equation that shows and prove how spirit goes into physical, Ancient Historical Facts, Anthropology Facts, Religious Philosophies, etc. that literally asserts the Black Man is God.

Now, with that said, let's get into the essay to see why I say the Black Man is the true and living Supreme Being, Almighty God on the planet earth and the heavens above.

Peace!

Manifest Supreme God-Allah

Atom or A.T.O.M.

The true and living God is Atom or A. llah T. he O. riginal M.an. What is an atom? Atoms are bundles of energy. They are the basic building blocks of all things that composed of several "subatomic particles."

In the nucleus (center) of the atom, there is the proton which is positive. The electron which is negative and the neutron which is neutral, it has no charge. It can go either way (positive or negative). Revolving around the nucleus (same as the planets revolve around the sun) are the electrons. The electrons travel close to, but never at the speed of light (186,000 m.p.sec) around the nucleus. There are an equal number of protons and electrons in the atom giving it a divine balance.

Now that understanding of the atom is understood, let's build on the subject more to see how it pertains to us (Asiatics) being God.

The first man in several traditions is therefore named atom or Adam or some variation thereof. (E.g. the creator God Atum was the first man in KMT).

Historian scholars George G.M. James in his book "Stolen Legacy", says the atom of science was named by the Greeks after this Egyptian God Man that evolved there from. He claimed that the name Atum means self- created; everything and nothing; combination of positive and negative principles; and the All.

The Supreme God of the Sumerians was called "Anu", which means in Sanskrit-atom. Charles Finch's book "Echoes of the Old Darkland", confirms that Adam is rooted in the Egyptian word Atum. The first man of the Greeks, Hebrew, Moabites, Hindus, Buddhists, Arabians, etc. was called Atum or Adam, or some form of it. God first existed as the uncreated, All father, which existed in the Black Womb (space), which was a hidden light. The Honorable Elijah Muhammad at the 1969 Savior's Day celebration said, "a little small atom of life rolling around in darkness ... building up itself ... just turning in darkness making its own self ... He is self- created."

The beginning consisted of a 3 stage darkness (or triple darkness). A force or power (energy) brought the light out of this darkness. One could not have come out of darkness unless force was in the darkness to bring it out. God as force (or energy) was already in the darkness, located in the triple darkness of the womb (space). At some point a primordial atom was created. (It's not recorded anywhere of Gods self- creation, why? Because God has no beginning or ending). The beginning was God creating self from atom of life. God is self- created because he alone created his own form or body from the atom. Our first Father formed and designed Himself, meaning God used the atoms (collectively) to build up his body. This motion was considered the beginning of time. If One was to do the science, you could easily see that the 1st act of creation narrated in Genesis 1:4, was Gods own emergence from the triple darkness as a brilliantly luminous man. The Genesis narrative describing Gods creation and vivification to give life of Adam is actually esoterically, a description of God's creation of and incarnation within His own Black body into Adam or Atum. Our 1st Father formed and designed Self. Think this over for a minute, a man being able to design His own form and He never seen another man before He saw Himself. This is pure power and by far a Supreme, Divine Design!

Being that God emerged from total darkness, naturally He would create Self totally dark. (It would seem logical right? Why would He create Himself any other color if Black was the only color in existence?) After Allah created Self, His 1st feeling was that of loneliness and His 1st desire was to reproduce Self. He began scientifically studying Self and found within Him a 2nd Self or the X chromosome. Allah the Original Man (A.T.O.M.)

proceeded to give that 2nd self an independent form. He had so much love and respect for womb (universe) from which He sprung, He put that same womb in the 2nd self that He created. Thus was born womb-man or woman. If you haven't figured out yet, the Original Black Woman is the 2nd self. Before the sun, moon, and stars, she was created.

A.T.O.M. and His Queen became the 1st Man and Woman or the progenitors of the whole human family. She is the co-creator with God. This is in accords with antiquity (ancient history). The law of Manu, after Brahma emerged out of darkness, he created from how own body "Vach", his female self. They were known as the 1st Man in woman in existence. Via, Vach, Brahma reproduces Self as "Vira" which means born again. The Sumerian Civilizations God was in the same form (man) and depicted as being Black. His name was Anu. He was the Father and King of all the Gods. His wife was Antu. The word An means man. All the other gods were his children Enki, Marduk, I Shtae, etc. who all were in human form. The Supreme God of Zarathustra (Zoroaster, an Iranian religion founded in 600 B.C. by Him) was named Ahura Mazda, and was depicted as a man with a dark blue/black body.

The best description of the whole self-creation of God is re-enacted during those 9 months a child develops in its mother womb. From one atom came millions of atoms to form the body of God. Just like we (humans) in our physical birth evolution in the womb of a woman, went from a single cell (atom) into trillions of cells that make up our physical body.

When pure spirit (energy) becomes matter (physical), this is a "fall" or descent. Thus, this first theological "fall of man" was the fall of spirit into matter. This information can be located in Eastern Philosophy, Christianity, Moorish Science Temple, etc. All it is-is spirit (energy) taking on a physical form. Now let's elaborate more on the topic of spirit going into a physical form…

E=MC2

"Who is that Mystery God?"

Albert Einstein, one of the greatest minds from out of the western hemisphere has ever produced, is most famous for his equation E=MC2, which revolutionized the world of physics. When properly understood, this mathematical equation provides the key to the nature of God.

A brief breakdown of E=MC 2:

The E stands for energy. All energy is conserved, meaning there is a set amount of energy in the universe and this amount is always constant. This energy cannot be destroyed and no energy can be created, it only transforms into different "types" (or solid, liquid or gas).

The symbol in mathematical terms mean equal (or: is). The M reference to the mass of an object. Mass and matter are used interchangeably here. Mass is defined as the measure of an objects' resistance to acceleration. When you try to push a big car, and can't, its resistance to your push is called mass.

The C 2 is the notation for the speed of light (186,000 m.p. sec) times itself. The significance of this famous equation is that it shows how energy and matter are the same.

When Energy (or E) is accelerated, it gains mass. The higher the velocity (rate of acceleration), the greater the mass. It becomes heavy. All objects and particles acquire mass when traveling at high velocities, e.g. a car gets heavier when in motion, than when it's parked. The C of the equation shows that there's an enormous amount of energy that goes into the creation of the tiniest particles of matter.

This is how matter is produced. All matter is frozen energy, and has an enormous amount of energy inherent within it. While this Energy is frozen in matter, it's called "rest energy". What scientists call energy, theologians call spirit. To me they are both the same. The key to converting energy (spirit) into matter (physical) according to E=MC2, is motion-high speed motion.

In the book of Genesis, when the spirit of God "moved", it began its process of materialization. As the spirit (energy) increased in velocity, it acquired more and more mass and became more dense. This is how energy becomes frozen in matter. Every particle of matter of imbued with an enormous amount of the energy which is frozen within it. This is why matter (phys.) is the conveyer of the spirit (energy), or better yet this is how God went from a single cell or atom to a physical form.

To be concise – THE ORIGINAL BLACKMAN IS GOD!!!

D.N.A.

What is DNA, and how does it pertain to the Original Blackman being God you ask?
Well, all DNA is only 10 atoms wide, Human DNA is 2 yards long (or 72 inches) and 10 atoms wide.

DNA's a chemical that can store information. Living organisms rely on the info stored in the DNA to control how they grow from a single cell to a complex, fully developed adult.

The DNA tells each cell what specialized features to develop (i.e. making 1 cell a nerve cell, another a liver cell, and so on).

DNA is the master molecule of life. It's the result of intelligence, not random chemical activity. Everything in life happens for a cause not because.

DNA is an abbreviation of the word "deoxyribonucleic acid". Deoxy is related to the Latin word "deus" meaning "god". Ribo is related to the Arabic (RB) written as "Rob" meaning, "the lord which nourishes a thing, stage by stage, during its evolutionary development towards perfection." Nucleic meaning center. Thus, DNA means that at the center of every cell there is God, the lord which nourishes stage by stage our human development towards the perfection of our being.

God is thus in our genetic make-up.

Christians and Muslims are not worshipping the Original God of their Religion!

"Can a Devil Fool a Muslim?"

It's a universally excepted by Christian theologians that God is an immaterial and formless spirit. Muslims don't call him "a spirit" but none the less will affirm that he is immaterial and formless, meaning God have neither a body nor substance.

Such an understanding of God does not derive from the Bible nor the Quran and Sunnah. But instead from later interpretations of these texts, who were influenced by Greek Philosophy, mainly by Plato and Aristotle who are largely responsible for the development of the idea of an immaterial and formless deity.

The God of the books (Bible, Quran) in their original language of Hebrew, and Greek for the Bible and Arabic for the Quran is neither immaterial nor formless. Like the Gods of the ancient Near East (KMT, Iraq, Turkey, Sumer, Canaan, Moabite, etc...), the God of the books is anthropomorphic (God possessing a human form) that is to say he has a form (morph) like that of a man (anthropos). The concept of a formless God was developed by Greek Philosopher who was repulsed by the anthropomorphic God's of the older Greek Pantheon (circle of God's).

Ionian Philosopher (a branch of Greek people named from Ion, 415 B.C., their legendary founder), Xenophanes (Greek Philosopher & Poet) was one of the earliest to reject the anthropomorphism and suggested God should be non-anthropomorphic.

Plato (428-348 B.C.) is pretty much the author of the Mystery God. Before Him it was recognized that all things, including spirit, was in some since material. The Greeks gave to the monotheistic (the doctrine that there's only one God), religions in particular, God, as a formless spirit. The Semitic tradition (Judaism, Christianity and Islam) possessed no such understanding prior to contact with Hellenes (daughter of Zeus and Leda – Greeks) or carriers of Hellenistic culture. This is why God of the Bible is 10 times explicitly called a man.

The God of the Hebrew Bible is without question a man. He has a human form, he has feelings (jealousy, anger, happy, etc…) It was the church fathers – Clement of Alexandria (A.D. 216), Origen (A.D. 185-253) and St. Augustine (A.D.354-439) who successfully brought the God of the Greek Philosophers (mystery God) into the churches. The writings of St. Augustine demonstrate that the indigenous Christians of N. Africa rejected the immaterial God of the Greeks and instead affirmed the anthrop. God of the Bible.

The church today therefore owes it – God to Plato and Aristotle, not to Jesus. Paulsen, D.L., book "Early Christians Belief in a Corporeal Deity" 1990, asserts: "the view that God is without body or parts …of Christians… in the beginning it was not so… the Christians or at least the first 3 centuries of the current era believed God to be corporeal (bodily; immaterial)."

St. Augustine 9A.D.354-430) born in Africa, is one of the pivotal fathers of the church. Besides Paul, his many works have influenced Christian though more than anyone else. St. Augustine said the reason it took Him so long to accept Christianity was because Christians, including his mom Monica, believed that God was in the form of man. It's evident that, up until Augustine, there were 2 strands of Christianity exclusive to each other.1 in Africa where it spread from the Apostles first, and one in Europe, interpreted via the Greeks. The African Christians God was in the form of Man. Even though St. Augustine was from N. Africa, He denounced the God of His native land, and embraced the God of a foreign land (Milan, Italy, 386

A.D.). The Egyptian Christians believed god the father to have, from the beginning, revealed himself in human form. The Africans held on to this belief all the way to the 5th Century. In the Book "the Christian Fathers" by London: Hodder and Stoughton, 1966, asserted: "the image of God which was not drawn exclusively or even primarily from scripture. Its primary source was the Graeco-Roman. It's not the description of God...from the bible... it comes straight from Patonic (Plato) tradition ..."

Noble Drew-Ali (Moorish Science) once said that "We strayed after the Gods or Europe of whom we knew nothing." I think it's evident his assertion was and is true from reading this passage. God, according to Muslims theologians is absolutely other (different) than immaterial. The Mystery God (formless God that can't be explained thoroughly) does not derive from the Quran or Sunna, but derives from later Greek inspired interpretations of the Quran and Sunnah. The Sunnah specifically refers to God as a person with a body. (Shakhs) The early Muslims understanding of these passages were to be taken literally as a description of God. It was non-Sunni Muslim groups, such as the "Jahmiyya and Mu'tazila, influenced by Greek Philosophy who rejected the anthrop. God of the Quran and Sunnah.

The Semitic and ancient near easterners (were Prophet Muhammad and Al-Islam derived from) all embraced anthropomorphism. The 99 attributes of Allah can be easily descriptions of a physical man.

Islams are most notorious advocates of anthrop. All were the 2 Brothers: Mugatil bi Sulayman (d.767) and Dawud al-Jawaribi, who affirmed that God was flesh and blood, human body and also affirmed that nothing, is like Him nor is He like anything else."

Mugatil said: "God is body in the form of a man, with flesh, blood, hair and bones, plus a hand, a foot, head, and eyes ..."from the book: Al Ash' Ari, Magalat al-

Islamiyyin. 152 f. on Mugatil. Another Muslim from the ancient era affirmed this assertion by the name of Muhammad b. Sa'dun better known as Abu Amin al-Qurah (d.524/1130), a famous and alusian theologian. He said, "In form however, God is like you and me..." cited by Goldziher, Intro., 93. Surah 38:75 speaks on Allah's 2 hands. 5:64 speaks on Allah having 2 hands again.20:39 speaks on Allah having eyes. 17:1 speaks on His ears and eyes. 55:2 speaks on him having a face. Hadiths speaks on Muhammad not only seeing God in his own vision (physical form), but he felt his hand and fingertips. The Sunnah even describes Allah as having human body parts including a chest, feet, hands, eyes, arms, elbows, lions, fingers, palm, etc. The concept of God as presented by the Muslim world today, as being invisible, incorporeal deity, is a foreign thing to Islam as laid down by the Quran and Sunnah. It's an import from Greece. Scripture calls God a divine man throughout the Quran. He is referred to as gibbor (mighty man), shakhs (personal/man), and shabb (young man). It seems to me that the Nation of Gods and Earths (God bodies) therefore represent a turning back to the God of Old, not the Greek God of the new. Blacks are the direct descendants of the original God who created everything in existence, making us the Original Man, or Gods of the planet earth.

The Near East's Black God

"Why did we take Jerusalem from the Devil?"

The Torah had multiple authors who wrote the books at different times and places (between 1000 B.C. - 586 B.C.) God of the Torah was a Black God. The Hebrew religion is a reworking of ancient KMT's wisdom.

When the opening verse speaks on God's creation, the heavens and earth in the Hebrew text (or in its original language) literally speaks of Gods shaping the pre-existing material into the heavens and the earth. One of the things that were shaped was the light that emerged from darkness. It's clearly unrelated to the sun, which wasn't created until day 4 according to scriptures. The light was God manifesting self (body) from the dark. Day 1 was thus the beginning of Gods visible corporeal man. He existed before day 1, but as a creative breath in the darkness.

According to esoteric tradition of Judaism, called Kabbalah, said the 6th day of creation is Gods self-revelation and His unfolding. Genesis 1 does not purport (to profess or claim) to describe the absolute beginning of things. I say that because before creation actually began on Day1, God already existed in the 3 fold darkness, which existed before the book of Genesis' accounts of things. Creation never began, it always been here.

On day 1, God's luminous form emerged from darkness, on day 6 that form incarnated in a black material body called Adam. In the Quran, the angels were made to bow down to Adam. Adam's body was made from Black clay or dust. Keep in mind science asserts the sun and planets was created from the unity of gases and "dust" via gravity.

God used the subsequent (coming later) atoms that developed from the first atom to build up his God-Body over time into a Divine Man we see today. God wrapped His luminous body in the black matter from which He initially emerged. Thus was born the BLACK GOD!

God has many names/titles but regardless of the form of semantics, they all are referencing to the same one reality. You may hear Him called Allah, energy, Holy Spirit, the breath, etc. It's all one in the same and from it sprung both matter and spirit. It's the same way that ice/steam is different forms of water. Energy revealed its form through spirit. Spirit revealed itself through matter.

Egyptian Theophile Obenga observes "the opposition between matter and spirit; does not exist in ancient Egypt where nature forms a whole matter and consciousness intermingled." The matter spirit opposition is much more recent. The civilizations of antiquity understanding of God was that He is spiritual manifested or conveyed Himself through the body of the Black Man. The Indus Valley Civilization, which is a sub-continent of India, was a great civilization and religious center established by the Black Man and Woman. They go back to 6-7,000 B.C. and reached its apex in Mohenjo-Daro around 3,000 to 2,500 B.C. They, as well knew God to be a Black Man.

Conclusion

"Why does the devil teach that a mystery God brings all this?"

The world in which we live is manufactured based off a lie designed by corrupt, devilish grafted minds. Back when we were world rulers (before the mystery God) we built unremarkable civilizations. Now since we been brain washed into "believing and putting all our faith into a mystery God to do those same things we did back then, we now can't even build a Tee Pee for ourselves, by ourselves (figuratively speaking). Back when we knew we were the true living Gods, our creations was unlimited, and history shows and proves this. With the mystery God ideology, our thoughts are now limited to a certain depth. The only how we as original people can become liberated is by returning back to our original state of mind (God), not this subservient, grafted state of mind that were in now (something foreign like the mystery God).

Any student of world religion or science should immediately see that the NGE's basic teachings are in complete agreement with the history of origins, as presented by the ancient religious literature and history texts, of the Black Man and Woman found all over the Earth. The knowledge of God has been a closely guarded secret for thousands of years. The secret was held by the mysterious and secret societies. The fact that the Original Black Man is God is not a new science. It was only being held amongst the select-elect until the advent of October 10th, 1964 A.D. in Harlem, N.Y. To a certain extent I can understand why some decided to keep the knowledge of God a secret. From observing, I seen how some people have taken the knowledge that the Black Man is God and either ended up becoming Black Devils or made Devils in the process (teaching their students). But there is no excuse for with- holding knowledge to the masses. With holding knowledge is a sin because it goes against the advancement of the human family. The reason were in the state that were in today is due to those with holding knowledge.

The knowledge of God is the highest form of Knowledge. Many get the knowledge without receiving a complete understanding of it, which is the reason there are "Black Devils". Understanding is the best part of knowledge and wisdom and understanding. The difference between God and man is that God is an immortal man and man is a mortal God. Man is a God whose 3rd eye is closed. God is a man whose 3rd eye is open.

If Prophet Muhammad was not "un-Islamic" for saying god came to him in the form of a man, then why should the Black Gods (NGE) be condemned for saying the same? Going back into the state of God, occurs not by memorizing degrees, or some form of teachings, but by years of discipline, self- denial, and spiritual development. Our lessons are only tools in assisting one with going back to our rightful places. It's not always about knowing something; it's about understanding and applying what you know.

Until next time we build, let this sit …

"What will be your rewards in regards to the destruction of the Devil?" Peace and Happiness!

Peace!

Manifest Supreme God-Allah

Sept. 20, 2008 A.D.

2:09 p.m.

References:

1. 120 Lessons
2. George G.M. James, "Stolen Legacy"
3. Charles Finch, "Echoes of the Old World"
4. 1969 NOI'S Savior Day Celebration-Elijah Muh. Speech
5. Godfrey Higgins, "Anacalypsis"
6. The Torah
7. Zechariah Sitchin, "The 12th Planet"
8. Rev. Ishakamusa Barashango, "God, the Bible, and the Black Man's Destiny"
9. "Essay on Egyptologist," by Theophile Obehga
10. Albert Einstein's E=MC 2 Equation
11. Writings of St. Augustine
12. "Early Christian Belief in a Corporeal Deity," by Paulsen, D.L.
13. "The Christian Fathers," by London: Hodder and Stoughton
14. "The Truth of God," by True Islam
15. "The Book of God," by True Islam
16. "The Moorish Holy Koran," by Noble Drew-Ali
17. Al Bakari-Hadith
18. Quran and Bible
19. Conclusion: Based on my personal thoughts

Contact Info:
http://TheIncarcerated7sBlog.Blogspot.com

Email: Incarcerated7s@hotmail.com

AUTHOR'S NOTE: MANIFEST SUPREME is a seasoned author and prolific Nation of Gods and Earths Enlightener. He recently wrote his 1st book called, "THE FIVE PERCENT NATION NEOPHYTES," which is available at M.A.P. CO., P.O. BOX 7430, MINNEAPOLIS, MN. 55407 for $16. Also, he is a writer in a book entitled, "KNOWLEDGE OF SELF-A COLLECTION OF WISDOM ON THE SCIENCE OF EVERYTHING IN LIFE," by Dr. SUPREME UNDERSTANDING ALLAH, SUNEZ ALLAH, CBS A LIFE ALLAH and LORD JAMAR (Manifest's article entitled, "THE TRUEAND LIVING" is on p.97 of that book) He is also the REGIONAL REPRESENT-ative for the Incarcerated citizens of the Nation of Gods and Earths in Region 7. He was appointed to that position by Religion 7 elder C-LATIFF ALLAH before he retired to the essence in June 2012.

From The Electromagnet Mind Of
Justice Universe Now Equality
Professor Born Supreme P.H.D. 7 Allah
Knowledge Understanding

A.W.M. YR 48

THE MASTERS CULTURE: AN INDEPTH ANALYSIS

Peace to the Nation Of Gods and Earths and all those that are actively seeking the Knowledge of themselves. Today's date in Gregorian calendar is June, 13, 2011. In the Nation Of Gods and Earths teachings called, THE SUPREME MATHEMATICS, Today's Mathematics is Knowledge (1) Understanding (3) all being Born to Culture/Freedom (4) (1+3=4). Applying my own Understanding to Today's Mathematics, I see this days Math as evidence that once the Blackman obtains the Knowledge and Understanding of how to restore himself to the position of one who controls the goods and resources of the World, only then can he truly express his culture freely on a Collective level.

In my eyes, even individual freedoms come in degrees and are earned just like the degrees in The Nation Of Gods and Earths Lessons. We earn our degrees 1 at a time by demonstrating that we are proficient at reciting them and applying them to life situations, as well as proving the historical accuracy or inaccuracy, of each degree through painstaking analysis and research. Not everyone who comes seeking to earn the right to wear the Universal Flag of Islam is patient enough to go through the required training. A lot of people come with good intentions but end up realizing that they are not ready for the labors required by those who guard our most sacred way of life.

The Elders who designed the structure of our curriculum Understood that it would be necessary to put certain safeguards in place to protect the integrity of what they established in 1964. They also knew that once they were not physically around anymore that those who did not have good intentions might attempt to infiltrate our Schools and dilute or graft what the Elders had put in motion.

To prevent this from ever happening, each God coming into the fold would have to show and prove his proficiency and sincerity by teaching civilizations human families without any form of monetary incentive. The sacrifice of time and effort was one of a few ways that they had learned to judge a person's sincerity level; since they knew that an insincere person most likely would never stick around to complete the basic requirements they had mandated.

Only after a person could recite and born an Understanding of every degree in The Nation of Gods and Earths Lesson called 120 Lessons was a person qualified to wear the Universal Flag of Islam. Those who took it lightly were quickly taught the weight of playing God and ran from amongst those who had dedicated their lives to the Culture. People either went home humiliated and studied to redeem themselves at a future encounter or removed the Flag from their body never to wear it again.

The tradition of vetting out the fakers is not a creation of the Nation of Gods and Earths. When one does research it's easy to find many examples in history that document this same practice in earlier societies. For example, the 1st degree in the Lost and Found Muslim Lesson No.2 of the Nation Of Islam explains the reason that the earliest documented Caucasians were put on the worst part of the Planet. This degree also explains why the 1st Caucasians were forbidden from accessing certain geographical locations in what is now the Middle East.

In the particular historical account, the Caucasians were ran across the Hot Arabian Desert after being given multiple opportunities to socialize with the indigenous people of that Region and committing acts that proved that they could not be trusted to act civil. Once the people of that region realized that they would not be able to teach them how to conduct themselves in a civilized way long term, the indigenous people of that Region were forced to restrict the Caucasians to the Hillsides of EUROPE. (4/114)

This pattern of behavior was repeated again as the Lost and Found Muslim Lessons Degrees progress until Muhamed IBN Abdullah learned that he couldn't reform them and decided that they had to be Murdered (10/114). This decision was made after he allowed some of them to come amongst his people and do some trading after they had studied how to do like them for 35-50 years (9/114).

This is an example of why Freedom has to be given in degrees to certain people. The same way that the Caucasian people of that time period were abusive of the freedom they had. People of today can and will abuse their access to the babies and the Lessons if they are just allowed to come amongst our Ciphers, without being observed and investigated. It's the equivalent of just allowing strangers to babysit your children!!! We as Gods and Earths have to start investigating unfamiliar people that start lingering around or seem over anxious for our Jewels. We also have to question people, as we give them Knowledge from our Books of Life. A person shouldn't mind telling you why they want a specific piece of information you have and it's not impolite to ask them, "Why do you want this Knowledge?" and watch their reaction. This was common practice back in the day.

In these days and time, we have to renew our knowledge of the practices and techniques of the Elders when they taught this Knowledge. Some of their techniques were unorthodox but highly effective while others may have been effective for that time but primitive for these days and times. One will never know unless he or she takes the time to research some of the Greats who taught this Knowledge on the Street in the 1960's and 1970's, such as PRINCE ALLAH, C-LATIFF ALLAH and others. PRINCE ALLAH (Allah's 3rd Born of the 1st 9 Born) created a technique that he used to teach the illiterate students he taught. It's amazing that he was able to teach the LESSONS to people who couldn't even read. Our culture calls it teaching MOUTH TO EAR. It's a technique in which a student is taught strictly through oral presentation and everyday life examples (ACTION TO EYE). These students would go on to completely memorize and internalize 120 Lessons this way and then could be taught how to recognize the words on paper, by comparing what they had memorized to what was written. See what I mean about the benefits of studying the methods of the Elders!! The good thing is that a lot of the methods and techniques of the Elders, as well as their personal philosophical views are preserved in writings on the Internet or at various Nation of Gods and Earths Learning Institutions. A few of the Elders are still alive today and write in the FIVE PERCENTER NEWSPAPER, the CREAM CITY NEWSPAPER and a few other publications of the culture.

In closing, today's Mathematics is Master; all being Born to Divine or Destroy, in the SUPREME ALPHABET of the NATION OF GODSAND EARTHS. A Master is one who knows and Understands everything within his circumference and one's culture, must be Divine meaning pure and refined in order to Destroy all Negativity. Peace to the Enlighteners who teach civilization for free and to all those who sacrificed their lives, so that I could have what so many of us take for granted.

Proper Education Always Corrects Errors
Professor Born Supreme P.H.D. 7 Allah

From The Electromagnetic Mind Of
Master Allah Why
Professor Born Supreme P.H.D. 7 Allah
Wisdom Power/Refinement

A.W.M. YR 47

WISDOM POWER/REFINEMENT

Today's Mathematics manifests as Wisdom Power/Refinement for this days rotation. It's all being Born to GOD. To Wisdom ones Power is to put that power in Motion from a potential State of being. This is how the process of Refinement is initiated. Refinement can't and will never take place without action. Merely thinking about how you should REFINE a thing is indeed a start b.u.t. that is only the 1st (Knowledge) step in the process. As Gods, we teach our CULTURE best by our Wisdom/ways and acts in our daily interactions with others. A person may learn best seeing the POWER of REFINEMENT by observing you REFINE something instead of hearing you quote the words of the degree in the Supreme Mathematics. One of the best Questions you can ask yourself and the GODS in your Cipher are: "HOW ARE YOU LIVING OUT TODAY'S MATHEMATICS THIS ROTATION?"

We show and prove that we are God's by strategically using the POWER inside of us to REFINE any behavior that is counterproductive to our growth and development as individuals and as a nation. We come to the people as the people to show them that it is possible for them to WISDOM their own POWER and REFINE anything that they decide needs Refinement when we do so ourselves.

We aren't some "Holier than Thou" types who never get into Negative situations or fall victim to vices that we may develop. We show and prove our POWER by overcoming these various obstacles and challenges in our own lives as the evidence of what's possible, when we apply Mathematics.

Now that we have identified some of the problems and mechanics, let's manifest solutions and move from the Knowledge to the Wisdom or application stage. 1 of many ways to live out Today's Math is to start with small steps instead of setting yourself up for disappointment by making an attempt to solve all the problems of the world in 1 day with 1 move. You can WISDOM (2) your POWER (5) to REFINE a thing today with something simple like abstaining from cursing for this rotation or abstaining from eating just for today as do-able examples. Abstaining from any habit that you see as counterproductive can be your own individual way of living out Today's degree in the Supreme Mathematics in your own Life/Cipher.

These examples also are a creative way of showing 85ers the POWER of our CULTURE. They will surely see that you are serious about this way of life. If you are the only one not eating at the table - you explain why, when they ask. Keep in mind that your sincerity may be the spark that motivates the next man or woman to seek the Knowledge of Self and realize themselves to be God or Earth.

PEACE
Professor Born Supreme P.H.D. 7 Allah

Contact Info:
http://TheIncarcerated7sBlog.Blogspot.com
Email: Incarcerated7s@hotmail.com

HOW TO BEGIN TEACHING

Before a person even receives the Supreme Math, the Enlightener (who must be able to recite 120 lessons by heart and explain the history of the NGE on a basic level) should wait at least 6 weeks. During this time, He has to spend time examining the potential newborns' ways and actions as well as his philosophies, social interactions, learning abilities and responses to criticism to know if his teaching style is compatible with the personality of the potential attribute.

One of the best ways to start is by giving the said individual books about specific topics and then discussing the contents with the person to see how they process information. The Enlightener, also will want to see how the person interacts with the cipher he's (The Enlightener) in. Is the person disruptive, rude, and inconsiderate of how the other Gods view things? These are things you'll want to investigate early in order to know if the person is Community oriented or self-centered. A lot of people can't function in groups effectively based on their past family experiences. So wise elevators have to study things over time and the cipher is the best place to get a lot of good feedback.

The other gods should be told that the person is interested in Building immediately once the person makes it known because 1 or more Gods may already know the person from past dealings. All this should be asked and discussed before the person is even allowed to attend a build session as an observer.

The ideal situation is to take it on as a family responsibility so that the person will always be interacting with one of the Gods in the 6 weeks. This way everyone will be able to observe his ways and actions over that period of time and Build with each other about his progression.

After the 6 weeks, the cipher should vote as to if the person is ready for the next step or not. If so the next step for the person is the 3 day fast. This is not like the Muslim Ramadan Fast. The NGE fast is 3 days with NO FOOD AT ALL (Liquids are permitted) Every person coming into the fold as an Active Citizen must do the fast and be witnessed as having complete it by one or more of the gods in the cipher he is entering, that have knowledge of 120 Lessons.

The newborn is now to receive a set of "The Self Government Rules and Principles" and after they are explained agree to accept them as law in resolving disputes among the Gods in his immediate cipher. He should also receive the meeting/cipher protocols, so he understands how the cipher functions right and exact. This particular social model is for the Gods/Earths laying the foundation in Prison, if it's not structured yet or the structure isn't working. Refer to the actual Self Government Laws and Principles 120 Class and Meeting/Cipher Protocols for the actual details (see attached documents).

It's encouraged that the newborns (as well as anyone who hasn't already) take on a righteous Attribute as a serious step. Also, do not tell the potential builder that if he waits 6 weeks, he'll go to the next level etc… This idea is for The Enlightener to have the information as a measuring tool; in 6 weeks a person will lose interest, if they aren't sincere or they won't be able to keep up any façade they're putting on for that long. Especially if they don't know how long they have to fake it. So be wise and use this information wisely to protect your culture and avoid a lot of bullshit. 6 is the minimum it can be (longer if need be) before you a give a person our Math and include them in the decision making of the Cipher.

Complied by Professor Born Supreme P.H.D. 7 Allah

Contact Info:
http://TheIncarcerated7sBlog.Blogspot.com
Email: Incarcerated7s@hotmail.com

Source: Street Academy of Cream City

GENERAL MEETING
PROTOCALS

- Open up by stating the date and number of the meeting (this is very important for your records).

- Then proceed to ask the secretary to read the last MEETING'S MINUTES, (or whoever is designated to record minutes can read the last meetings minutes).

- After the minutes from last meeting are read, ask are there any questions about last meeting's minutes.

- GENERAL REPORT: The general report includes reports from other cities and states. Report must include report on your own city (things going on or plans to do something). If there are any questions or statements on general report keeping, asking until there are no more questions or statements.

- COMMITTEE REPORTS: Each CHAIRPERSON of each STANDING* COMMITTEE makes their committee report (*standing means, ongoing committees, example: 120, finance, earths, etc.). After each committee report ask if there are any questions, or statements on committee reports. (Ask until there are no more questions or statements)

- ASK IF THERE ARE ANY QUESTIONS OR STATEMENTS ON ANYTHING. EVEN IF IT WAS NOT ON THE AGENDA. (THIS ISVERY IMPORTANT! AT THIS TIME ANY PROBLEMS THAT NEED TO BE ADDRESSED CAN BE ADDRESSED, AND EVERYONE HAS A RIGHT TO BE HEARD ON ANY ISSUE)

- THE DAY'S MATHEMATICS AND DEGREES*

  - *(Those present build on the day's math and degrees) Chairperson can assign math and degrees to be built on. 1-10, 1-36, 1-14, AF, or SF, or a combination of all or any of them, after math is built on.

- *(Recommendation: Let those who will build, know what degrees they will build on before the meeting begins).

  - Also as a strong recommendation, a new agenda should be made and written out for each meeting, as opposed to going off of the same agenda from the previous meeting.

Source: Street Academy of Cream City

Protocols for 120 Classes*

1. Chairman opens class with peace, and then states the class number, the year, month and date.

2. Chairman builds on their name and that day's mathematics (That day's degree is optional).

2a. the participants within the class build on their name and that day's mathematics.

2b. the new participants must state their name, who and where they received this
    knowledge.

3. After all participants have given their introduction, the chairman then gives a summary and conclusion of that phase of class. (Summary and conclusion consist of building on the class number, the month, the day's mathematics, etc.)

4. Chairman states that the next phase is when we have the participant who is on the lowest degree, to state the degree that they are on and quote the degree before that, then give their understanding.

4a. All participants must state the degree they know, so the chairman will know where
    There at in 120.

5. The chairman asks if there are any questions or comments on their statements, after each participant has finished quoting and giving their understanding.

5a. All participants within the class at higher degrees have an opportunity to ask the Participant questions on their degree.

6. After all participants have gone through their degrees, the chairman asks the Co-Chairman **if they have any questions for any participants.

7. If there are no further questions or comments, the chairman asks the participants if they would like to advance to their next degree. (The Chairman and Co-Chairman make the decision of whether they should receive their next degree).

8. After each participant of the said ability has received their degree, the chairman asks them to read the degree they received for the purpose of clarity.

9. After all participants have received their degrees, the time remaining is open or any other questions or comments.

10. Chairman closes class at proper time.

**Co-Chairman are those who knowledge 120 →
*Class should not last longer than 90 minutes.

Contact Info:
http://TheIncarcerated7sBlog.Blogspot.com
Email: Incarcerated7s@hotmail.com

Source: National Office of Cultural Affairs

SELF GOVERNMENT LAWS AND PRINCIPLES

Supreme Revelation of love! Allah's wisdom on basic principles, of Activation within the Power percent nation, with unique design to preserve and maintain for the trust of our existence, is to establish universal Government upon the foundation of peace. On the day of Wisdom during the course of parliament procedures, the God Nation as one, agreed to endorse the following procedures and principles of law to act as god rules. Also, Born through the order of Truth, to all hereafter, shall be enforced, as law in the regulation of Activation of the Power Percent Nation for all to see.

1st LAW – each being representing the purpose for his existence through an attribute of Allah shall perform his duties according to the degree of Born or leave Allah's world.

2nd LAW – no one shall participate in the decision making procedures of the God Nation, without first being recognized by the God Nation as an active attribute in the furtherance of growth and development, of the Nation as a whole.

3rd LAW – no individual coming in the name of Allah shall dare play god. His word shall be his bond and failure to fulfill the commitment of his word giving shall cause penalty to be forced upon him.

4th LAW – it shall be incumbent upon each and every individual active within the God Nations cipher to record to memory the teachings of Life (Knowledge Wisdom Cipher). The order shall be no less than a degree a day.

5th LAW – **Every** individual expressing the will to add to the God Nation shall be subject to an examination by a screening board. Elected, selected and approved by the God Nation as whole.

6TH LAW – **If** an individual is to be subjected to the degree of exile, the Nation shall hold a parliament to discuss before the whole the cause there and define the terms of exile to which the individual subjected shall be ordered to comply with.

7th LAW – **Where** discussions occur between two individuals and each has been recognized by the God Nation as God and the discrepancies are restored between the two, neither shall serve physical justice to the other, but bring the degree of discrepancy before the Nation for resolution.

8th LAW – It shall be **the responsibility of each** God individual and one collective upon detention of lying or backstabbing by one or more within the bounds of the righteous to bring such degree to the attention of the cipher.

9th LAW – **No individual in the name of Allah** shall activate within a potential state of his being ill thought of hate, lust, envy, or any negative degree against another attribute of Allah without bringing it to the attention of that individual person or the nation as a whole for resolution. 10th LAW – **Each** individual shall be forwarded to any god within the cipher (of his choosing) an address of any individual to contact in the case of emergency.

11th LAW – **Word is Bond** and must be enforced by all those in knowledge of the law or degree of self.

12th LAW – **No one** shall be exempt from contributing to Zakat.

13th LAW – **All** gods shall give at least Justice minutes of and from his daily schedule toward an examination to determine for elevating his reading comprehension ability, the amount of equality to be given by the nation to make up for that which is lacking of that individual.

14th LAW – **Respect** each brothers greeting of Peace and extend the same.

15th LAW – fast understanding, days before parliament.

16th LAW – **All** who comes in the name of Allah shall be enforced upon the principles and order of law Governing the Power Percent Cipher here at this part of the planet and any other refinement matters relating to our policies.

There shall be no amendments to our universal self - governing laws, Hell constructs upon the foundation of imperfection. In the parliament, there is peace which is the absence of confusion. Peace is not a password so stop and build. It can hold on to your knowledge and save your life.

A) Education Department

B) Economic Department
C) Physical Education Department
D) Nation Representation
E) Security Department

These functions are to establish our growth and development as a nation. If done right and exact on the security, the best effect for us is to set it up in a form of business and hire ourselves out as security guards that can be our job and training at the same time.

Contact Info:
http://TheIncarcerated7sBlog.Blogspot.com
Email: Incarcerated7s@hotmail.com

IN THE NAMEOF MANIFEST SUPREME #1 GOD ALLAH

Q: "WHY DOES MUHAMMED MAKE THE DEVIL STUDY FOR 35 – 50 YEARS BEFORE HE CAN CALL HIMSELF A MUSLIM SON AND WEAR THE GREATEST AND ONLY FLAG KNOWN IN THE UNIVERSE AND WHY MUST HE ADD A SWORD TO THE UPPER PART OF THE HOLY AND GREATEST UNIVERSAL FLAG OF ISLAM?"

ANSWER

"So that he can clean himself up" … He cleans himself up from the mental and physical state of cave-ism as well as the savageness they've accumulated within the 2000 years of living without the knowledge, wisdom, understanding, culture, and refinement in which caused them (like it would anyone else) to live a beastly life. The way of U.S. (Universal Saviors) is to civilize them or anyone around us, as long as they desire and strive for love, peace, and happiness which the end result is righteousness.

"A Muslim do not love the devil regardless of how long he studies" … We don't love the Devil because being that we made the Dirty – Evil, we (wise educators) understood / understand his nature, as well as his weak ways and actions being that he was grafted from the Original Man. Study What? Well, his grafted mind had to be refined from the devilment he was taught at birth. He had to study Islam (the science) under the enlightenment of the Prophet Muhammad. Their 1st civilized teachings derived from their civilizer who was the Prophet Musa (Moses) in the Torah in which due to this teaching they adopted the attributes "Hebrew' and "Jew" (short for Judah) meaning they studied and learned to do like the

Original man as well. It was due to the 10% holdings knowledge hostage all throughout Europe (just like during the Renaissance Era) that the Devils became in need of another "Divine Revelation" after Musa.

Much of the History inside of books that we read today was written and researched during a Victorian Age of High Christianity. This was done during a time when every theory or fact was bent toward a Christian point of view. The actual Religion known as Christianity by most is a grafted form of ancient African (Asiatic) History. Many historians, artists, builders, politicians, lay people etc... wanted to pass the truth on (that the Blackman is God and that there is no Mystery God b.u.t. they couldn't safely do it due to the powers that be (the 10%). This brought about the need to devise ciphers, codes, and symbolism for their own kind and future generations to decipher. Free-Masons took the Knowledge and wisdom from the Original Man in the East and brought it back to Europe and like now they would built on it in seclusion and secrecy.

"After he devoted 35 – 50 years trying to learn to do like the Original Man, he could come amongst us and do some trading" … The devil goes through many understudies to clean himself up mentally as well as physically which then enables him to get and understanding (3) of the power (5) of our teachings as well as see the power (5) of the cipher (0) so that he can Build (8) with the power positively and destroy the negative powers (5) Yakub taught him from birth. Through these studies, he gets the knowledge (1) and understanding (3) of our internal existence (Allah – God) as well as our righteous way of life = Culture (4) 35 + 50 = 85; 8 + 5 = 13;   1+ 3 = 4 or Culture/Freedom. The trade was the trading post of Knowledge and commodities such as spices, herbs, silks, metals, diamonds etc... in which is only grown or made in the best part back then. The trade aspect was to get closer to the root or best part due to its natural resources.

We (World Enlighteners) gave him civilized teachings from one of our books called the "Quran" and through this process they were able to become <u>Free</u>Masons who were specifically to become known as the "ANCIENT ORDER OF THE NOBLES OF THE MYSTIC SHRINE" (here on out referred to as A.A.O.N.M.S.) This order was instituted by the Mohammedan "Kalif Alee" who was the cousin/german and son in law of the Prophet Muhammed (as the A.A.O.N.M.S.) records it. It began as an Inquisition or vigilance committee to dispense justice and execute punishment upon criminals who escaped their just deserves through the tardiness of the courts. It was also to promote religious toleration amongst cultured men of all Nations, religions and those in High positions of learning and power. They build from their instructional book called "The Book of Constitution and the Regulations of the Imperial Council". All Muhammedans respect everyone who has made the pilgrimage to Mecca and those who repeat the formula of the creed: "There is no deity but Allah" without reference to what his private belief may be for they have a maxim which states "The interior belongs to god alone". They stand upright, feet as 45 degrees to show that they are perpendicular (T) to the square which they call knight of the Sun of Prince Adept". The Shriners to the date of this writing still live out certain good acts within communities like giving to hospital charities throughout the world in an attempt to do like us (righteous acts and deeds).

"And we would not kill them as quick as we would the other Devils. That is, those who have not gone under this study. After this labor of 35-50 years, we permit him to wear our holy Flag which is the Sun. Moon and Stars but he must add a sword to the upper part of the Flag…" Labor means: physical or mental work or it can mean a job or a task to be completed. The labor he goes through is the journey of righteousness. Just like us (The Nation of Gods and Earths) they weren't to receive a Flag until they complete their studies. Prior to this, they could only come amongst our ciphers but not participate within them (see 4/1- 14).

If they ever Borned this knowledge, they'd lose their heads!!! It was just like in our ancient Kemetic (Egyptian) Universities. The initiations into the Mystery Schools were a secret order and membership that were only gained through a pledge of secrecy. The sword is to make sure the Muslim Son keeps in mind that they got this Knowledge from and also their pledge to secrecy. Our Universal Flag of Islam (The Nation of Gods and Earths) does not contain a sword, why? Because we do not take an oath to conceal the truth. We are the movers and doers, as well as the light bearers, whose duty it is to bring forth the truth (16 – 20/1-40).

Muslim Sons/Masons study from 35 – 50 years and then they make their pilgrimage to Mecca to give their degrees. This movement was formed after Muhammad returned to the essence, so they could see their brother Muhammad spiritually and get an - Al, Medina, Mecca, Sword, Sun, Moon, Star, an Arabian Man, etc... above their Fez and Flags. The crescent is the master key to all wisdom according to Noble George Root of the A.A.O.N.M.S. He also asserts that for esoteric reasons, they hang the horns upside down with the points on the horns pointing downwards to represent the setting of the moon, of the old faith, at the moment of the rising sun of the new faith, in the brotherhood of all mankind. He says, "They have to also walk across the shifting sand of the desert which typifies ignorance and darkness into the halls of science until they stand in the light." Light is symbolic to intelligence or knowledge. He also went on to explain that the Fez is a part of the rich costume of Eastern characters made out of silk and velvet.

When the pilgrimages to Mecca were interrupted by the crusaders in about 980 A.D., the Mohammed and West

of the Nile River journeyed to Fez (also known as Fas) in Morocco. They wore the Tarboosh which is now known as the Fez. Moorish Americans of the Moorish Science Temple of America Inc. teach that the Fez symbolizes consciousness. The A.A.O.N.M.S. can't wear their Fez outside of the temple meetings. They created their 1st temple in New York
9-26-1872 and they call it Mecca just like us.

"The sword symbolizes Justice and was used by the original man in Muhammad's time. Thus, it was placed on the upper part of the Flag, so that the devil could always see it and keep in mind that if at any time he revealed the secret his head would be taken off by the sword." The history of I.S.L.A.M. teaches us that Muhammad propagated his religion at the point of a sword to all Christians, Jews and Pagans (as they identified them). The Freemasons/Muslim Sons could not go out and teach this knowledge because they had to 1st cleaned themselves up. I bear witness to the fact that a seed that sprouts before its scheduled time will bear no fruit. The secret of the secret rites is that the Blackman is God.

The Holy Flag of I – God S.L.A.M. is the Greatest and Only flag in the Universe. The Universe is everything: the Sun, Moon and Stars. Planets are something that's grown or made from the beginning. Holy is something that has not been mixed, diluted or tampered with in any form … Muslims Sons are white males (usually) who have climbed the ranks of Freemasonry (Scottish Rite or Knights Templars 32 Degrees) and then became inducted into the A.A.O.N.M.S. after they complete their studies and give their degrees (Quran). Planets are made or grown from the beginning. Made is the moon because it came to be from the Earth (It's made from the Earth). The Sun and Stars are Grown. Planets Build to be Born. Hydrogen divided and made Helium (8 to be 9) etc… A thing has to 1st grow and then from the growth it's made into whatever shape it's supposed to take on.

If one wants to study self, all they have to do is study the Universe. The Universe is always ever expanding even as U-N-I-verse at this hour. This is Nature's way of showing us that 1, 2 and Supreme 3 must constantly continue to expand. The Universe is always building (adding on) so why are we "chillin" (destroying). The 10% teaches daily to secure his luxury in which I'm sciencing this up as we (the poor, righteous teachers inside and abroad) must teach hourly. The Universe is Universal and it doesn't deny any energy so it's evident, we must teach all from the Knowledge seeds to the culture seeds (Black people to white people) along with any other shades in between. Within Man, Woman and Child, the universe lives. Religions are not for us, they are for our sons and daughters!!! It is for the Freemasons, Jews, Muslims Sons, etc… to help them become one or to re-align/re-ligion their own selves back to the origin of all things in existence which is Allah – God!!

They (our Sons) submit to the will (choices) of Allah (the Original Man/Mind) when they studied and learned to do like the Original man who is Allah – God (1/1-10). In Allah's – Truth (120), the 1st degree, we learn that we are Gods of the Universe, not any Muslims or submitters to what we created. As Allah – God, we control the forces of the Cosmos instead of being a slave to them. Only until you get to this degree in Allah's (1) Truth (20) do we ever hear of a Muslim. The honorable Elijah Muhammad (PBUH) seen Self as a Muslim dealing in Supreme Wisdom. The True and Living Gods see self as Allah – God living with Supreme knowledge, wisdom and most importantly … Understanding.

PEACE TO ALL WHO LIVE OR STRIVES TO LIVE AN
UPRIGHT, RIGHTEOUS LIFE OUTSIDE
BOUNDARIES AND WITHOUT MEASURE!!!
PROVE EVERYTHING ALLAH CREATED EXISTS!!!
(PEACE)
Manifest Supreme Knowledge God Allah

References: The Ancient Arabic Order of the Nobles of
Mystic Shrine (1930) revised 2002 by Noble George L.
Root of Mohammad Temple in Peoria, Illinois, Cream City
Newsletter 8–2010, from Allah School in Cream City
(Milwaukee, Wisconsin) Book of Life/120 Lessons of the
Nation of Gods and Earths, Secret Societies by Phillip
Gardiner (2007), the Enigma of the Freemasons by Tim
Wallace – Murphy (2006) The Sun of Man Newsletter 5 –
2010, The Immortal Birth by Allah Jihad (2007)

Contact Info:
http://TheIncarcerated7sBlog.Blogspot.com
Email: Incarcerated7s@hotmail.com

AUTHOR'S NOTE: MANIFEST SUPREME is a
seasoned author and prolific Nation of Gods and Earths
Enlightener. He recently wrote his 1st book called, "THE
FIVE PERCENT NATION NEOPHYTES," which is
available at M.A.P. CO., P.O. BOX 7430,
MINNEAPOLIS, MN. 55407 for $16. Also, he is a writer
in a book entitled, "KNOWLEDGE OF SELF-A
COLLECTION OF WISDOM ON THE SCIENCE OF
EVERYTHING IN LIFE," by Dr. SUPREME
UNDERSTANDING ALLAH, SUNEZ ALLAH, CBS A
LIFE ALLAH and LORD JAMAR (Manifest's article
entitled, "THE TRUEAND LIVING" is on p.97 of that
book) He is also the REGIONAL REPRESENT-ative for

the Incarcerated citizens of the Nation of Gods and Earths in Region 7. He was appointed to that position by Religion 7 elder C-LATIFF ALLAH before he retired to the essence in June 2012.

THE CROSSINGOF THE BURNING SANDS

"Why Did We Run Yakub and His Made
Devil From the Root of Civilization
Over the Hot Arabian Desert, into the
Caves of West Asia as they now
Call it Europe?"

By

Manifest Supreme #1 God [in the name of] ALLAH

12/13/2009

The Book of Genesis

To truly understand the Bible, we have to realize
that 90% of the text is parables used to describe certain acts
lived out by individuals, or a body of people who
performed a specific duty. One has to be able to draw the
parables up and learn not to take everything in the Bible on
face value. The Bible is a book of recorded events (history)
that was made by the Original Man who is Allah. Even
though, the Bible may have been re-written thousands of
times by those who did not have its best interest at hand, if
righteously understood and deciphered, one could see that
is still contains many truths within its stories. The first 5

books of the Bible is the teachings and laws of our Prophet Moses (Musa) given to the grafted man while located in the hills and mountains of Europe over four thousand years ago. It's been thought that Moses was an ancient KMT (Egyptian) Priest of the Mystery Schools, and that he taught the savages in the Book of Exodus the science he grew up under, which was the science of the Original Man.

The teachings of KMT Universities derive from the ancient Anunian (Ethiopian/Axum) knowledge and wisdom, which derive from Central Equatorial Asia (Afrika) and was migrated all over the planet Earth. Some call Moses teachings "The Torah", in which means "the law or teachings". These were the 1st civilized teachings & laws the colored man in the caves ever received.

The Greeks named the 1st book Genesis in which derives from the Hebrew word "bereshit" which both means in the beginning. In the beginning of what? Anything that have a beginning, have an ending, so it cannot be the beginning of God, and it cannot be the beginning of the Original Man because Genesis 4:17 confirms that there was many people on earth existing within these first 4 chapters of Genesis. So how can this book describe the Origin of the Original Man or God, whose essence exists within infinite blackness? This beginning in Genesis is the making of the grafted man or Yakub grafted devil of the planet earth. Grafting is a scientifically/medical process which separates germs. Grafting is used today on plants, animals, foods, lab mice, monkeys, etc…

In order to graft, you have to begin by making something from the original. Biblical scholars agree that the 1st man was named "Adam" (even though the Bible doesn't assert this). In Hebrew, the attribute Adam means red, ruddy, or all human beings. Adam is the title used to describe all the hue-man families that was made on or after 4004 B.C. in which the Bible teaches us that sin and death came into existence from these men. The Bible is silent on what happened to Adam and Eve after they were exiled from the holy land. In Paul L. Guthrie's book "Making of the Whiteman", claims that they were forced to live in the caves and mountains not only by force b.u.t. because of shame and disgust. They were run across the hot Arabian Desert, into the caves of W. Asia, as they now call it Europe by a Black Arab named Chief Monk-Monk. Genesis 3:24 says, "After We drove them out, Cherubim was stationed with a revolving sword to guard the way." This is why Freemasons practice the ritual of walking across the hot sand in their customs.

In the 19th century, scholars in Ethiopia allegedly discovered a document called "The Book of Adam and Eve" in which many scholars include it as part of the Lost Books of Eden. It was originally scribed in Arabic, b.u.t. the text had long ago been translated into Ethiopic. This book picks up where the book of genesis leaves off. If describes how Adam & Eve was forced to walk across the hot desert. The book said "…when Adam looked at his flesh that was altered, he wept bitterly, he and eve, over what they have done. Adam said: "Look at this cave that is to be our prison in this world, and place of punishment …" In my sentiment, this book is a must read.

Mind detect Mind

Genesis 1:26-27 says God made man in our image & our likeness. Image is a reproduction of the form of a person or object. Likeness is similarity, resemblance, an imitative appearance or semblance. These hue-mans was grafted or made from the Original Man, the Asiatic Black Man who is Allah. We made them in our likeness, our image meaning our physical structure/form. Also, they possess our same mental capacities, just only in a weaker, mixed diluted & tempered form due to the lack of melanin or their pineal glands being calcified, in which is the reason they do not have high degrees of melanin, life's chemical building block. He only has 6oz of brains while the Original Man has 71/2. The Father Clarence 13X (who knowledge and understand the Unknown 13X) righteously known as Allah always taught us that: "Son, if you cannot speak the language, than you shouldn't live in the land."

Genesis or Gene and –sis:

Genesis consists of these two words. Gene is a cell or the life germ in which an organism can undergo mutation. –sis is a suffix used to form verbs like action, process, state, or condition. This genesis is referring to the process or condition of undergoing a mutation of the Original Germ (or taking the germ from its original sate of black, to its last state and weakest state which is white). In the book 'Knowledge of Self' by Supreme Understanding – Allah, the God Shaikhi Teach Mathematics Allah, in Virginia stated:

"In the book of genesis, it is revealing the beginning or origin of the devil … through a genetic process, whereas something is being grafted or made out of something else."

Peace to the God! I personally couldn't break it down or draw it up any better. Always remember that anything made from the Original is a devil. The nature of something depends on the essence of how it's made. Being that they are made from the original, automatically makes them (or anything) a devil, by nature not by anyone's personal feelings or thoughts ---b.u.t. by NATURE! Question: Who made this man?

YAKUB (Jacob)

It was predicted in the year one of this Asiatic Calendar Year that Sun would live this act out of making a new man. The Bible calls this parable 'Jacob' in Hebrew. In Arabic it's Yakub. The word Jacob in Hebrew means to

Supplant or to be a supplanter, which means 'to take the place of another by scheming, force or strategy' the suffix – ER means to designate (to select for a duty or purpose) either persons, or things. Yakub was designated or selected by the 23 scientists to replace one thing (the black germ) by or for something else (white germ) by means of scheming, strategy, or force (force: 30/1-40). See 28/1-40 and Genesis 30:25, Jacob outwitting Laban. God is known by His ability to show and prove look up the following words: "lamb, sheep, livestock, goat, rod, flock." Now read Genesis Chapter 30, verse 28 – 43. Then read Chapter 31:3-10. Notice how Yakub receives abnormal colored sheep (people) that was spotted and streaked with white in it (if it had white in it, than what color was it originally?), see how Yakub didn't want the dark sheep, only the spotted ones, in which verse 39 confirms they mated and brought forth speckled kids (grafting process) etc…

The NOI (Nation of Israel) was synthesis of heterogeneous (completely different) tribal elements who, combining their oral histories in a consistent manner with the common denominator being the patriarch Jacob (Yakub), who was able to unify the divided people into a single nation. The Hebrews were allied with the 'Hyksos' (shepherd kings) who were supposed to be an Indo-Aryan People, who once inhabited and almost destroyed KMT at one hour. In Theophile James Meeks book called the **Hebrews Origins**, pp. 17 mention the fact the one of the Hyksos kings was named Yacub-har. W.F. Albright in his literature called: From the Stone Age to Christianity, pp.242 confirmed the same that Ya'cob har is Jacob who made the Hebrew/Hyksos people into a single nation. KMTic Historian Manetho in his works 'Manetho, with an English translation by W.G. Waddell' says that the Hebrews are identified with the Hyksos, in which he describes them as descending from lepers (a person affected by leprosy). Of course many Israelites were Black because they was fathered by an Original Man (Jacobs), now at the same time the grafted ones took after their founding father's name Israel and began living out what He taught them, via his literature. Remember the suffix –ITE means follower or adherent of. These people eventually became civilized via the teachings of their teacher. Now who taught them civilization?

MOSES (Exodus)

The word exodus means departure. This chapter is breaking down the departure of the colored man/grafted man from the mountains or hillsides of Eu-rope.

This is the chapter were Moses gave the Israel – ites at Mt. Sinai the laws on how to live a respectable life, how to build a home for themselves, and a little of the forgotten trick knowledge Yakub taught them. Prophet Moses (PBUH), in this degree, first task was to unite a divided people (Exodus 3:15). Moses re-taught them the trick knowledge in which they never forgot, only we seem to have, which is why we still continue to fall for all. What Moses taught them went on to become what is today known as Freemasonry. Moses is credited with providing the necessary leadership, dietary, hygienic, civil and criminal code of laws which were to assist in the governing of the nomads, now called Hebrews (Habari).

Exodus 7: 1 confirms Moses was a God and his physical brother Aaron was his prophet. Exodus 2:10-11 skips from Moses being a baby adopted by Kmt's, to an adult. It seems like the re-writers is striving to leave something out. What? Probably the actual fact that Moses, their civilizer/enlightener taught them ancient Asiatic (Afrikan) science, and that their foundation originates in Afrika (E. Asia). This was their ploy to erase the history of Blacks in Biblical terms and antiquity in general. Exodus 2:23-25 explains how the 23 scientists gave him the knowledge of the devil living in those caves. Exodus 3:1-3 says, God came in the form of a burning bush. We know this is only a parable, and that this burning bush is only one of the 23 who was on fire/upset at how the cave people was living and realized the duties of a civilized person is to teach he who is a savage civilization, righteousness, etc. Exodus 6:12 and 6:30 confirms that Moses was a poor speaker, which is why He had to use some of the forgotten trick knowledge to secure his safety. Exodus 6:30 also is the devil in the hillsides. Exodus 12: 37 builds on the devil coming out the mountains after 2,000 years of being roped in by the Cherubim (angels/physical men). Exodus 19:10-15 the 23 scientists is teaching Moses the instructions on how these devils is to live if they are to come back to our Holy Lands of the East, (example: #10 says he has to wash his clothes). Exodus 20:1-17, they receive their laws, in which many of them still follow them today (Jews). These laws derive from the 42 precepts, or law of Maat. Musa only gave them 10 of 42. Acts 7:22 confirms Moses was a KMT Priest, so it's only natural he taught them KMTic (Original Man) sciences right? In Leviticus, Moses taught them proper eating habits, to always stay in the state of purity (refinement), sacrifices, etc. May Supreme Peace Be Upon the Prophet Moses (MUSA; Akhenaton)!

Conclusion

The lessons of the NGE are the literal words of our Prophet W.F. Muhammad and The Honorable Elijah Muhammad form the period of 1933 – February 20, 1934 A.D. in Detroit, Michigan. W.F.M. taught Elijah M. astrology because our history and mathematical make up is written in the stars, and He used methodology, esoteric stories, and parables throughout his teachings to give the student a clear understanding of his overstanding. The same as Jesus spoke using parables, or our ancient ancestors used parable

(Asar/Osiris), etc. . . This is only an ancient Asiatic tradition. We in the NGE (and the Nation of Islam) use the parable/story of Yakub/Jacob to describe how the fourth family came into existence from the original (Black, Brown, Yellow). As the book of Revelations teaches us, this devil was manufactured (or a Man-U-Factured – factured mean made), on the isles of Pelan, which today is called turkey and Greece. After they was completely grafted, they came back to our land, and as loving people, we accepted them into our homes. We bathed, clothed, and fed them, and gave them the best, best of our best part – the understanding of our supreme sciences. And what did they do in return, they caused chaos and confusion amongst us, causing us to fight and kill one another.

We never assumed them to be the cause of all confusion because they always stepped in as the middle man acting as if they are trying to solve the problem they secretly created (same as today). As Allah is truly All Seeing-All knowing, we quickly discovered they were the cause of all this chaos. We then rounded them up and took everything from them such as our books, food, clothing, shelter, etc. and left them with nothing b.u.t. their own language of telling lies and stealing. We drove them across the hot Arabian desert into the caves of West Asia as they now call it Europe (Genesis 3:23-24). They remained in that condition for 2,000 years. In Greek, the word EU was changed to mean' Good'. I science that up as it was good we roped them in when we did or surely Now our Nation would've came to an End.

Through Moses civil eye, he civilized the uncivilized. Revelation 13:18 says: "Wisdom is needed here; one who understands can calculate the number of the beast, for it's a number that <u>stands for a person. His number is 666."</u> (Emp. Added)

Question: Who's the only said person that exists with a 6 oz. brain? What man can change 6 colors (brown, when he tans, green when he's sick, blue when he's out of air, red when he's angry, pink when he blushes, and back to black, his origin, when he returns to the essence)? According to scripture, what man did it take 600 years to make? What man governs 6 million miles of land? In closing, I want to give honors to <u>ALL</u> of Master Now (MN)'s, First Borns here in the high north who taught one, who taught another one, in return eventually taught me. There righteous attributes are: Black, Sha Grace, Ali Quan, Universal, Mahdi, Nackream, Powerful (Excellent Life), I-Love, Divine Savior, C.I. Black Mind, Sincere and Gifted Self-Allah and I Sure Supreme Being God-Allah. Peace to the Gods!

I'm leaving your mental in the same signs I

came into it which is Freedom, Justice, Equality

and most importantly:

P.rove E.veryday A.llah's C.ulture E.xists!

Manifest Supreme Knowledge God-Allah

WHAT MAKES RAIN, HAIL SNOW & EARTHQUAKES?

What makes rain, hail, snow & earthquakes? First & foremost we must come to an understanding of the many & or different ways that this can be expressed. Rain, hail & snow form in the atmosphere of the planet earth & earthquakes are the trembling movements of the earth's surface & core. The earth is approximately covered under water ¾ of its surface. Just like the Asiatic BlackWomen should be covered ¾ mentally as well as physically. First, her God gives her the knowledge of how to understand (3) her culture (4) which is covering her mentally with water (Wisdom). Wisdom is the wise words & actions that is used by an intelligent earth that knows & understands that God is no mystery & is none other than the Asiatic BlackMan of the planet earth.

Her culture is Islam (I-Sincerely-Love-Allah's-Mathematics) which is love, peace & happiness within her cipher & within the kingdom of God which is both he & her home/Universe. The Sun & Moon attraction powers on our planet while it is making a terrific speed of 1,037 1/3 miles per hr. on its way around the Sun. Man & woman possess attraction powers by showing & proving through their ways & actions that they both are not mixed, diluted, or tampered with in any form, such as obtaining the devils "Trick knowledge" within their cipher or square. These attraction powers are Freedom, Justice & Equality towards one another, as well as Love, Peace & Happiness.

The Sun draws this water up into the earth's rotation which is called gravitation into a fine mist that the naked eye can hardly detect. Meaning God is constantly observing, respecting & collecting this knowledge & purify this water (Wisdom) for the Earth to distill back on her planet (mind) to bring forth life mentally & physically. The gravitational pull, that's the love (10) right there &

sometimes is come in the form of a fine mist that the naked eye can hardly detect because love can be expressed in many ways & has many different aspects. Seeing love with the 3rd eye, which is the mind, that understands (3) the true essence, the highest elevation. But as this mist ascends higher & increases with other mist of water in different currents of the atmosphere until it becomes heavier than gravitation, then it distills back to the earth in the form of drops of water, or drops of ice which depend on how heavy the mist was in the current of air it was in.

I see these different currents of the atmosphere as being symbolic to different emotions, feelings & or controversies within Gods cipher. Once the Son of Man acknowledges his light (Power/Effect) reflecting off the moon, Justice is now served (Reward/Penalty) because this is His ways & actions (cause/effect) being manifested through His Wisdom (Forms of Water) There are some layers of air real cold & warm & some very swift & changeable. I relate this to the 12th degree in the Supreme Alphabets being Love, Hell, Right. These layers & currents can be situations that get out of hand. Cold & cruel, comments and/or actions towards one another out of anger, but love has to go through hell & be purified before any relationship can have an understanding & come out right. These layers & currents also show & prove how God & Earth can be swift & changeable, yet still remain on the foundation of Islam. Born-U-Truth when this water (Wisdom) strikes a cold current it becomes solid ice, meaning your wisdom is frozen (32°) & unable to free her from the triple stages of darkness or the devils un-civilization. This water is never been drawn above six miles from the earth's surface by the Sun & Moon, because this is the Black Woman's limitation. Earthquakes are caused by the Son of Man "Experimenting" with high explosives, in fact, all the above is caused by the Son of Man. Experimenting with high explosives means a test is demonstrated or made to demonstrate an actual finding of truth. This is why the Son of Man must remain all wise & forever righteous in his nature, because anytime he acts other than his own self, which is falling victim to the devils un-civilization & mentality. He can destroy & or does destroy civilizations mentally as well as physically. Born-U-Truth Allah can destroy the devil's mentality in one day, meaning in an instant, because Allah is God, always has been & always will be. Experience is the best qualified teacher for learning, so if the earth is giving off negative vibrations or shifting in her core, you (God) are the only one who causes all of this to happen.

MANIFESTED FROM THE DIVINE MIND OF –
SINCERE BUILD EMPIRICAL ALLAH

Contact Info:
http://TheIncarcerated7sBlog.Blogspot.com
Email: Incarcerated7s@hotmail.com

THE ELEMENTS OF THE UNIVERSAL FLAG OF ISLAM

Peace to the Gods!!

Today, a True and Living God sat down and asked me a question that sparked the Wisdom on this paper. The Question he asked was: "Does the Universal Flag Of Islam consist of anything "Universal" and if so, what is it and if in fact this Universal Element exists what would be the weight of it on the Flag?

As you can see this is a very deep question so as a Wise Man, I did the knowledge to the question before I spoke. I was about to ask him a question to obtain a better Understanding of his Words B.U.T. I instead applied the knowledge of Almighty God Allah when he once said, "Ask not a Question B.U.T. answer the one I've asked". Since a Wise God once told us that it's improper to answer a Question with a Question. Knowing this information, I sat in silence and began to Born an answer in my own Mind by applying Mathematics. As I was involved in this process the God rose up, patted me on my back and said, "You'll figure it out, it's all Math" and then he left my physical presence.

As I sat alone I began to dissect every word and then it hit me - Universal – Something "Universal" as in an Element!!! That took my attention to the Periodic Table of Elements since there is both GOLD and BLACK (CARBON is BLACK) on the Universal Flag of Islam. This is how I came to see the answer is yes Emphatically (Why Equal Self). Let's explore ALLAH'S TRUTH (120) and the way the knowledge of the Elements of the Flag came to be shown and proven by Self.

On the Periodic Table Elements, We see the Elements of what we represent. This degree should bring to life the importance of the Culture to explore and apply new ways of learning, teaching and speaking Mathematics.

GOLD

Symbol AU, Atomic Number 79, Atomic Weight 196.967, Outer Configuration 5d10, 6S1, Periodic

The 8 Points of the Greatest and Only Flag of the Universe (Universal Flag Of Islam) represent the ever expanding Universe and the rays of the Sun as well as the speed and distance that the Truth is capable of travelling. The Right side of the Eight Points is Gold (AU 79). This represents or symbolizes the Brown, Red and Yellow seeds. It is our duty to reunite these seeds as one - A.U. (Allah's Universe) 79 (God Born). ALLAH is the Supreme Being Blackman from Asia, the Sole controller and Ruler of the Universe. The Bold Gold Shine that you see from the Universal Flag of Islam was crafted by ALLAH himself.

The GOLD shine is Light/Truth which travels at the rate of 186,000 miles per second. This light destroys all attempts of the Devil as he attempts to keep our people blind, deaf and dumb to the knowledge of who they are. The Universe is everything, the Sun, moon and starts. ALLAH is the sole controller and ruler of the Universe. Universe is 21 because when you Wisdom (2) your Knowledge (1) you bring forth Understanding (2 + 1= 3). The Understanding of our Flag and the Elements on the Periodic Table are Universal.

The Atomic weight of GOLD is 79. God (7) is Allah who is the Supreme Ruler of the Universe which he crafted with 1 thought. Born (9) is the completion of all in existence to manifest from Knowledge to Born (1-9). In order for one to express his or her culture in its proper form, one must know and Understand who he is in this Universe and beyond!!! The completion of all in the existence has to begin with knowledge in order to progress to the next stage.

The Atomic weight of GOLD is 196.967 which is part of the answer to the question proposed in the beginning. Knowledge (1) Born (9) Equality (6) Born (9) Equality (6) God (7). When U add these #'s, you will come to Understand Build meaning the GOLD in the Flag you will Understand how God himself built it if you use Wisdom. Understanding (3) and Build (8) gives you Knowledge (1) added on to Knowledge (1) (8+3=11). ALLAH being the sole controller and ruler used his Knowledge to bring forth Wisdom of the True and living light Bearer. Here we travel to the outer configuration number 5d10 6S1. D here represents the transition Elements. (See Periodic Table of Elements) Also, D is the Neutrons charge. (Neutrons Mass: 1,839 charge D lifetime in seconds 8.89×10 to the 2nd power – Electron Mass: 1, Electron Charge – 1, Lifetime in seconds stable-Proton Mass: 1, 836, charge +1, lifetime in seconds stable). The Atomic Number of an Element Represents the Protons in an Atomic Nucleus, so in GOLD that would be (79). The #'s on the outer configuration represents the neutrons 5d10 (to the 10th power) (d being a transition element) The Electrons 6S1 (to the 1st power) so 5d to the 10th power, we see POWER (5). POWER is the force or creative energy. This force was used to create the elements that have to be regardless to whom or what. D to the 10th power is DIVINE is to be pure and refined in order to Destroy all Negativity. (10) JUSTICE/KNOWLEDGE CIPHER: JUSTICE here would be you reward or penalty for wearing GOLD and either failing to or Understanding its Nature.
KNOWLEDGE CIPHER (10) is to aid your Cipher with the Knowledge of this Element. Now, Wise Elevators see 6S1s this # represents the Electron which is 6, its charge 1 and life time in seconds. (S = Stable) (Just as 5 represents the neutron Mass with a charge of D lifetime in seconds 8.89×10 2 or d 10). Here wise educators see equality being done. The equality of base elements as GOLD is used

Universally for adornment, monetary value and a variety of Electrical and Mechanical usage. The S or Self-Savior is the Knowledge of Self. This is what makes you Savior of Self by borning Self or completing Self. ALLAH is just that – SELF SAVIOR!! The only God is the Sun and Man and we will waste no time searching for that which does not exist.

The KNOWLEDGE (1) above S1 is knowledge is the accumulation of facts through observing, learning and respecting. Knowledge is the foundation of all in the existence. Do you agree? YES (WHY EQUAL SELF)!! Last, Wise Educators see the #6 again to the far left (see Periodic Table). This #6 represents the highest occupied Electron Level. It's the 6th Row out of 7 Rows in which GOLD rest in the 2nd group # column. GOLD is the 11th Element out of this 6th Row. GOLD as defined by Webster's Dictionary is: A soft, yellow corrosive resistant, highly malleable and ductile metallic Element that is used as an international monetary standard in jewelry for decoration and as a plated coating on a wide variety of Electrical and mechanical components: Atomic #79, Atomic Weight 196.967

Back to the question at hand; Does the Universal Flag of Islam consist of anything Universal? YES!!! And if so, what is it? (GOLD) If in fact there is, then what would the weight of the Flag be? The GOLD present in the Universal Flag of Islam is seen on the Right side. Its weight is 196.967. So now we move to the next Element of the Universal Flag which is CARBON.

CARBON

The 8 Points of the Greatest and only Flag of the Universe represent the ever expanding Universe and the Rays of the Sun as well as the speed and distance that the Truth is capable of Traveling. The left side is Black/Carbon. In physics, colors are understood to be waves of radiant energy projected from the Sun and made visible by refracted light which stimulates the retina of the Human EYE.

Sciencing things from this perspective, one can easily see that BLACK is not a refraction of Light at all!!! It is the state of being from and by which colors are made manifest. The BLACK present in the Universal Flag is the very essence of Life itself. It is the 1st with no beginning nor ending. It is the foundation of all existence!! See/Cee is to Understand ones true sight with his 3rd Eye which is the Mind.

ALLAH sees everything with a wise eye. The Foundation of all things in Life (Our Universe) is BLACK!! The sky is never actually Blue. It is actually Black. It appears blue due to refracted light. 6 is Equality in the Supreme Mathematics of the Nation of Gods and Earths. Equality means to be Equal in everything which is perfect for this Element. For more in depth information one can refer to a Build by Earth Sci-Honor devotion in the Book called Knowledge of Self – A Collection of Wisdom on the Science of Everything in Life by Dr. Supreme Understanding. The exact page is page 103. Carbon is the basis for all organic life. It's the Ying and Yang (The Balance). Carbons distribution in the Universe is even which makes Carbon the only element with this attribute. Black/Carbon is the foundation and fundamental priniciple of the basis of Life as stated above. This is the Essence of the Original family. ALLAH stated: "AS ABOVE, SO BELOW." It's BLACK above, so be it below!!

The Atomic weight is 12.01111of Carbon on the Periodic Table of Elements (Knowledge (1) Wisdom (2). Cipher (0) Knowledge (1) Knowledge (1); When you add these #s, you come to Power which ALLAH has shown and proven to U-N-I-. Power is Force or Creative Energy. The Original Man didn't lay this Blueprint by chance, NOW Cipher (NO)!! ALLAH knew very well of his actions.

Here we travel to the outer configuration which is 2S2 2p2. In this case, we have Wisdom (2) which is wise words being spoken or to speak knowledge as well as a wise dome meaning a wise mind acting accordingly to it. This science was manifested from ALLAH's wise dome/Supreme Mind.

Self Saviour or S2 is your Knowledge being used in its proper form. The 2 above the S is that Wisdom that has to "BE." Carbon must exist which it does. Within our physical makeup, Carbon is a driving force within us that most of us don't acknowledge or see. Again, Wisdom (2) is that which must BE regardless to whom or what. P is POWER , 2 Being. This POWER must BE because our wisdom is even Divine in its least popular form. This is our Culture.

Lastly, CARBON is found in the 2nd Row 4th group number. The 2 on the far side left represents the Electron level. The Wisdom needed to figure this out has to be of a Divine Nature. Carbon is the 4th Element on the 2nd row. Carbon as defined in Webster's Dictionary is: A naturally abundant nonmetallic Element that occurs in many inorganic and organic compounds. Carbon exists in amorphous, graphitic and diamond allotropes and is capable of chemical Self bonding to form a large number of chemically, biologically, commercially important long chain molecules. This basically answers the Gods question. The answer is YES the Universal Flag of Islam contains Elements Carbon and Gold and both can be weighed and the combined weight of both is the weight of the Flag.

Proper

Education Always Corrects Errors

Divine

All Wise Allah

Interior

Cipher, Ohio

THEY ARE ORIGINAL PEOPLE TOO

The title above is taken from the Nation Of Gods and Earths LESSONS which contain a series of essays with Questions asked by W.F. Muhammad and answered by Elijah Muhammad. In one LESSON in particular (Lost and Found Muslim Lesson No. 1); the 3rd degree speaks about Christopher Columbus and the true history regarding his so called discovery on America. The Lesson Goes on the explain that the Indians who he found her had been exiled 16000 years from the date the Lesson was manifested (1934) and that they are also BLACK/Original people contrary to the general perception that the Native Americans are not a shade of the BLACK peoples of the World.

The information presented in the work of renowned author and scholar IVAN VAN SERTIMA has shined a bright light to evaporate the lies of deception introduced to the American public to cause division amongst not only the Indian /Native American population with the people of India but also created a bridge through its examination of historical data and the accuracy of what's being taught thru the American lens of Euro - centricity in Schools and books.

For so long, the actual events of history regarding the origin of the Indians found in North America has gone unchallenged or un-reviewed due to the writers of said books slam-ting the versions of the each event to glorify themselves no matter the cost. The LESSONS/120's are one of many tools that on people have been given (Black people) to accurately interpret the events that led up to the present since the wise men of the East anticipated/predicted the events that we are experiencing in these days and times in advance and prepared for the loss or distortion of our history by preserving the true narrative of events in unconventional ways as a safeguard. Now Let's Build on the actual title and explore now THEY ARE ORIGINAL PEOPLE TOO.

THE LOST AND FOUND MUSLIM LESSON NO.1 3rd degrees give us a brief synopsis of the history involving Columbus as a guide to further exploration. The degrees in the LESSONS are unlocked through the sciences which include objective Epistemology. The Lessons are only a guide and require one to research what's being said for a more in depth Understanding of each degree in our 120 LESSONS. We learn from IVAN VAN SERTIMA'S book THEY CAME BEFORE COLUMBUS, some of the deeper details of this degree that are not spoken of in this degree, so if you haven't read/studied this valuable jewel yet, get the book and review it and then reread this build.

The Indians were exiled from India 16,000 years before 1934 because they began to worship idols and strayed outside of themselves. The known blueprint amongst civilized people (which they were at the time) was that the Original Man is God. This was the knowledge that protected the people by preventing them from losing time searching outside of themselves for something that does not exist. The Indians that were exiled fell victim to this false idea and went savage as a result of exhausting their Minds and resources looking for this Mystery God and had to be exiled from the Holy Land once they began to live as savages.

In 1939, in the jungles of Vera Cruz, archaeological finds seemed to be the most startling in "American History." A head made of Black features (full lips, flat wide nose) was found. It was 6 feet high, 18 feet in circumference and weighed over 10 Tons!!! The find follows a slab of stone with dots and crosses which when it was deciphered gave the date of 11-4-291 B.C. This was the earliest date then known of American history; however, larger heads with earlier dates etc... were yet to come. This find was contrary to the misinformation taught in the American School system and still is to this day.

Other "Negro Heads" 8 feet tall were found. Specifically, 3 more with vivid details that were unlike any American art at that time. There was 1 that was 8 feet high and 22 feet in circumference. All faced East toward the Atlantic. This is the birth place of Man that is now called Africa. These stones of "Negro Heads" support the title of this build because THEY ARE ORIGINAL PEOPLE TOO. When Black people see our Mexican brothers and sisters or any other Latinos, it is almost a mirror image. They resemble us and may have the hue of our skin, similar noses, our lips, our body types, etc... Where does this come from and how is the same art (pyramids, paint, education, monuments, religion, culture, etc...) found in ancient Egypt, Nubia, and also Mexico, South America etc...? The Europeans in America will say that the Negro presence in Ancient America is found in stone. There's over 140 figures that are mostly Negroid type and Negroid – Mongoloid mix.

Egyptian influences on Pre = Christian America is Ancient itself. There is obvious Negro – Egyptian contact with the Olmec Culture. The pyramids are one example. A specific type (the step Pyramid) can be traced to Ancient Babylon and Egypt. It's also known as the ZIGGURAT STEP PYRAMID. This is a distinct Religious architectural structure such as a Chinese Pagoda or an Islamic Mosque. Nowhere in the history of American Architecture will you find anything close to this before what is known in history as "the contact period"(800-680 B.C.). The 1st American Step Pyramid was found at Laventa which is the site of those colossal Negro Heads." Other notable America pyramids are Choluda which was dedicated to Quetzalcoatl (150 B.C.) and the Pyramid of the Sun near Mexico City.

This contact period brought the culture to our own also that had been lost in the Wilderness of North America.

Wise Elevators are here to teach knowledge, wisdom and Understanding to the uncivilized people who are blind, deaf and dumb.

Our brothers of the brown seed were lost only to be found, "THEY ARE ORIGINAL PEOPLE TOO!! The pyramids of America/Egypt are not identical by design; they are identical in how they function. They are constructed to the stars with an identical shape and religious attributes. What is interesting is that the Egyptian step Pyramid age was long over during this art in America but no in Nubia!! THEY ARE ORIGINAL PEOPLE TOO. The Wisdom is passed on as those who study 120 LESSONS see the connections that are hidden to the blind, the deaf and the dumb.

Wise Educators know that 1 +1=2 regardless to whom or what. This knowledge is what makes your foundation secure in any form of testing. THEY ABSOLUTELY ARE ORIGINAL PEOPLE TOO!! It is a known fact that the Indians in Mexico also used Mummification techniques that were nearly identical to those used by the Ancient Egyptians. One such artifact corroborating this statement of fact is the one found in the Sarcophagus at Palenque. Multiple features show the Blackmans influence on the burial process.

First is the Jade mask on the face of the dead. Another is the flared based of the actual Sarcophagus which was first used by the Egyptians to facilitate Vertical Burials. The Mexicans adopted this very same practice of burying their dead as an option to Horizontal burials. These Mummification techniques were mastered in Mecca also known as East (Africa) and then exported to this part of the world. The same technique is used in PERU. The chemical technique embalms and purifies the dead Kings of PERU are identical to those used in Ancient Egypt. How else could this be?

Maybe it's because: THEY ARE ORIGINAL
PEOPLE TOO!!! The Egyptians buried parts of the corpses
in 4 jars called "HORUS JARS" to show and prove 4
Cardinal points. Certain organs were placed in all
directions. Specifically, the SMALL VISCERA (NORTH),
the STOMACH (South) as well as the LARGE
INTESTINES, the LIVER and GALL (west) and in the
East Jar the HEART and LUNGS. In addition to this
practice, Colors were assigned to each point. RED for
NORTH, WHITE for SOUTH, DARK COLORS for
WEST such as BLACK for EGYPT and BLUE for
MEXICO and GOLD for the EAST or YELLOW in
MEXICO. It's simply impossible for all this to be a
coincidence in places so far apart!!!

Wise Educators are here in North America to bring
the fruits of Allah to our people of all shades on the
Universe Flag of Islam. In the 3rd degree of the Student
Enrollment Lesson of the Nation of Gods and Earths 120
LESSONS, the population of the Indians in the Wilderness
of North America is 2 Million. You can use your wisdom to
Understand that the total population was the Original
people all over the planet is Culture (4) Culture (4) which is
all being born to Build using the science of Supreme
Mathematics. (4+4=8) The beginning of that is 17 million
(Knowledge God) all being Born to Build/Destroy (1+7=8).
This was the duty spoken of in the Lost and Found Muslim
Lesson 17th degree applying the science of the 120's to the
topic at hand. (See 17th degree in Lost and Found Muslim
Lesson No.2).

The duty of those exiled 16,000 years ago is to
rebuild their civilization and reclaim their Original attribute
of God. In order to do so, one has to 1st Knowledge (1) God
(7) in order to Build (8) with Divine Wisdom. This is what
will bring about a righteous culture here in North America
and Worldwide. The 3rd degree in the Student Enrollment
specifically states that there are 17 million Originals with

the 2 million Indians making it 19 Million Originals in North America and all over the planet there are 4 billion, 4 hundred million.

Obviously, THEY ARE ORIGINAL PEOPLE TOO!!! The OLMECS followed the Egyptian tradition of mummifying Dogs (Nubian Horses). The Olmec's began art sculpting Dogs on the wheels of their chariots. In PERU, mummified dogs have been found during excavations.

These Dogs however, do not look like "American Spits or Husky types. They look just like the Basenji which was the Egyptian Dogs revered by the Pharaohs at certain points in history.

A surviving species of this Dog is found in Africa today used by the Pygmies of Iturbi forest to track game. The Dog stands with its feet apart and its ears taut like webbed antennas. This however, is not as surprising as the fact that this particular breed of Dog has no body odor and makes no noise!! The Dog is known as the "Barkless Dog" and it was this actual breed that inspired the mold for the Dog Headed God of Egypt named ANUBIS. Columbus himself sent a report about the "Barkless Dog" during his voyages to the Caribbean. Other similarities indicating that the influence of the Original people was present were the GOLDEN MUMMY MASK aka CHIMU MASK OF PERU and the GREEN STONE in the mouth of the dead. Both Egyptians and Mexicans saw this "GREEN STONE" as a symbol of the heart and a prolonged of Life.

This could possibly mean that … THEY ARE ORIGINAL PEOPLE TOO!!! Take note of the fact that there are many Black Indian Chiefs as well as whole Indians tribes that have Moorish names such as BEY, EL, or ALI showing and proving our ties and links, from the Pacific to Mexico and South America.

Wise Elevators can prove what they say to people and don't need gimmicks. Rituals practiced by the

OLMECS are almost the same ones practiced in Egypt. The Color Purple as a Royal Color, the incenses used, the wearing of false beards by High Priests, the Umbrella and the Bird – serpent to name just a few. The beard worn by Kings and Priests is a Mystery within itself, being that the Mexican Native Americans were depicted as hairless on their chins in most drawings that they left behind except in ceremonies. The donning of the beard by the men in Egypt represented one of high office.

As for the Umbrella, the Mexican Umbrella was a Royal expression to be compared with one hovering over a tomb painting in HUY over a Nubian Prince. The color purple as an expression of the Religious hierarchy was an ancient industry in Mexico also. No other place will you find anything so far away from each other that are so close to each other.

Wise Educators must Understand in detail what our true way of life is to live out our Culture. The Universal Flag of Islam which is the express intellectual property of the Nation of Gods and Earths has given us a history that is accurate, so that we can reconnect the Human families in their proper order. In the Gold that's present, we learn that our family is the 1st of the Black to the last of the Yellow seeds as Original people and the significance of unlocking and retracing our Bloodlines.

Please Educate Allah's Children Everywhere
DIVINE ALL WISE ALLAH

Contact Info:
http://TheIncarcerated7sBlog.Blogspot.com
Email: Incarcerated7s@hotmail.com

EUGENICS

Produce epic artistry creates elegancy
Today's mathematics manifests as understanding
Cipher all being born to understanding. Let's touch on
today's reality and eugenics. If we understand our cipher,
Wise Elevators know how Yakub made the devil by
grafting, or separating, the germs, etc.; applying eugenics to
this ° is as follows:

First, eugenics – from the Greek EU (well), and
Gens (to produce); eugenics refers to the manipulation of
the process of evolutionary selection in order to improve a
particular genetic stock or population. This may be
achieved either through 'negative' eugenics (for example,
the provision of screening facilities to pregnant mothers, in
order to detect and prevent the inheritance of deleterious
recessive genetic conditions), or through 'positive'
eugenics, in which certain groups may be selected for, or
prevented from, producing. The latter is generally
considered ethically unacceptable. The former is an area of
ethical controversy.

The Eugenics Society achieved notoriety in the
early years of this century, for advocating various forms of
'positive' eugenics in order to improve the genetic quality
of the national populations in Britain and the United States.
See also, Darwinism; Gene African Psychology Pg. 11. It
was probably no accident that shortly after the U.S.
emancipation of African slaves, Sir Francis Galton (1869),
proposed the development and implementation of a
"science of heredity" (i.e. eugenics).

England's "Good Knight" believed that Black
people were a race grossly inferior to "even the lowest of
any white people." The above mentioned is explained in
our Wisdom (28th) and Understanding (30th) Cipher °s. In
the Understanding (30th) Cipher °s, it explains how there
are two genes/germs, a black and brown gene, which

Yakub manipulated, which falls in the place of 'positive eugenics' (only allowing selected groups that were producing, or not); which in the Wisdom (28th) Build ◦ is destroying the alike and saving the unlike.

In 1869, Galton published his major work on "hereditary genius" and argued that, based on his "scientific scale of values" (racial values), he was able to conclude that the average intellectual standard of the Negro was at least two grades below that of whites. In which 1st of all, is emphatically now cipher; Born Universal Truth, the devil teaches trick knowledge. He desires to make slaves out of all he can. (Cee 1/14◦s, (6th) Equality◦, (7th) God◦, (8th) Build◦, all dealing with lies)

Now Darwinism or Social Darwinism is the belief in the theory of evolution by means of natural selection. The most well-known manifestation of this social Darwinist movement was eugenics (Going by (120 Lessons) Allah's Truth, the natural selection is destroyed by the grafting process due to its very nature being unnatural). In its most extreme manifestation, members of the "eugenics society" wrote pamphlets variously advocating compulsory sterilization and the incarceration of large sub-groups of the population while advocating selective breeding among the rest; in order to improve the genetic quality of the population as a whole.

Note most "scientist" (so-called) are now convinced that Darwin's theory is insufficient. Galton, who was reportedly Darwin's cousin, was adamant in promoting the idea of racial improvement through selective mating and sterilization of the "unfit". This was used in Yakub's 600 year process of black to brown, brown to yellow, and yellow to white! Selective mating was killing the black babies, saving the brown babies. The proof of Allah's truth is everywhere. This is the science and trick knowledge that Yakub left behind. So, today's reality shows/proves Wise Elevators must understand our cipher. Here, the ◦ s bring

Universal Saviors into a state of Building the uncivilized cipher.

P.E.A.C.E. 7 Divine All Wise Allah

Contact Info:
http://TheIncarcerated7sBlog.Blogspot.com
Email: Incarcerated7s@hotmail.com

<u>2200 MILES</u>

Power Self, King!
Provide Encouragement and Create Equality!

"And I, Divine All Wise Allah, who am also your Brother and companion in tribulation, in the kingdom and patience of the original man, was in the isle called the, Interior Cipher, for the word of, I stimulate life and matter, and the testimony of Arm, Leg, Leg, Arm, Head."

In order for universal saviors to grow and be fruitful, wise elevators must understand each letter of each word with supreme intelligence, with not one word being taken at face value! (If one states 1+1 = 2, hold up two fingers before being satisfied). With that being said, I would like to add on, and bring about a higher glorious level of understanding. . .

"Why did we run Yakub and his made devil from the root of civilization, over the Arabian Desert, into the caves of West Asia, as they now call it Europe?" This is explained within this °, Born Universal Truth, what is not spoken on is this "Hot Arabian Desert." This (or these) deserts, spoken on, are the Al HiJaz and the An Nafud deserts. These are the deserts unnamed in this °. The Al Hijaz located in West Saudi Arabia, along the coast of the Red Sea. These desert lands stretch from the Northwest region of Arabia, down to Mecca and run into the Asir Mountains. Northeast of Al Hijaz is the An Nafud desert land, which is about 500 miles North of Mecca.

"The root of civilization is in Arabia, which means where the knowledge and wisdom of the original man 1st began when the planet was found ..." First, the word "root" has many definitions. Here, root is used as: [Source, origin: ancestry; the essential cure – establish] Mecca – West Saudi Arabia, containing the Great Mosque of Islam, where the population is 366,801. If one follows the "Islamic

Faith", Mecca is the "Holy Land" for him or her. This is a
"Place on a map for them." Born Universal Truth, U-N-I
was born! The Universe itself is Mecca. This is where U-N-
I- got our 1st name, "Atom", which was perverted by
European scientific fabrication to be, spread as "Adam,"
the so-called 1st man! The 1st (knowledge of the original
man) life began as a single atom (thought). Knowledge is
the accumulation of facts. This fact, at this stage, was total
darkness.

One becomes two, with the study of self. Through
this process of self - study [(self – savior)], Atom (U-N-I)
generated an image of a woman ("The wisdom of the
original man"). [Remember, knowledge = man/wisdom =
woman. This ∘ Wise Elevators are building on is the 4th
∘/culture ∘ in the Divine Culture of the True and Living.
Mecca is the "Root" [Source, Origin, and Ancestry] of our
civilization. Civilization is, one having 1,2,3,4, Refinement
and is not a savage in the pursuit of happiness.

Mecca is: Master Equality Cee Cee Allah. In order
to master your 6, you must cee who Allah really is, Sun! He
is No mystery or spook that is hard to find, etc…
Emphatically now, Cipher, the truth, or square is in our
face, King! Wise Elevators have to really attack and
understand in full color Allah's truth (120 Lessons)

We ran the devils over the hot Arabian Desert! This
running over the hot Arabian Desert is stated in Genesis
3:24. The pursuit of happiness, by this grafted people was
of the savage type and had no place in, or around
civilization of the righteous nature. So, they were placed or
chased into caves or Europe; E.U. means: Hillside, Rope
means: to bind in. They were bound into the hillside.

It was 2,200 miles. 2,200 miles from Mecca? Why
Equality Self (YES) From Mecca, on your map to the
Caucasus is roughly about 1,500 miles from Mecca to the
Caucasus border. Then it is another 700 miles to the exact
location of the caves spoken on in the Said, ∘! The path is

from the Al Hijaz Desert which runs through Mecca, at the Southwest, the travel would be North through the An Fud Desert. The areas of these mountains are 700 miles long and 120 miles wide. So the exact place and cave area is made up of the extra 700 miles; it takes 1,500 to be in the Caucasus region. It was 2,200 miles, within that 2,200 it was 1,500 then 700 (1,500 + 700 = 2,200).

So, as the original man took this devil away from the best part (Mecca), the travel alone was symbolic, if you are a Wise Elevator. Cee, the first 1,500 miles, the devil was to (1) knowledge the (5) power of the (0) Cipher. Knowledge is the foundation of all in existence. Power is force, or creative energy. Cipher is completion. So the foundation of all (1) had to show its (5) power, which was a creative force, to travel and place this savage away from universal saviors and our (0) existence.

Along the travel, once our knowledge (1) had been acknowledge, through the (5) power of our (0) cipher (1,500 miles), Wise Elevators found an exact location, and cave area, to settle the devil in. This took an additional 700 miles; which bore the lesson of (7) God's Cipher being all wise, just and true for His was and actions were right and exact. It was 2,200 miles; which means the wisdom added brought forth a savage culture, cipher that had no place among U-N-I!

So why Equality Self, it was 2,200 miles! Mecca is the mind, if you are 2,200 miles away from anything. No wisdom will bring forth a culture (2 + 2 + 00 = 4). Mecca is the mind that has no beginning, nor ending! The mind is infinite. In order to understand Allah's truth, one has to research every word.

~ Peace 7 Divine All Wise Allah ~

PLUS THOUGHT

Mecca is a state of mind. U-N-I along with the whole of our nation, must make our pilgrimage to. This is a pure and refined state of mind and body. This is the birth place of the "Prophet" in one's mind, where he/she figures if he/she has set out on righteous endeavors, or not. You are your own Prophet, Non - Muslims are not allowed into that city. The eighty-five percent, or bloodsuckers are not allowed there.

Wise Elevators destroy negativity, meaning all non-cipher acts are nowhere around universal saviors. Here, the sacred shrine exist [the brain and its 7 1/20z.]. God (7) knowledge (1) wisdom (2) and put forth that which He acknowledges to work. Nearby is the Holy Zem-Zem Well. Holy is something that has not been mixed, diluted, or tampered with in any form. The mind itself is Holy until non-cipher ways and thoughts mix, dilute and tamper with it. Zem Zem is a well which contains Holy water (So they say, Zem Zem water is pure).

That is the fluid which is within you heard. It's pure holding the brain which contains the functional Holy City of Mecca.

Peace,
D.E.M.A.L.E. All Wise Allah
(Divine Being Short for Demale)

PROPERLY ENLIGHTENED ALLAH CONTROLS EVERYTHING

The science of I.S.L.A.M. through the Eyes of Divine Truth Allah … (I) ntensify – 9, (S)urrounding – 19, (L)imited – 12, (A)tmospheric – 1 (M)echanics – 13

Islam is the science of the Properly Enlightened Always Controlling Existence so the word ISLAM must have a scientific and a Mathematical explanation to which Wise Elevators and Born a True Understanding of Proving Everything Allah Created Exists. Let's 8…

(9)INTENSIFY: is to strengthen and increase. Strength is power which the culture must utilize to uplift our Nation into the Sate of Being conscious. By having an Understanding of Power being the Truth and the Light, what is used to raise our Nation into the State of Awareness is Nothing other than Knowledge!! The only truth is obtained through Knowledge and the only light that is righteous is Knowledge being manifested. Each one should teach one according to their own knowledge!!

(19) SURROUNDING: is the state of existence. The state of existence is both mental and physical. Mental existence is the level of intelligence one possesses. Physical existence is the actual environment that the body rotates. Everything is a physical manifestation of the Mental existence because it all became from a single thought. It does not matter what the actual physical state may or may not be, for the only factor or any relevance is how one's Mind perceives the situation. Positive Evaluation Allows Correct Equations of the Mind equals Paradise!!

(12) LIMITED: are the restrictions that hinder one from being at his or her ability to build and destroy depending on their Supreme Intelligence. With such limitations, one cannot have Knowledge, Wisdom and Understanding of everything within their circumference. Most allow their current physical limitations to dictate their

true selves by not living our natural way of life which is ISLAM without conflict!!

(1) ATMOSHERIC: is the completion of Celestial bodies (man, woman and child). This is a clear manifestation of your Universe. The unified Black family is the vital building block of this beautiful Nation (NGE). The wisdom of one's knowledge brings forth a brighter level of Understanding … just as when U N I verse. Gravity is the force that attracts and balances these Celestial bodies within the Universe… Gravity is the knowledge and wisdom of the Human families which brought into existence Understanding. It's no mistaking why Understanding is the best part of life because our children are the link to our future … loves them!!!

(13)MECHANICS: is the science of matter, the essence of why things exist and the function of it in its existence. Universal Saviors are the only ones qualified to born the Divine answers of a Mechanic for Allah is the Supreme Being Blackman with the Knowledge of Self and Everything in existence!!

Wise Elevators live a life of I.S.L.A.M. not as a religion b.u.t. as a scientific manifestation of Perceiving Errors as Creative Energy!! Once Wise Elevators strengthen and build the uncivilized brothers and sisters into civilized men and women in a Divine state of being pure and refined destroying the physical limitations so that the Celestial being can elevate to the highest level of awareness… thus showing and proving the mastery in the science of matter. I+S+L+A+M = Power Culture. The empowerment of your culture to born it in the Power Equality Allah Cees Everything state of NGE. The phrase "Mind over Matter", is the manifestation of the Celestial being that Elevates and destroys physical limitation … if one's mind is mastered, so is the physical. If you don't Mind – then it don't matter!!

PROPERLY ENLIGHTENED ALLAH CONTROLS EVERYTHING
DIVINE TRUTH ALLAH PROVIDE ENCOURAGEMENT AND CREATE EQUALITY

The science of ISLAM through the Eyes of 7 Divine All Wise Allah; (S)cience (L)ogic (A)nalysis (M)athematics (9) ENTELLIGENCE: The capacity to acquire and apply Knowledge – Intellect (according to Webster's Dictionary)
Intelligence is Knowledge in motion as an art form. "I" is Self-who's True Culture is ISLAM. The Intelligence that Allah expressed has not said beginning or end. Islam is older than the Sun, Moon and Stars. This is the (9th degree) of our Student Enrollment Lesson. In our Alphabet, 9 is I which is ISLAM and its timeline is explained in plain English. The Intelligence in Allah's Truth has shown us how to be our Self, the science of the Germs of Life (Black/Brown), the Grafting Process, the Process of Rain, Hail, Show and Earthquakes, the measurements of our Earth etc… Wise Elevators apply 1 and 9 to our 4 regardless of whom or what.
(19) Science – The study of Natural Phenomena or the Knowledge so acquired. Any branch of Knowledge, an activity requiring study or method (according to Webster's Dictionary). The science of our Intelligence is in full bloom in what Wise Elevators call Plus Degrees. Here the True Science is shown/proven or Knowledge is Born (19) so let's make 19 using the science of the 10th degree 1-40 Lesson. Q: Who is that Mystery God? There is no Mystery God. The Sun of Man has searched for that Mystery God of trillions of years and was unable to find that so-called Mystery God. So they have agreed that the only God is the Sun of Man, so they would lose no more time searching for that which does not exist (using the 3rd definition of science which is an activity requiring study and method le's see).

Holy Bible: Psalms 82:6 I myself have said, Ye are Gods.
John 10:34, Jesus answered them, "Is it not written in you
Law I said, Ye are Gods". Now let's make 19: Psalms 82:6
8+2+6=16 1+6=7 and 7 = GOD so using this science one
must understand that you have to build on your wisdom in
order to make your knowledge known to your cipher (10).
8 + 2=10. Then, you show you've dealt equality (6) when
you do you will know or knowledge your equal aspects in
life. This is the action of God!! John 10:34 shows how our
righteous brother Knowledge (1) to his cipher (Chapter 10)
which he made an Understanding (3) to his Culture (4)
(verse 34) 3 + 4 = 7, 1 + 0 + 3 + 4 = 8. Only God can
righteously build on the Positive and Destroy the Negative.
Science makes your Knowledge (1) Born (9) 19.

(12) LOGIC: The study of reasoning, valid
reasoning (according to Webster's Dictionary). Reasoning
is to reach a conclusion by Logical thinking which is shown
in our 8th degree of the 1-40. The process of Rain and the
water cycle that continues to bring rain by a natural process
is not a Supernatural phenomenon. The 14th degree in the 1-
40 uses logical thinking and the processes of Inductive and
Deductive reasoning to define a slave of a mental death and
power, when one doesn't know their true origin in this
world and in fact has no knowledge (1) of his Culture (4)
i.e. 14th degree. See, this is Logic unspoken that Father
Allah gave Universal Saviors as a blueprint. All Wise
Elevators have to do is follow it by using your knowledge
and wisdom to bring forth understanding.

(1) ANALYSIS: The separation of a whole into its
parts for study and interpretation (according to Webster's
Dictionary). Here one sees our whole 8 points of Self
Awareness or Allah's Truth, Book of Life, the Foundation,
120 Lessons, etc… One has to understand one vibration at
a time before the next. You must learn how to speak our
tongue 1st because if you can't speak the language, you
can't live in this land. One has to 1st get Knowledge of each

degree and then the wisdom to finally get the understanding. This is the proper order to science a thing properly. This is the Jewel of Life. Knowledge (1) Arm, Leg, Leg, Arm, Head, the foundation or the Found Nation once the Knowledge is Understood.

(13) MATHEMATICS: The study of Numbers, forms, sets, etc... and their associated Relationships (according to Webster's Dictionary). This is to Manifest from Knowledge to Born in order to be complete. Mathematics is used in all and is the unit #1. Due to the fact that it is the Foundation (Found Nation of 1) of all in existence, through Supreme Mathematics, man sees his mental elevation, his relationship to our Universe and beyond his relationship to animal, pant, insect, etc... his relationship to his counterpart (woman) and a lot more. Through the mechanism of Mathematics, wise elevators can see with our real eye, the all Seeing Eye!! Math is our knowledge (1) Understood (3) which is the very essence of our culture (1 + 3 = 4). Mathematics is not to be confused with Numbers!!! Mathematics is of God himself, while Numbers can be used and have been use by Devil to keep us Blind, Deaf and Dumb. For example; the 2000 U.S. Census placed Latinos and Hispanics in the category of "White" to boost their Numbers!!! Eurocentric Propaganda and other deliberate revisions come as Whites are about to officially be recognized as the minority. Here, the Colored Man (Caucasian Man) used Numbers to attempt to keep us illiterate of his actions, while he lives in luxury b.u.t. the True and Living knows the Mathematics will show/prove his Numbers are on a decline. Always has been and always will be!! Also, the so-called Latinos/Hispanics are our people (Original People). Most are just as dark, if not darker than those already recognized as Black. They simply speak a different language due to Europeans enslaving our people in different places over time and impressing their language and cultures on those they conquered. They are

those who are present in the Universal Flag of Islam, as the Right Side of the 8 Points as Yellow or Brown (2nd seeds). "I Fast and Build" that you acknowledge this and bring understanding to your understanding, providing encouragement and Creating Equality.

PEACE
DIVINE ALL WISE ALLAH

Contact Info:
http://TheIncarcerated7sBlog.Blogspot.com
Email: Incarcerated7s@hotmail.com

Actual Facts Plus Gem

1.) **The Pacific Ocean covers 68,634,000 miles:** The Pacific Ocean is the 1st (knowledge) / biggest ocean on the Earth's surface. Ferdinand Magellan gave it the name from the Latin word, Pacificus (which means, pacify, in English), because of its tranquil appearance to him. This ocean is between Asia, and the so-called American continents. It occupies approximately 1/3rd of the Earth's surface, between the West coasts of North and South America, and the East coasts of Australia and Asia, to be specific. This has a maximum width of 11,000 miles; a maximum length of 9,000 miles; and a maximum depth of 36, 198 feet, in the Challenger Deep in the Marianas Trench, 250 miles Southwest of Guam. Along the Eastern shore, there is a narrow continental shelf, and high mountains rise abruptly from a deep sea floor. A series of volcanoes, the so-called "Ring of Fire," rims this ocean. The Asian coast is low and fringed with islands rising from a wide continental shelf.

2.) **The Atlantic Ocean covers 41, 340,000 square miles:** The Atlantic Ocean is the 2nd (wisdom) / biggest ocean on the Earth's surface. It separates North and South America from Europe and Africa. It is narrowest (1,600 miles) off Northeast Brazil and deepest (28,000 feet) in the Milwaukee deep North of Puerto Rico. The generally narrow continental shelf reaches its greatest widths off Northeast, North America, Southeast, South America and Northwest

Europe. This ocean is divided, lengthwise, by the mid-Atlantic ridge; a submarine mountain range, 300-600 miles wide, that extends 10,000 miles from Iceland to near the Antarctic Circle. This ridge which has a few peaks that emerge as Islands, is constantly widening, filling with molten rock and pushing the bordering continents further apart (look up plate tectonics).

3.) **The Indian Ocean covers 29,321,000 square miles:** The Indian Ocean is the 3rd (understanding) / largest ocean; located between South Asia, Antarctica, East Africa, and Southwest Australia. It is 4,000 miles wide at the Equator and reaches a maximum depth of 25, 344 feet in the Java Trench, South of Indonesia. Its major arms include the Arabian Sea, Red Sea, Gulf of Aden, Persian Gulf, Bay of Bengal and Andaman Sea. A complex series of mid-oceanic submarine ridges intersected to enclose deep-sea basins; their summits rising to the surface in places to form the Andaman, Nicobar, Seychelles and other island groups.

4.) **Lakes and Rivers cover 1,000,000 square miles:** A "Lake" is: A body of standing water occupying a depression in the earth. Most lakes are freshwater bodies; a few (e.g. The Great Salt Lake, The Dead Sea), however, are more salty than the oceans. The Great Lakes, of the United States and Canada are the world's largest system of freshwater lakes. The Caspian Sea is the world's largest lake. Most lake basins were formed by the erosive action of glaciers on bedrock. Other sources include volcanic calderas, natural and human-made dams in streams and rivers. Lakes are transient geological features, eventually disappearing because of climatic changes, erosion of an outlet and eutrophication (Look it up).

A river is: A stream of water larger than a brook or creek. Runoff after precipitation flows downward by the shortest and steepest course. Runoffs of sufficient volume and velocity joined, to form a stream that by erosion of underlying earth – rock deepens its bed. It becomes perennial when it cuts deeply enough to be fed by ground-water, or when it has an unlimited source (e.g. the "Saint Lawrence" flowing from the "Great Lakes"). Sea level is the ultimate base level for a river but the floor of a lake, of a basin, where a river flows, may become a local, temporary base level. Rivers modify topography by both erosion and deposition (Look up Delta).Young streams have steep sided valleys, steep gradients, and irregularities in the bed. Mature rivers have valleys with wide floors and a more smoothly graded bed. Old rivers have courses graded to base level and run through broad, flat areas.

5.) **Hills and Mountains cover 1,910,000 square miles:** a <u>Hill</u> is: A natural raised part of the Earth's surface, often rounded and it is smaller than a mountain. A <u>Mountain</u> is: A high land mass projecting above its surroundings, usually of limited at is summit. Some are isolated but they usually occur in ranges. A group of ranges, closely related in form, origin and alignment is a mountain system. An elongated group of systems is a chain; and a complex of ranges, systems and chains, continental in extent is a coroillera, zone or belt. Some mountains are remains of plateaus dissected by erosion (Look up Butte and Mesa). Others are cones of volcanoes, or intrusions of igneous rock that form domes. Fault-block Mountains occur where huge blocks of the earth's surface are raised relative to neighboring blocks. All the great mountain chains are either, Fold Mountains, or complex structures in which folding, faulting, and igneous activity have taken part. The ultimate cause of mountain building has been a source of controversy. The concept of plate tectonics (Look it up), is the 1st reasonable unifying theory hypothesizing that the earth's crust is broken into several plates that side-swipe each other, or collide (Look u the Continental Drift), compressional stresses are generated along the margin of the plate containing a continent, causing deformation and uplift of the continental shelf and continental rise, where accumulated sediments become complex folded and faulted mountain chains. Mountains have important effects on the earth's climate, population, economics and civilization of the regions where they occur. Major mountains ranges include the Alps, the Andes, the Caucasus, the Himalayas, the Pyrenees and the Rocky Mountains. The highest elevation on earth, above sea level, is the peak of Mount Everest.

6.) **Deserts cover 14,000,000 square miles:** A
desert is: An arid region <u>usually</u> partly covered
by sand supporting a limited and specially
adapted plant and animal population. So-called
"Cold Deserts," caused by extreme cold, and
often covered perpetually by snow and ice, form
about 1/6th of the earth's surface. Warm deserts
form 1/5th of it. The world's largest desert areas
lie between 20∘ and 30∘ North and South of the
Equator, in regions where mountains intercept
the paths of the trade winds, or where
atmospheric conditions limit precipitation. An
area with an annual rainfall of 10 inches or less
is considered a desert; although some deserts
and semi-deserts exist in areas of higher
precipitation where moisture is lost by runoff, or
evaporation. The 2 (wisdom) largest deserts are
1) the "Sahara" in Africa and 2) the "Great
Desert" of Central and West Australia.

7.) **Mount Everest is 29,141 feet high:** Mount
Everest is the highest mountain in the world. It
is located in the Central Himalayas on the
Tibet/Nepal border. It's named after, Sir George
Everest. It was first climbed in 1953 by,
Edmund Hillary and Tenzing Norkay, after at
least 8 earlier attempts to climb it had failed.
These 2 men calculated its height at 29,002 feet
high and this triangulation figure had been
accepted since 1850. In 1954, the Surveyor
General of the Republic of India set the height
at 29,028 feet, plus or minus 10 feet because of
snow. This figure was also accepted by the
National Geographic Society. In 1999, a team of
climbers, sponsored by Boston's Museum of
Science and the National Geographic Society

measured the height, at the summit, using sophisticated satellite based technology. This new measurement or 29, 035 feet was accepted by the National Geographic Society and other authorities, including the U.S. National Imagery and Mapping Agency. By May 31, 2007, over 50 years after the 1st climbers reached its summit, some 2,765 more had followed and about 193 had died in the attempts.

8.) **Sound travels at a rate of 1,120 feet-per-second:** Sound is produced by vibrations of an object and is transmitted by alternate increase and decrease in pressures that radiate outward through a material media of molecules – somewhat like waves spreading out on a pond, after a rock has been tossed into it. The frequency of sound is determined by the number of times the vibrating waves undulate per second, and is measured by cycles-per-second. The slower the cycle of waves, the lower the frequency. As frequencies increase, the sound is higher in pitch. The human ear is usually not sensitive to frequencies of fewer than 20 vibrations-per-second – although the range varies among individuals. Intensity or loudness is the strength of the pressure of these radiating waves and is measured in decibels. The speed of sound is generally defined as 1,088 feet-per-second, at sea level, at 32°F. It varies in other temperatures and in different media. Sound travels faster in water than in air; and even faster in iron and steel.

9.) **Light travels at 186,000 miles-per-second:** Light is a form of electromagnetic radiation, similar to radiant heat, radio waves and x-rays. It is emitted from a source in straight lines and spreads out over larger areas as it travels. Light per unit area diminishes as the square of the distance. The English mathematician and physicist, Sir Isaac Newton (1642-1727), described light as an emission of particles. The Dutch astronomer, mathematician and physicist, Christian Huygens (1629-1695), developed the theory that light travels by a wave motion. It is now accepted by most that these two theories are essentially complementary, and the development of Quantum Theory has led to results where light acts like a series of particles in some experiments and like a wave in others. The speed of light was 1st measured in a laboratory experiment by the French physicist, Armand Hippolyte Louis Fizeau (1814-1896). Today, the speed of light is known very precisely as 299,792,452 km-per-second, or 186,282.396 miles-per-second in a vacuum; in water, the speed of light is about 25% less and in glass 33% less.

10.)   **The Earth is 93,000,000 miles away from the Sun:** Since we know that light travels at 186,000 miles-per-second, **approximately** calculating the Earth's distance through the Sun's light is one way to figure out how far they are apart from each other. It takes about 8 minutes and 3 seconds for the Sun's light to reach the Earth, normally, so if light travels 186,000 miles per second; it travels 11,160,000 miles per minute (186,000 x 60, since 1 minute = 60 seconds). 11,160,000 x 8.3 = 92,628,000 or approximately 93,000,000 miles.

11.) **5,280 feet equals 1 mile and 1760 yards equals 1 mile:** There are 3 feet in 1 yard, so 1760 x 3 = 5,280 feet. To get yards you can divide 5,280 ÷ 3 = 1,760 yards. 1 foot is 12 inches. 1 yard is 36 inches. 1 mile is 63,360 inches.

12.) **The Arctic Ocean covers 390,000 square miles;** The Arctic Ocean is the world's smallest ocean; centering on the North Pole and connecting with the Pacific Ocean through the Bering Strait, and with the Atlantic Ocean through the Greenland Sea. It is covered with ice, up to 14 feet thick, all year; except in France areas. Contrary to the calculations in 120 Lessons, most Geography books and scientific calculations list the Arctic Ocean as covering 5,500,000 square miles, with an average depth of 3,407 feet. In 120, subtract 1, 2 + 3 in Actual Facts from total mileage of water on earth.

13.) There are 12 trillion, 478 billion, 118 million, and 400 thousand inches on the planet Earth. There are 12 inches in 1 foot and 5,280 feet = 1 mile. The Earth has 196,940 square miles. According to the 120 Lessons (See 5/110; 4/140). So it's 196,940,000 x 5,280 x 12.

Compiled by Professor Born Supreme P.H.D. 7 Allah

Contact Info:
http://TheIncarcerated7sBlog.Blogspot.com
Email: Incarcerated7s@hotmail.com

AFTERWORD

Well, if you're reading this then you obviously have this book in your possession Right? The Question is: Now, What are you going to do with all the information in it? I wrote the essays and compiled this book in my prison cell, as an example of how this Culture has impacted my thinking and changed my World view for the better. I know that this is just a start for me toward my life long journey toward the knowledge of Self but every journey begins with the 1st step. This just happens to be <u>BIG</u> 1st Step.

The main thing I want people to know is that your life isn't over once you are given a prison sentence. It's all about how you decide to react to the circumstance. You can hate the World and let bitterness overcome and consume you or you can strive to find a way to make a productive and Positive Contribution from where you are starting Right Now. I've decided to do just that so this is my way of showing the World what type of Mind I have. The Physical limitations on my Movement are simply an obstacle to be overcame for a person who knows their own potential like Myself. I'm planning a lot of Business moves this year and you'll be seeing a lot more from me and the Incarcerated Gods and Earths in the near Future so be on the lookout. You can also go to THE INCARCERATED 7'S BLOG online at http://theincarcerated7sblog.blogspot.com, if you want to keep up with the movement. There will be unpublished writings and information to contact the writers directly to give them input and feedback as well as other Gems. I've enclosed a National Gods and Earths Directory which many be updated by going to http://atlas.allahsnation.net online. I've also included the entire INTELLIGENT TAREEF ALLAH (ITA) case and decision that set the standard for Nation members to receive Culture Accommodations pursuant to the U.S.

Constitution. This case can be modified slightly in any state since it is a Federal Decision. For those Nation Members that are either familiarizing themselves with or seeking deeper insight into our History, Supreme Mathematics, Supreme Alphabets and 120 Lessons, I've enclosed 10 Quizzes on these topics. Do the research to answer every Question and I guarantee that you will see a lot of growth in your Knowledge. Don't forget that the goal is to use what you know to make a Positive impact on your environment so use the contacts and ask questions. The majority of the proceeds from this book will be used to finance the Gods that are fighting for Cultural Accommodations from Prison Administrations across the U.S., materials to educate more people in these prisons and I want to do something special for my Mother because she's been my rock over these last 10 years and my beautiful babies whom I am striving to be a better Father to. If either of my Babies' Mother's is reading this, Yall Aint't Getting Shit!!! Ha Ha! Seriously, I love you both and I know that it took a lot to put up with me before I grew into this Knowledge. Maybe now I can make you all proud of me which is all that I ever wanted to do. It's not a gimmick and it took some time for me to truly appreciate what I have. To BORN KING ALLAH and the Gods and Earths at the National Office of Cultural Affairs, thanks for all that you do for the Nation Members in Prison.

Proper Education Always Corrects Errors
Professor Born Supreme P.H.D. 7 ALLAH
Aka
Born

To all my brothers and sisters that are Incarcerated in Ohio as well as State and Federal Prisons, throughout the United States and beyond: ITS TIME TO LET THEM

KNOW WHAT WE CAN DO FROM BEHIND THESE WALLS! So make your presence known by purchasing this book and passing it around in them Segregation and Restrictive Housing Units!! I Plan to donate copies to the Juvenile Facilities because the babies are the ones that we can reach before it is too late. Walk with me and watch what happens!

RECOMMENDED READING

1. The Immortal Birth, by Allah Jihad available at Amazon.com $20
2. The Five Percenter Newspaper, (January 1996 to December 1996 issues have the entire 120 Lessons printed in them) $2
3. ASIA Journal 1, ASIA Journal 2 and ASIA Journal 3, by Saladin Quanaah (available at http: //www.atlantischool.blogspot.com) Love, Hell or Right $20
4. Tales of an Urban Sufi, The Mental Health of The Nation of Gods and Earths by Saladin Quanaah (available at http:// www.atlantischool.blogspot.com) $20 a piece
5. Knowledge of Self-A Collection of Wisdom on the Science of Everything In Life, by Lord Jamar, Sunez Allah, C'BS Alife Allah and Dr. Supreme Understanding available at Supreme Design Pub, P.O. Box 10887, Atlanta, GA, 30310 $13
6. 9 Points of Recognizing a Good Enlightener (article written by Saladin Quanaah at http://www.atlantisschool.blogspot.com
7. Five Percent Nation Neophytes by Manifest Supreme Knowledge God Allah available at M.A.P. Co., P.O. Box 7430, Minneapolis, Minnesota, 55407 $15
8. National Office of Cultural Affairs (N.O.C.A.) Self Help Civil Litigation Manual available at N.O.C.A., P.O. Box 2145, Lexington, Kentucky, 27293 $2 (Money Orders made out to NOCA info C/O BORN KING ALLAH

9. THE GREATEST STORY NEVER TOLD by Beloved Allah (Google it or write the Allah School in Mecca at 2122 7th Ave, N.Y., N.Y., 10027, phone (212)865-4175 ask for it) This is the information to order the 5%er newspaper also

10. Awaken the Giant Within by Anthony Robbins available at Amazon.com

11. The Sun of Man Digest available at Audubon Station, P.O. Box 372, N.Y., N.Y., 10032 $35 per year or $4 per issue

12. Pedagogy of the Five Percent by Sujan Kumar Dass (This is a Doctoral Dissertation at Argosy University for a Doctorate Degree on the culture and History of the Nation) 131 The Cream City Paper $5 per issue

RESOURCES FOR THE INCARCERATED

1. T.I.F. Services LLC, P.O. Box 903, North Fork, CA, 93643. This business does all types of research online for a small fee, sets up email and manages it as well as a lot of other services. Write and ask for a price list. They have a website online (www.TheInmatesFriend.com) email is inmatesfriend@yahoo.com

2. Center for Constitutional Rights, 666 Broadway, N.Y., N.Y., 10012, phone (212)614-6464, online: www.ccr.ny.org, this spot will mail you a free Jailhouse Lawyers Manual, if you are in the hole or wherever and a free copy of the U.S. Constitution. Write them and request both-may also, send free cases from all Courts still.

3. Prison Legal News, $2 per issue or $24 per year, P.O. Box 2420, West Brattleboro, VT,053030, phone (802)257-1342 online: www.prisonlegalnews.org, info@prisonlegalnews.org (This publication lets you know what is going on in Prisons across the U.S., new Legal cases that might affect your state, etc… it is worth **every** penny, so get it! They also have a raw booklist, so ask for 1 when you write or contact them online.

4. KYTE MAGAZINE/FACEBOOK or KYTE MAGAZINE, P.O. BOX 190382, ROXBURY, MA,02119

5. Justice Denied, P.O. Box 68911, Seattle, WA, 98168 online: www.justicedenied.org this place is a National Forum for the wrongfully convicted to be seen and their stories heard. If you are innocent of your crime, write them with your evidence and if it is convincing, they will help you network and get your story seen by people with resources to make a difference. They also have a good book selection. So write and ask for a booklist.

6. Reach Out Transportation, 4758 Ridge Road 278, Cleveland, Ohio, 44144 online: www.ReachOutTransportation.com to ask prices call (216)367-5652 ext. 102 and (216)367-5651 ext.101. This place provides rides for the families of the Incarcerated to visit to and from their houses for a fee.

TEN TESTS CONCERNING THE SCIENCE OF 120 DEGREES, OUR HISTORY AND CULTURE

I have composed the following as instruments in which one can exercise the knowledge gained in regards to our lessons ... Mathematics, Alphabet, 1-10, 1-36, 1-14, 1-40, Actual Facts and Solar Facts. I have also included a test on one's knowledge of our Universal Flag as well as on the Father and our Nation's history. There is no time limit on this test for it is meant to develop, refine and hone one's understanding of 120. One should only deal with the test that is reflective of where one stands in their lessons... If you're in the 1-10 don't try to answer questions for the Actual Facts section, though you may be able, this is not the focus. Mathematically we ALWAYS build from knowledge to born to in all things remain within the context and parameters established by that. These questions are in NOWAY all there is to understanding any component of our culture... borning universal truth; they will set you upon the path to engage in further and more in depth research.

TEST I: THE FATHER'S AND THE NATION'S HISTORY

1. What month, day and year was the Father born on?
2. In what city and state was he born in?
3. At what age did the Father migrate to New York? In what year was that?

4. What was the name of the woman whom the father had his first seeds by?
5. In what year did the father enter the service? What branch was it?
6. How many brothers and sisters did he have?
7. What war did he see action in?
8. As a result, did he receive any commendations? If so for what?
9. What skills did he also acquire while in the service?
10. When did he enter the Nation of Islam? And what or who prompted him to do so?
11. In what year did he receive his attribute "Abdullah" from Elijah Muhammad?
12. Why was The Father expelled from the Nation of Islam?
13. Who left the temple with him and remained with him for the remainder of his life?
14. What is year one for the Nation of Gods and Earths?
15. Name the nine first Borns.
16. Why was the Father placed in Mattawan? What year was that?
17. When was the first attempt made on his life and by whom?
18. When did the Father return to the essence and what were the circumstances surrounding his death?
19. When was the first Show and prove held? How about the first Universal Parliament?

TEST II: UNIVERSAL FLAG

1. How many degrees are between each short point? Between each long and short point?
2. What color should the moon be? And why?
3. How many points should be on the seven? And why?
4. How many total points are on the flag? How do you cee that?
5. Should any portion of the moonrise above the seven? Why?
6. In what year was the flag manifested and by whom?
7. Give two things that the eight points represent.

TEST III: SUPREME MATHEMATICS

1. Explain briefly in your own words the meaning of "In the Name of Allah".
2. Write a short history of Supreme Mathematics.
3. Explain what is Mathematics.
4. What is meant by "Mathematics is the truth and can only be used by the Sun of Man?"
5. What makes up Mathematics?
6. Explain briefly what is living Mathematics?
7. What is the mathematical science of self-creation?
8. Why does mathematics go from knowledge to born?

9. What is the natural order of mathematics and what would happen if wisdom were placed before knowledge?
10. Explain briefly the nine laws of mathematics.
11. Write a manifestation which includes within itself every mathematical unit of Living mathematics.
12. What are the essential life forces of Mathematics?
13. Write the name of at least 12 sciences which are ramifications of Mathematics.
14. Why is mathematics the key of life?
15. Explain the mathematics of 360 degrees.
16. What is the meaning of Bio-chemical reconstructive terms of mathematics?"
17. Explain briefly why one must know the day's mathematics.

TEST IV: SUPREME ALPHABETS

1. Explain briefly is your own words the meaning of "Supreme Alphabets".
2. What is the meaning of language of God?
3. What makes up the Supreme Alphabets?
4. What does wisdom one's knowledge mean?
5. What does the language God use indicate?
6. What does A-Z knowledge born mean to you?
7. Write a brief autobiography of your God/Earth self.
8. List three sources for increasing one's vocabulary.

TEST V: STUDENT ENROLLMENT 1-10

1. How do you cee the words Original, Asiatic, Maker, Owner and Cream of the Planet Earth?
2. How do you cee "Colored"?
3. What is meant by the term "Grafted"?
4. Explain briefly the origin of the word Caucasian.
5. If the Indians are also original people, why is their population given separately?
6. What is the ratio of Colored People to Original People all over the planet Earth?
7. How does one arrive at the total square mile of the planet Earth?
8. What is the useful land that is used every day by the Original Man?
9. What are TWO examples of the useful land that is used every day by the Colored Man?
10. Show and prove Buddhism too be 35,000 years old.
11. What is the PRESENT age Buddhism?
12. What is the year of birth for Christianity? Who was responsible for making is so?

TEST VI: ENGLISH "C" LESSON NO.1 1-36

1. Who is W.F. Muhammad?
2. What is the birth date of W.F. Muhammad?
3. What is his father's name? His mother's name?
4. What date is 379 years from the date of THAT writing(the 1-36)

5. Who exactly was the slave trader, and how did he go about his task of bring the Uncle over here?

6. Who is W.F. Muhammad's uncle and exactly why is he his uncle?

7. What is his uncle's own language?

8. What are some methods and tactics the devil used to put fear in them when they were little boys?

9. What are some examples of the "wrong foods"?

10. What is the above _question_ number 10?

11. Who exactly are the Muslim sons referred to in the knowledge god degree?

12. Exactly what happened 60 years ago from the date of that writing?

TEST VII: LOST FOUND MUSLIM LESSON NUMBER 1:1-14

1. Why do we say Musa is Half-Original?

2. What is a prophet?

3. Exactly how many square inches are there on the planet Earth?

4. Why do we say Columbus was Half-Original?

5. Why were the Indians exiled from India 16,000 years ago from the date of that writing?

6. What date was that when the Indians were exiled?

7. When was Yacub born physically?

8. When did he return to the essence?

9. How long were the devils in the root of civilization causing trouble amongst the righteous before we ran them out?

10. If Yacub was an Original Black man and the Father of the devil ... Does that make him a devil? Explain.

11. What date was 6,019 years ago from the date of that writing?

12. Why is Yacub said to have been run across the Hot Arabian Desert? Was he alive at that time?

13. Name some methods used to master the Original Man?

14. What is Jebus, Salem and Oriel?

15. Exactly, who took the city from the Devil, what date was 750 years ago from the date of that writing and also what major event was taking place?

16. Name some methods the devil uses to keep our people blind to themselves?

17. When did Asia begin to be called Africa?

18. When was the prophet Muhammad born? When was Elijah Muhammad Born?

19. If you have heard that your word shall be bond regardless to whom or what ... is it necessary to say, "Word is Bond," "That's my Word!" or even "I promise?"

20. How do you cee the "Fruit of Islam?"

21. Who is the Capt? Who is the Lieut? Who are the private soldiers? 22. Should the education of the Black woman be limited to those topics in the knowledge culture degree?

TEST VIII: LOST FOUND MUSLIM LESSON
NUMBER 2:1-40

1. It is said the Qur-an will expire in the year 25,000; 9,080 years from the date of that writing ... do the math, is that correct? If not why?
2. How do you find the circumference of the planet Earth?
3. Show and prove on the total weight of our planet.
4. Show and prove our planet travels at the speed of 1,037 1/3 mph.
5. The above speed refers to what motion?
6. What science deals with rain, hail and snow? What science deals with earthquakes?
7. Name the different parts of the Earth's atmosphere.
8. Exactly how far does the Earth's atmosphere extend?
9. How fast does the Earth travel around the Sun?
10. Answer the question to the 14th, 15th, 16th, 17th, 18th, 19th and 20th degree using the mathematics of each said degree.
11. What is meant by "blood suckers of the poor?" How do the 10% suck blood from the poor? 12. If a civilized person does not perform his duty, what is the severe punishment he/she receives?
12. Give a brief biography of Yacub. Including birth and death dates.

13. How do you cee "born twenty miles outside the Holy City of Mecca?"

14. "Who was the founder of un-like attract and a – like repel" is the wisdom knowledge degree in the 1-40, add on to how you cee that.

15. What is some other of Yacub's rules and regulations that are not mentioned in the wisdom build degree?

16. It tells us in the wisdom born degree that Yacub didn't build prison houses to imprison his people; why were they built then?

17. Does the brain weigh seven and one half ounces? IF it doesn't then why is that said?

18. It is said that we cannot reform the devil, so he must be taken off the planet. How do we go about doing so?

19. It is said the devil's civilization expired in the year 1914 … did it end then? If not why? When will it?

20. What is the exact number of years, months and days of YOU being birthed on the planet?

21. How do you cee "I fast and pray" in the understanding born degree?

TEST IX: ACTUAL FACTS

1. How are the measurements obtained for the oceans?

2. How deep is each ocean?

3. Why are not the seven seas mentioned in this lesson?

TO BE CONTINUED

UNITED STATES DISTRICT COURT

FOR THE SOUTHERN DISTRICT OF NEW YORK

RASHAAD MARRIA,

Plaintiff,

- - against –

- - DR. RAYMOND BROADDUS, et al.,
- - Defendants.

97 Civ. 8297 (NRB)

2003 U.S. Dist. Lexis 13329

July 31, 2003, Decided

July 31, 2003, Filed

OPINION AND ORDER

NAOMI REICE BUCHWALD

UNITED STATES DISTRICT JUDGE

Plaintiff Intelligent Tarref Allah, formerly known as Rashaad Marria n1 (hereinafter "plaintiff"), has been an inmate in the custody of the New York State Department of Correctional Services ("DOCS") since June 1995. For the duration of his incarceration within DOCS, plaintiff has been a member of the Nation of Gods and Earths ("Nation"), which he joined in August of 1994 while awaiting trial at Rikers Island. Defendants are DOCS employees sued in their individual and official capacities: defendant Glenn S. Goord ("Goord") is current the Commissioner of DOCS; defendant Dr. Raymond Broaddus ("Broaddus") was the Deputy Commissioner for Program Services of DOCS at all times relevant to this action; defendant G. Blaetz ("Blaetz") was a Senior Counselor and the Media Review Committee Chairperson at DOCS' Green Haven Correctional Facility ("Green Haven"); and defendant Warith Deen Umar ("Umar") was the Coordinator for Islamic Affairs at DOCS at all times relevant to this action (collectively, "defendants" or "DOCS").

Plaintiff challenges DOCS' policy classifying the Nation as an "unauthorized" or "security threat" group and DOCS' consequent prohibition on his receipt of Nation materials and literature, including the group's central texts and its newspaper, and ban on formal gatherings with other members of the group. He seeks declaratory and injunctive relief pursuant to 42 U.S.C. § 1983, alleging violations of the First and Fourteenth Amendments to the United States Constitution, the Religious Land Use and Institutionalized Persons Act of 2000 ("RLUIPA"), the New York State Constitution, and state law. Plaintiff's federal due process and analogous state law claims were dismissed on qualified immunity grounds at the summary judgment stage of this case. See Marria v. Broaddus, 200 F. Supp.2d 280, 301-302 (S.D.N.Y. 2002).

The Court held a five-day bench trial during which the parties presented evidence bearing on the issue of whether plaintiff's beliefs as a member of the Nation are entitled to Constitutional protection and, if so, what proper the scope of protection would be. Having reviewed the testimony and evidence that has been presented, we find that plaintiff's sincerely-held beliefs as a member of the Nation are entitled to First Amendment and RLUIPA protection, and thus grant plaintiff's requested injunctive relief in part and remand in part for further consideration and action by DOCS not inconsistent with this decision. n2 Our findings of fact and conclusions of law are set forth below.

BACKGROUND

The Nation's history, teachings, and practices are largely not contested, nor are the existence and application of DOCS' policies concerning the Nation.

A. The Nation of Gods and Earths

The Nation, whose adherents are commonly referred to as "Five Percenters," the "Five Percent", or the "Five Percent Nation," was founded in New York nearly 40 years ago. The Nation traces its roots to the Black Muslim movement that emerged in the mid-twentieth century and most directly to the Nation of Islam ("NOI") - a group that DOCS classifies as a religion pursuant to the settlement in Muhammad v. Coughlin, 1998 U.S. Dist. Lexis 10134, No. 91 Civ. 6333 (S.D.N.Y July 8, 1998), and one with which the Nation shares some teachings and its central text (known to Nation members as the 120 Degrees). n3 See Trial Tr. at 162:11-17; Trial Tr. at 56:18-23. The concept of the "Five Percent" from which the Nation derives its colloquial name was first set forth by NOI leader Elijah Muhammad, who separated the world's population into three categories: the Five Percent, the Ten Percent, and the Eighty-Five Percent. See Trial Tr. at 54:6-20. According to Elijah Muhammad, the Ten Percent teach the Eighty-Five Percent to believe in the existence of a "mystery God" and thereby keep the Eighty-Five Percent enslaved by having them worship something that they cannot see. See id. Muhammad characterized the remaining Five Percent as the poor, righteous teachers who do not believe in the teachings of the Ten Percent and instead teach the identity of the true and living God, as well as freedom, justice, and equality to all human families of the planet earth. See id. The term "Five Percenter," while commonly used to describe members of the Nation, can be used more generally to describe a person who subscribes to the belief that humankind can be broken down into the Five Percent, the Ten Percent, and the Eighty-Five Percent. Thus, not all people who might nominally identify themselves as "Five Percenters" are necessarily members of the Nation of Gods and Earths. See Trial Tr. at 55:15-25.

The Nation of Gods and Earths began in 1964 when its founder Clarence 13X Smith broke with the NOI. See Trial Tr. at 56:18-23. In contrast to the NOI's belief that Allah (God) appeared on Earth solely in the person of its founder Master Fard Muhammad, Smith and his followers professed the central belief that every black man is an embodiment of God with the proper name Allah and that every black woman is "Earth," from which life springs. See Trial Tr. at 56:24-57:7. Thereafter, with the assistance of the City of New York and the Urban League, Smith and his followers created the "Allah School in Mecca," a headquarters that also houses the "Allah Youth Center in Mecca," in Harlem, New York as a street academy designed to bring the Nation's message to urban youth. See Trial Tr. at 56:18-23; see also generally April 30, 2001 Decl. of Elise Zealand ("Zealand Decl.") Ex. N (article discussing the history of the Nation); April 27, 2001 Decl. of Rashaad Marria ("Marria Decl.") P 15 & Ex. D (discussing the Nation's relationship with the Urban League and New York City). The Center, which enjoys 501(c)(3) not-for-profit tax status and a favorable ninety-nine year lease from the City paid at the rate of twenty dollars per month, continues to operate in Harlem as do several similar centers elsewhere. See Trial Tr. at 316:9-13. Among the activities sponsored by the Allah School and Youth Center are substance abuse programs, after-school tutoring for children, and youth trips to show children that "there is more to life than what they see in the ghettos." See Trial Tr. at 313:17-315:21. Aside from its headquarters in Harlem, the Nation does not have a formal stucture or hierarchy beyond preaching respect for "elders" - i.e., those with the most extensive knowledge of the group's beliefs and lessons. See Trial Tr. at 94:12-24.

As we previously mentioned, some of the Nation's beliefs and practices overlap with those of the NOI as a result of the two groups' shared belief in the lessons that comprise the 120 Degrees. Both groups, for example, believe that the black man is the "original Asiatic man." Both the Nation and NOI also believe that the white man is "the devil," made through a selective breeding process referred to as "grafting," as all of these teachings are set forth in the 120 Degrees. See Trial Tr. at 165:12-21; Trial Tr. at 302:15-20; Pl. Trial Ex. 180 (anthropological "syncretism" created by plaintiff witness Ted Swedenberg comparing the Nation of Gods and Earths to various religious traditions); Blocker Decl. P 8. Members of both groups also observe dietary restrictions, such as refraining from eating pork, and fast on holy days. n4 Finally, the Nation's emblem, known to members as the "Universal Flag," is reminiscent of the one used by NOI. Compare Pl. Trial Ex. 1 (cover of Five Percenter newspaper containing the "Universal Flag") with http://www.noi.org/ (visited May 26, 2003) (NOI web page displaying crescent emblem).

Although plaintiff asserts that his belief system as a member of the Nation would be commonly understood as a religion, he and other nation members reject the label "religion" in describing the Nation because they believe that the term "religion" connotes "belief in the mystery God" - i.e., the false religious belief systems promulgated by the Ten Percent to enslave the minds of others. See Trial Tr. at 106:13-16. Therefore, plaintiff and other Five Percenters commonly describe the Nation as a "way of life or culture," not a "religion." See Trial Tr. at 58:2-13.

The 120 Degrees, along with two numerology devices known as the Supreme Alphabet and Supreme Mathematics, forms the core of the Nation's literature. The 120 Degrees are lessons arranged in a question and answer format that represent the teachings of NOI founder Master Fard Muhammad and Elijah Muhammad. The Supreme Alphabet and Supreme Mathematics assign a word to each letter of the alphabet (almost all of which begin with the letter to which they correspond) and ten "righteous" principles to each number from 0 to 9. They are used as the keys "to understanding man's relationship to the universe and Islam," as well as to understanding and interpreting the 120 Degrees. n5 Marria[Decl. P 13. There is no dispute that the Supreme Alphabet and Mathematics have not changed since they were created by Clarence 13X Smith in the 1960's and are made widely available by the Nation and others. Members of the Nation use these sources in conjunction with one another to attain "knowledge of self," which is central to their membership in the Nation, and they must be understood and applied on a daily basis in order to live righteously. Hence, just as Nation members are required to fast on holy days and follow dietary restrictions, they are also required to study the lessons in these teachings on a regular basis both individually and in group sessions. The Nation's beliefs are also based on the Koran and the Bible, which serve as secondary texts, see Trial Tr. at 65:7-66:15, and "plus lessons" consisting of written commentary by Five Percenters aimed at fostering further insight into the group's texts and teachings. See Trial Tr. at 64:17-20, 64:25-65:6.

One additional piece of Nation literature specifically at issue in this case is The Five Percenter, a monthly newspaper published by the Allah Youth Center. It contains articles about current events relevant to the Nation, information about community activities, letters to the editor, editorials, and Five Percenter lessons and "plus lessons," including teachings from the 120 Degrees, the Supreme Alphabet, and the Supreme Mathematics. See e.g., Pl. Trial Ex. 3 (copy of the October 1995 issue of The Five Percenter received in evidence); Pl. Trial Ex. 6 (copy of the June 1996 issue of The Five Percenter received in evidence). Some of The Five Percenter's content is directed specifically towards prison inmates, including messages advising them to better themselves and follow prison rules while incarcerated. n6 Plaintiff asserts that The Five Percenter also serves as the principal and vital link for him to communicate with members of the Five Percenter community outside prison. See Trial Tr. at 69:24-70:17; see also Trial Tr. at 154:24-155:6 (plaintiff's expert anthropologist Ted Swedenberg explaining that The Five Percenter shows Nation members how the group's abstract principles can be applied in life); Trial Tr. at 292:17-293:15 (Nation representative Cee Aaquil Allah Barnes discussing the importance of The Five Percenter as a link to the community for prison inmates who are members of the Nation); Pl. Trial Ex. 4 (December 1995 issue of The Five Percenter containing a "Correspond with a God Column" for readers who wish to correspond with incarcerated members of the Nation).

Practicing members of the Nation also have various congregative gatherings. For example, the Nation conducts "Civilization Classes," in which more senior members - i.e., those who have studied the lessons longer than others - educate newer members about the lessons and how they can be applied. See Trial Tr. at 291:17-23. Such classes are held regularly at the Allah Youth Center. See Trial Tr. at 314:25-315:3. Nation members also gather regularly for "Parliaments" and "Rallies." During these gatherings, members come together to help one another learn their lessons, to educate one another by conversing about the lessons' meaning and application (which they call "building"), and to make decisions as a community. See Trial Tr. at 59:25-60:10; Trial Tr. at 287:25-288:8; Trial Tr. at 291:2-10.

Finally, as we mentioned earlier, the Nation has an official symbol referred to as the a Universal Flag, consisting of an eight-pointed star containing a number 7, a crescent, a smaller five-pointed star, and the words "In the Name of Allah." See Trial Tr. at 155:16-23.

B. DOCS' Policies Concerning the Nation

DOCS deems the "Five Percenters" to be an "unauthorized" or "security threat" group, which is the nomenclature that DOCS uses to describe a gang or other group that it views as an organized threat to prison safety and security. n7 As a result, though DOCS' correctional philosophy is primarily "behavior based," Nation members like plaintiff are regarded as gang members within the New York State correctional system and are consequently prohibited from receiving or possessing any of the group's literature or symbols, as well as from engaging in any organized activities associated with the Nation.

DOCS' policies concerning the Nation stem from its non-recognition policy designed for security threat group management, which seeks to diminish gangs' power and importance by refusing to legitimize their existence. DOCS does not officially recognize unauthorized or security threat groups, even by tracking their activities internally, because it believes that "to do so would give them undue credibility and attention and embellish their importance." Def. Findings at P 45 (citing Trial Tr. at 340:18-341:19). Pursuant to its non-recognition policy, and to further prevent the growth and/or proliferation of security threat groups through recruiting, DOCS implemented Rule 105.12 of its Standards of Inmate Behavior, which states that inmates "shall not engage or encourage others to engage in unauthorized organizational activities or meetings, display, wear, possess, distribute, or use unauthorized organizational insignia or materials." Def. Trial Ex. I. Rule 105.12 defines an unauthorized organization as "any gang, or organization which has not been approved by the Deputy Commissioner for Program Services." Id. Materials violating Rule 105.12 are considered contraband and are not subject to the "Media Review" process DOCS has implemented for determining the acceptability of the majority of other printed and written materials received by prisoners. See Trial Tr. at 360:21-361: 9. DOCS has also implemented a zero-tolerance gang policy, under which any kind of behavior deemed to be part of gang activity, including possession of written materials or gang-associated emblems or logos, will subject an inmate to discipline. See Trial Tr. at 342:13-19.

Applying its complete ban on "Five Percenter" literature pursuant to its non-recognition policy, DOCS forbids plaintiff from having lessons from the 120 Degrees, possessing the Supreme Alphabet and Mathematics, or receiving or possessing The Five Percenter and other materials that are either associated with the Nation or contain its symbols. n8 DOCS' designation of the Nation as an unauthorized group also means that plaintiff can meet with no more than four other Five Percenter inmates at a time, and can only do so sporadically. See Trial Tr. at 63:6-18. He is thus prohibited from attending or organizing Civilization Classes, Parliaments, or Rallies. Finally, plaintiff is not permitted to eat his meals after sundown on fast days or to meet with other inmates on those days in order to break the fast, privileges that are extended to inmates who adhereJuly 16, 2003 to authorized religions like Nation of Islam members and Orthodox Muslims. See Trial Tr. at 62:11-63:5.

Because DOCS' procedures for becoming "authorized" explicitly exclude religious groups, there does not appear to be an established process by which an unrecognized group like the Nation can attain recognition as a religion from DOCS in order to avoid gang treatment. n9 We surmise from the trial testimony, however, that a religious group could become effectively "authorized" in a manner equivalent to becoming an authorized group directly through the Department of Program Services by attaining a favorable recommendation for accommodations from DOCS' Division of Ministerial and Family Services that is subsequently approved by executive level DOCS officials. See Trial Tr. 525:25-526:15, 530:3-6 (former Director of Ministerial and Family Services John LoConte describing his role in investigating and making subsequent recommendations to executive level DOCS officials concerning inmate requests for religious accommodations). It has apparently been DOCS' practice upon receiving an inmate request for religious accommodations to attempt to "verify the religious practice, whether or not it is something that is understandable in light of organized operational religious communities," Trial Tr. 512:17-21, and to "reach out to the outside religious community of the inmates [making the claim]" in order to confirm the practices' legitimacy and seek assistance in providing accommodations. Trial Tr. at 513:1-2. However, DOCS did not introduce any evidence to indicate that it has made such investigative or outreach efforts with respect to the Nation, despite having received a number of requests for religious accommodation. n10 Moreover, in defending this lawsuit, DOCS has consistently avoided this issue by insisting that plaintiff cannot seek religious recognition because the Five Percenters are, in its view, a gang and not a religion.

C. Conflicting Claims About the Nature of the Nation

While plaintiff claims that DOCS' ban on Nation materials and gatherings violates his free exercise rights under the Constitution and RLUIPA, DOCS argues that his beliefs and practices as a member of the Nation are not protected because they are not sincere or religious in nature, and in any event that its ban of the Nation's literature is justified by violence associated with Five Percenter inmates. The parties' conflicting claims boil down to widely disparate characterizations of the nature of the Nation of Gods and Earths.

DOCS, on the one hand, takes the position that "the Five Percenters," including purported members of the Nation of Gods and Earths, is a violent organization that, like some other gangs, utilizes symbols and seemingly innocuous literature touting the group's positive aspects to identify its members and "territory," as well as to recruit new members into its violent and illegal activities. n11 Such activities include assaults, intimidation, extortion, drug dealing, and retaliation against fellow members who attempt to leave the group or act against other Five Percenters. See Def. Findings PP 56-58. DOCS additionally asserts that Five Percenters utilize the Supreme Alphabet and Mathematics as a code in furtherance of its disruptive activities. See Def. Findings PP 61-63, 103-104. DOCS' stance in this case represents a shift from its previous litigation position that the content of the Nation's literature itself is dangerous. n12 Here, DOCS concedes that the Nation's literature is innocuous, but claims that its ban on Nation materials is still necessary to preserve prison safety and security because the materials are used to facilitate the recruiting efforts and illegal activities of a violent and disruptive organization. Furthermore, according to DOCS, it would give the Five Percenters and other security threat groups increased legitimacy and status, contrary to its non-recognition strategy, if inmates were permitted access to the groups' materials. See Def. Findings PP 42, 52, 90-92, 94-95 (outlining this justification for DOCS' non-recognition strategy in general and for its specific application to the Five Percenters).

Plaintiff, on the other hand, asserts that the Nation is not a gang, but rather a legitimate religious group whose beliefs extol lawfulness, righteousness, freedom, justice, equality, and peace and whose literature focuses largely on positive messages, such as education, self-improvement, self-worth, and responsibility. See Pl. Proposed Findings of Fact ("Pl. Findings") PP 19-21, 35-36. According to plaintiff and other Nation members, "any purported member who engages in violent or disruptive activities is violating the tenets of the Nation." Pl. Findings P 35; see also Trial Tr. at 287:9-288:8. He further asserts that the Supreme Alphabet and Mathematics are a religious numerology system, not a secret code, see Pl. Findings PP 16-19; see also Trial Tr. 47:13-16, and that Nation members are allowed to leave the group without reprisals. n13 See Pl. Proposed Conclusions of Law ("Pl. Conclusions")26; see also Trial Tr. at 96:4-23; Trial Tr. at 385:6-386:11. Plaintiff thus argues that allowing him to receive the group's literature poses no threat to prison safety or security.

In evaluating these contradictory positions, we make further factual findings below as they become relevant.

DISCUSSION

A. Sincerity and Religious Nature of Plaintiff's Beliefs

As a threshold matter, we discuss DOCS' position that plaintiff may not seek the protections of the First Amendment or RLUIPA because he has failed to demonstrate either the sincerity of his professed beliefs or that they otherwise merit religious protection.

The Second Circuit set forth the scope of this Court's inquiry into a plaintiff's beliefs in Patrick v. LeFevre, a previous free exercise case brought by a Five Percenter inmate, by emphasizing the "limited function of the judiciary in determining whether beliefs are to be accorded first amendment protection" as follows:

It cannot be gainsaid that the judiciary is singularly ill-equipped to sit in judgment on the verity of an adherent's religious beliefs. Mindful of this profound limitation, our competence properly extends to determining "whether the beliefs professed by a [claimant] are sincerely held and whether they are, in his own scheme of things, religious."

Patrick v. LeFevre, 745 F.2d 153, 157 (2d Cir. 1984) (quoting United States v. Seeger, 380 U.S. 163, 185, 13 L. Ed. 2d 733, 85 S. Ct. 850 (1965)). Hence, a court's scrutiny of whether a plaintiff deserves free exercise protection "extends only to whether a claimant sincerely holds a particular belief and whether the belief is religious in nature." Jolly v. Coughlin, 76 F.3d 468, 476 (2d Cir. 1996) (discussing this standard in the context of a free exercise claim brought under the Religious Freedom Restoration Act). Sincerity analysis "seeks to determine the subjective good faith of an adherent in performing certain rituals" and can be guided by such extrinsic factors as a purported religious group's size and history, whether the claimant appears to be seeking material gain by hiding secular interests behind a veil of religious doctrine, and whether the claimant has acted in a manner inconsistent with his professed beliefs. Int'l Soc'y for Krishna Consciousness v. Barber, 650 F.2d 430, 441 (2d Cir. 1981). However, "courts are not permitted to ask whether a particular belief is appropriate or true - however unusual or unfamiliar the belief may be." Jolly, 76 F.3d at 476. Patrick v. LeFevre further instructs us that deciding such subjective issues as the sincerity and the perceived nature of beliefs requires the factfinder - the Court in this case - to assess the claimant's demeanor at trial and "delve into the internal operations of the claimant's mind and in turn assess the sincerity of the held beliefs and the place occupied by such beliefs in the plaintiff's life." Patrick, 745 F.2d at 158; see also id. at 159. In this regard, the Circuit has cited with approval the definition of religion espoused by philosopher William James - "the feelings, acts, and experiences of individual men in their solitude, so far as they apprehend themselves to stand in relation to whatever they may consider the divine." Id. at 158 (quoting W. James, The Varieties of Religious Experiences 31 (1910)). Having heard plaintiff's testimony and observed his demeanor throughout the week-long trial, we find that plaintiff meets the two Patrick v. LeFevre, 745 F.2d 153 criteria.

i. Sincerity Analysis

We find that the trial record contained ample evidence of plaintiff's sincerity in his beliefs and that DOCS' arguments to the contrary are unpersuasive. Plaintiff, who is incarcerated for murder, testified that the Nation had "resurrected" him "from ... a life of total unrighteousness." Trial Tr. at 100:8-9. He also described the manner in which his life is guided by his Five Percenter beliefs - specifically the 120 Degrees, Supreme Alphabet, and Supreme Mathematics - and his efforts to conform his life to his beliefs as follows:

When I look at that first degree in the student enrollment [the first few lessons of the 120 Degrees] and I see the black man is the God of the universe, it's endowed me with the power to know the sky's the limit. I manifested, I make changes in my life. I don't do things I did before. I became a vegan, stopped eating animals. I enhanced my discipline level. My mother's, she's amazed I've been locked up so long and haven't even had a fight. I learn to conduct myself in matters where people respect me for who I am. I don't have to be bothered no more because people respect intelligence, and once they see you living what you say, they respect that. And I learn to conduct myself in a manner which I don't put myself in predicaments that would lead to altercations and things of that nature.

Trial Tr. at 100:14-101:1. He reports that in doing so he has gone from being a person who was "trying to take things to the extreme, you know, on a negative aspect" to being a "very disciplined person, a person that's constantly striving to obtain righteousness" who has "learned and grown to have respect for other people's feelings." Trial Tr. at 43:5-17. Examples of ways in which plaintiff has conformed his life and daily activities with his beliefs as a member of the Nation include memorizing and studying his lessons to the extent possible under DOCS' complete ban, eschewing pork and pork byproducts, fasting on holy days, and officially changing his name from Rashaad Marria to a "righteous" one reflecting Nation values and custom (Intelligent Tarref Allah), not to mention diligently pursuing this litigation since 1997 and engaging in a letter-writing campaign to recover confiscated copies of The Five Percenter prior to that. See Trial Tr. at 38:14-18; 100:17-20. When one considers the totality of plaintiff's testimony, it is apparent that he has structured his daily lifestyle in conformity with the rigors of membership in the Nation for some time. This conclusion is underscored by plaintiff's record of conduct as a prisoner, which includes earning his GED, participating in numerous other classes and programs, serving on the Inmate Liaison Committee, n14 and no incidents of violence or disruptive conduct. See Trial Tr. at 126:12-14; June 18, 2001 Reply Decl. of Rashaad Marria Exs. F-J (certifications and letter of commendation documenting various classes and programs in which plaintiff participated while incarcerated).

Plaintiff's sincerity was further substantiated at trial by the largely unchallenged testimony of Cee Aaquil Allah Barnes and Born Justice Allah, representatives of the Allah Youth Center, concerning the Nation's apparent legitimacy outside prison. n15 See Trial Tr. at 296:17-298:13 (DOCS' extremely limited cross examination of Mr. Barnes); Trial Tr. at 323:10-12 (DOCS declining to cross examine Mr. Justice Allah). There was no suggestion by DOCS that either of these representatives was involved in a criminal organization. Nor did DOCS contest the testimony that the Nation's non-incarcerated members include police officers, doctors, lawyers, and other professionals who would presumably not be part of a violent gang. See Trial Tr. at

294:17-21. Moreover, the Allah Youth Center's 501(c)(3) tax status and the favorable lease that it continues to receive from New York City, neither of which DOCS disputes, are strong indications that the Nation itself is not believed to be a criminal organization outside prison. n16 The various community-oriented programs and activitie the representative described as taking place at the Allah School and Youth Center are also consistent with plaintiff's claims that the Nation is a sincere, legitimate religious group. See Trial Tr. at 290:16-25 (Cee Barnes testifying about health and book fairs taking place at the Allah Youth Center), 292:1-16 (Cee Barnes testifying about the Nation's prison outreach and assistance given to former inmates); Trial Tr. at 313:17-315:19 (Born Justice Allah testifying about the youth programs run at the Allah School).

The Nation thus appears to be in the somewhat unique position of having a legitimate existence outside prison while being classified exclusively as a security threat group within DOCS. n17

In support of its position that plaintiff is insincere, DOCS makes a series of unpersuasive arguments. Several concern instances in which DOCS claims plaintiff did not conform his conduct to his professed Five Percenter tenets and thereby suggests that he is essentially faking them in order to gain the legitimacy that religious protection would afford his gang participation. See Def. Findings PP 21-32. DOCS first cites three instances in which plaintiff was disciplined by prison authorities for nonviolent conduct: (1) giving false information to a corrections officer, to wit, falsely telling the officer that he had received legal pads from the prison commissary; (2) failing to obey a direct order from a guard who apparently told him to stay away as he was attempting to observe another inmate's grievance meeting in the sergeant's office as the representative of the Inmate Liaison Committee; and (3) possessing an "altered item" - a toothbrush that plaintiff testified he used as a makeshift screwdriver by outfitting it with the sliding metal piece from the inside of a pair of headphones - that could be used as a weapon. See Def. Findings PP 29-31; Trial Tr. at 124:22-129:9. Whether or not one believes plaintiff's assertions that he was disciplined unjustly in the first two instances, they are a far cry from the kind of marked or regular departure from professed beliefs that would lead us to find a plaintiff insincere. Cf. Int'l Soc'y for Krishna Consciousness v. Barber, 650 F.2d 430, 441 (2d Cir. 1981) (citing, as an example of the type of inconsistent act that would lead a court to find an adherent insincere, a Jewish adherent claiming a free exercise violation from being compelled to appear in court on the Sabbath who otherwise works on Saturdays). In the case of the altered item, which no one disagrees constituted contraband, we find credible plaintiff's explanation that he was simply using it as a makeshift screwdriver, given that he did not alter the rounded, blunt tip of the headphone piece and made no real attempt to conceal the item, which was found in a bucket filled with radio parts and other knick-knacks where it was regularly kept. See Def. Trial Exhibit OO (photocopy of "altered item"). n18

Other evidence of inconsistent conduct, according to DOCS, includes plaintiff's mentioning only that the Nation's dietary restrictions require him to eschew pork while Cee Barnes testified that the Nation's tenets require one "not to eat pork and if you go a little bit further ... not to eat any type of scavenger, and a scavenger is like shrimp or tuna fish," Def. Findings P 28; see also Trial Tr. at

.

287:7-8, plaintiff's allowing his subscription to The Five Percenter lapse for a time in 1996, see Def. Findings at P 26, and plaintiff's adopting a NOI religious designation during a period in which he attended a number of NOI services. See Def. Findings P 27. The purported inconsistencies raised by the first two arguments seem sufficiently minor that we need not address them in detail here, except to note that DOCS does not contest plaintiff's testimony that he has adhered to a vegan diet since becoming a Nation member (meaning that he does not eat shrimp or tuna) and that the lapse in plaintiff's subscription occurred during a period in which DOCS began to confiscate the newspaper as illegal contraband. n19

With respect to DOCS' argument about the NOI designation, plaintiff testified that he sporadically attended both NOI and other groups' services while remaining a member of the Nation in order to "get an understanding of what separates the two and why people think the way they think," Trial Tr. at 67:3-5, but that NOI was the only group for which DOCS required him to sign a religious designation form in order to be allowed to attend the services. See Trial Tr. at 67:22-68:16. He emphatically, and credibly, denied that his attendance at any other group's services constituted a commitment to be a part of a religious community other than the Nation. See id. We find it unsurprising that a member of the Nation, which builds on related religious traditions, like plaintiff would seek to attend NOI services and correspondingly sign up as a NOI adherent when DOCS treats the Nation itself as an unauthorized group, especially since this is exactly what DOCS encouraged him to do in response to his requests for religious accommodations. n20 Cf. Campos v. Coughlin, 854 F. Supp. 194 (S.D.N.Y 1994) (finding "not persuasive" DOCS' attempt to cast doubt on the sincerity of Santeria adherents' religious beliefs because they had previously self-identified as "Catholic"). Moreover, DOCS' argument that we should find plaintiff insincere because he signed up for and attended NOI services is in tension with its claim, discussed infra, that plaintiff's beliefs are not substantially burdened by its policies because he can gain access to the Nation's lessons through the NOI (presumably in part by attending their services).

Ultimately, the point of sincerity analysis is to "provide[] a rational means of differentiating between those beliefs that are held as a matter of conscience and those that are animated by motives of deception and fraud." Patrick, 745 F.2d at 157 (citation omitted). Having engaged in such an analysis, and while we do not find it inconceivable that a gang or other group might seek to cloak itself in a purported "religion" in order to increase its legitimacy, we find DOCS' attempt to cast doubt upon the sincerity of the plaintiff's beliefs in this case singularly unpersuasive.

ii. Religious Nature of Plaintiff's Beliefs

DOCS' claims that plaintiff's beliefs are not "religious in nature" are similarly unpersuasive. DOCS' argument on this issue throughout this litigation has been a semantic one, focusing on plaintiff's and other Nation members' reluctance to call the Nation of Gods and Earths a "religion." See Marria v. Broaddus, 200 F. Supp.2d 280, 292 (S.D.N.Y. 2002). DOCS asserts that Nation members' refusal to call the group a "religion" indicates that it should not be treated as one and that plaintiff's statements that he believes that the Nation fits the legal definition of a religion are merely a self-serving tactic to further this litigation. See Def. Findings PP 3-7, 23-25. In support of this argument, DOCS notes that plaintiff stated at his first deposition that the Five Percenters are not a religion, but rather a way of life. See id. P 24; see also Feb. 12, 2001 Decl. of Dale Artus Ex. Q (issue of The Five Percenter with headline and article entitled "We Are Not A Religion").

The weakness of DOCS' semantic argument is evident. While it is somewhat understandable that a group that refuses to describe itself as a "religion" did not inspire immediate outreach from DOCS officials, the law of the Free Exercise Clause does not turn on mere semantic distinctions. Cf. Graham v. Cochran, 96 Civ. 6166, 2000 U.S. Dist. Lexis 1477, at *30 (S.D.N.Y. February 14, 2000) (Ellis, M.J.) (noting, in a similar case brought by a Five Percenter inmate, that "just as calling one's beliefs a 'religion' does not make it such for constitutional purposes, failure to label one's beliefs a 'religion' does not prohibit constitutional protection"). The significance of plaintiff's beliefs in his life is considerably more relevant than what plaintiff and other members of his community choose to call their beliefs - "a rose by any other name," as the saying goes, "would smell as sweet." As already described in some detail, plaintiff has submitted substantial evidence that he has been a practicing member of the Nation since August of 1994 and that he lives by the Nation's teachings and observes the Nation's holy days to the extent possible under DOCS regulations. Furthermore, plaintiff, the Allah School representatives, and an expert cultural anthropologist all testified that the Nation carries the same significance for its members as Christianity, Judaism, and Islam do for their adherents, and that the Nation's contrasting belief system means that one could not be a part of those religions and the Nation simultaneously. Overall, plaintiff has convincingly demonstrated the central significance of the Five Percenter belief system in his daily life and his understanding of that which he considers divine, which is in accordance with the William James definition of religion. Finally, it would be incongruous for us to reject the notion that the Nation's belief system is "religious in nature" when it is, in several respects, more orthodox in both its practices and notions of the "divine" than the belief systems espoused by other groups that currently receive religious protections. n21

For these reasons, we find that plaintiff's beliefs as a member of the Nation of God's and Earths are both sincere and "religious in nature" and therefore entitled to RLUIPA and First Amendment protection under the free exercise clause. Cf. Patrick v. LeFevre, 745 F.2d 153 (2d Cir. 1984) (finding for summary judgment purposes that an inmate's beliefs as a Five Percenter were constitutionally protected); Breland v. Goord, 1997 U.S. Dist. Lexis 3527, No. 94 Civ. 3696, 1997 WL 139533 (S.D.N.Y. March 27, 1997) (same); Graham v. Cochran, No. 96 Civ. 6166, 2000 U.S. Dist. Lexis 1477, (S.D.N.Y. February 14, 2000) (same); Lord Natural-Self Allah v. Annucci, 1999 U.S. Dist. Lexis 7171, No. 97 Civ. 607, 1999 WL 299310 (W.D.N.Y. March 25, 1999) (Heckman, M.J.) (finding, for purposes of a preliminary injunction, that "Five Percenterism, in its pure uncorrupted form, represents a system of beliefs which, outside the prison context, does not advocate or promote violence").

B. Religious Land Use and Institutionalized Persons Act

Congress enacted the Religious Land Use and Institutionalized Persons Act ("RLUIPA") in response to the Supreme Court's holding in City of Boerne v. Flores, 521 U.S. 507, 138 L. Ed. 2d 624, 117 S. Ct. 2157 (1997), declaring unconstitutional the Religious Freedom Restoration Act ("RFRA"), 42 U.S.C. § 2000bb-1(b). n22 RLUIPA applies both to programs or activities that receive federal financial assistance and to substantial burdens on religious exercise having an effect on interstate commerce. 42 U.S.C. § 2000cc-1(b). Although other courts have debated the statute's constitutionality, see e.g., May Weathers v. Newland, 314 F.3d 1062. (9th Cir. 2002) (finding RLUIPA constitutional); Madison v. Riter, 240 F. Supp.2d 566 (W.D.Va. 2003) (ruling that RLUIPA violates the Establishment Clause), defendants in this case have never made such a constitutional challenge, RLUIPA's constitutionality, moreover, was assumed in our earlier opinion at the case's summary judgment stage, see Marria v. Broaddus, 200 F. Supp.2d 280 (S.D.N.Y. 2002), without subsequent objection by either side, and we maintain that assumption for purposes of this decision. RLUIPA provides:

No government shall impose a substantial burden on the religious exercise of a person residing in or confined to an institution ... even if the burden results from a rule of general applicability, unless the government demonstrates that imposition of the burden on that person -

(1) is in furtherance of a compelling governmental interest; and

(2) is the least restrictive means of furthering that compelling governmental interest.

42 U.S.C. § 2000cc-1(a). Under RLUIPA, once a plaintiff produces prima facie evidence to support a free exercise violation, the plaintiff bears the burden of persuasion over whether the regulation substantially burdens his or her exercise of religion and the state bears the burden of persuasion on all other elements. 42 U.S.C. § 2000cc-2(b).

By its terms, RLUIPA is to be construed to favor broad protection of religious exercise. See 42 U.S.C. § 2000cc-3(g). The statute defines religious exercise as "any exercise of religion, whether or not compelled by, or central to, a system of religious belief." Id. § 2000cc-5(7)(A). This reflects an extension of the definition provided in RFRA, which defined exercise of religion as "the exercise of religion under the First Amendment to the Constitution." 42 U.S.C. § 2000bb-2(4); Kikumura v. Hurley, 242 F.3d 950, 960 (10th Cir. 2001) (noting the change in definition); Henderson v. Kennedy, 347 U.S. App. D.C. 340, 265 F.3d 1072, 1073-74 (D.C. Cir. 2001) (noting that the definition of religious exercise in RLUIPA expanded upon the protections of RFRA). The otherwise similar language of RFRA and RLUIPA, however, suggests that cases decided under RFRA may guide this Court's inquiry in this case. See Wyatt v. Terhune, 315 F.3d 1108, 1115 (9th Cir. 2003) (noting that RLUIPA "provides rights similar to those delineated in RFRA").

In seeking to defeat plaintiff's RLUIPA claim, DOCS argues that the record does not establish that its ban on Five Percenter literature and gatherings substantially burdens the exercise of plaintiff's beliefs. See Def. Findings PP 9-20. DOCS further asserts that its regulations are in furtherance of a compelling governmental interest in prison security and that the ban on Five Percenter literature and congregative gatherings is the least restrictive means of effectively controlling security threat group behavior. See Def. Findings at 24-25.

C. Evaluating DOCS' Treatment of the Five Percenters Under RLUIPA

i. Substantial Burden

Like its predecessor RFRA, RLUIPA requires a plaintiff to demonstrate that his right to free exercise of religion has been substantially burdened. The Supreme Court has defined a substantial burden in this context as "where the state ... denies [an important benefit] because of conduct mandated by religious belief, thereby putting substantial pressure on an adherent to modify his behavior and to violate his beliefs. While the compulsion may be indirect, the infringement upon free exercise in nonetheless substantial." Thomas v. Review Bd. of the Indiana Employment Sec. Div., 450 U.S. 707, 717-18, 67 L. Ed. 2d 624, 101 S. Ct. 1425 (1981); Jolly, 76 F.3d at 477 (citing this passage of Thomas with approval in considering Rastafarian inmate's RFRA claim). Despite DOCS' treatment of the Nation exclusively as a security threat group and complete ban on Nation materials and literature, defendants argue that plaintiff's Five Percenter beliefs are not substantially burdened because he can still practice certain aspects of his beliefs. These include possessing the

Bible and Koran, gathering informally with five or fewer Five Percenters at certain times of day, learning the Supreme Alphabet and Mathematics orally, gaining access to lessons through NOI, celebrating certain holidays informally, and communicating with Nation members outside prison (though not through the Five Percenter newspaper). See Def. Findings PP 9-20.

Defendants' arguments are untenable. Throughout this litigation, plaintiff has credibly maintained that the study (alone and with others) of the 120 Degrees, Supreme Mathematics, the Supreme Alphabet, as well as other lessons found in The Five Percenter, is an integral part of the daily practice of the Nation's beliefs, and his testimony was substantiated by that of other Nation representatives. Furthermore, in a religious community that lacks both a formal organizational structure and a fixed place of worship, The Five Percenter newspaper serves as a central link and mechanism of communication, clearly falling within RLUIPA's broad protections of religious exercise "whether or not compelled by, or central to, a system of religious belief." 42 U.S.C. § 2000cc-5(7)(A). There is no question that under DOCS' regulations plaintiff may not possess these materials and study them with other inmates and is denied the opportunity to gather with other Nation members other than informally. n23 The evidence at trial also established that the Bible and Koran serve only as secondary religious sources for Nation members, refuting DOCS' argument that plaintiff can meaningfully practice his religion while possessing only these texts. n24 Finally, DOCS' contentions that plaintiff is able to obtain the 120 Degrees through NOI and fast on holy days contradict the evidence that plaintiff cannot receive the lessons from NOI without being an official member registered with an NOI temple outside prison, n25 see Trial Tr. at 57:8-15; Blocker Decl. PP 10-11, and that he is not permitted to eat his prison meal after sundown on holy days or gather for that meal (as are NOI and Orthodox Muslim inmates), but must do so using food he has saved from the prison commissary. See Trial Tr. at 62:11-63:5.

We thus find that plaintiff's free exercise of his religious beliefs are substantially burdened by DOCS' current policies concerning Five Percenters.

ii. Compelling Interest and Least Restrictive Means Tests

Moreover, DOCS has failed to establish that its complete ban on Five Percenter materials, literature, and activities furthers a compelling security interest and is the least restrictive means of doing so under RLUIPA. It is undisputed that maintaining the safety, security, and internal order of prisons is a compelling governmental interest. See Campos v. Coughlin, 854 F. Supp. 194, 207 (S.D.N.Y. 1994) ("prison security and penological institutional safety goals are indeed a most compelling governmental interest"); Muhammad v. City of New York Dep't of Corrections, 904 F. Supp. 161 (S.D.N.Y 1995) (finding compelling interest in internal order in prisons); Breland v. Goord, 1997 U.S. Dist. Lexis 3527, No. 94 Civ. 3696, 1997 WL 139533, at *4 (S.D.N.Y. March 27, 1997) ("there is no question that prison safety and security are legitimate penological interests"). We are also mindful of the well-established judicial tradition of giving heightened deference to the experience and judgment of prison officials on such "central" issues in the context of inmate First Amendment claims. Duamutef v. Hollins, 297 F.3d 108, 112 (2d Cir. 2002) (citing Giano v. Senkowski, 54

F.3d 1050, 1054 (2d Cir. 1995) and Thornburgh v. Abbott, 490 U.S. 401, 415, 104 L. Ed. 2d 459, 109 S. Ct. 1874 (1989) quoting Pell v. Procunier, 417 U.S. 817, 823, 41 L. Ed. 2d 495, 94 S. Ct. 2800 (1974) for the proposition that prison security is "central to all other corrections goals"). However, it is equally well-established that "prison walls do not form a barrier separating prison inmates from the protections of the Constitution," Turner v. Safley, 482 U.S. 78, 84, 96 L. Ed. 2d 64, 107 S. Ct. 2254 (1987), and our tradition of deference on security matters does not require this Court to altogether abdicate its role in constitutional cases brought by inmates. Hence, while prison officials "must be given latitude to anticipate the probable consequences of certain speech, and must be allowed to take reasonable steps to forestall violence," Giano v Senkowski, 54 F.3d 1050, 1055 (2d Cir. 1995), they "cannot merely brandish the words 'security' and 'safety' and expect that their actions will automatically be deemed constitutionally permissible conduct." Campos, 854 F. Supp. at 204. Cf. Jolly v. Coughlin, 76 F.3d 468, 479 (2d Cir. 1996) ("The DOCS policy is not insulated from scrutiny merely because the defendants brandish the concepts of public health and safety."). Congress also made it clear in enacting RFRA/RLUIPA that "inadequately formulated prison regulations and policies grounded on mere speculation, exaggerated fears, or post-hoc rationalizations will not suffice to meet the Act's requirements." Campos, 854 F. Supp. at 207 (quoting the Senate Report to RFRA); Jolly, 76 F.3d at 479 (1996) (same). Even the less restrictive test set forth in Turner v. Safley that governed prisoner free exercise claims prior to the enactment of RFRA/RLUIPA recognized that deference is not warranted when a prison regulation represents an exaggerated response to security objectives. See Turner, 482 U.S. at 97-98 ("No doubt legitimate security concerns may require placing reasonable restrictions upon an inmate's right to marry, and may justify requiring approval of the superintendent. The Missouri regulation, however, represents an exaggerated response to such security objectives.").

Here, DOCS proposes to treat exclusively as a gang a group that has had a law-abiding existence outside prison for the better part of 40 years, that is an offshoot of another group that DOCS considers a religion, and that has practices that largely resemble those of recognized religious groups, with the consequence that DOCS has banned literature which it concedes is facially innocuous as well as any other expression of religious identity associated with the group. In order for such a ban to be upheld, there ought to be some sense that DOCS is substantially correct in its decision to treat the group exclusively as a gang and not a religion. Cf. Jolly, 76 F.3d at 479 (holding in a RFRA analysis that "the connection between the application of a policy to an individual and the furtherance of the government's goals must be clear"). n26 The evidence DOCS presented at trial, however, failed to justify such treatment.

First, DOCS failed to provide any evidence that its decision to treat "Five Percenters" as a security threat group was either reasoned or informed. The trial record is almost entirely devoid of evidence concerning DOCS' initial decision to treat the Nation as a gang and not a religion. DOCS possesses no records whatsoever setting forth the basis for its decision or even documenting its decision-making process concerning the Five Percenters. None of the DOCS officials who testified at trial were the decision-makers, nor could they do more than speculate about who the decision-makers were, when the decision was made, how it was made, or what information was deemed relevant. n27 Moreover, DOCS admits that its classification of Five Percenters as a security threat group is not based on any guidelines or specific criteria. See Trial Tr. at 340:16. Nor, pursuant to its non-recognition policy, does DOCS maintain statistics concerning gang activity or even the rough number of gang members in the system. See Trial Tr. at 341:16-19, 345:10-13. Rather, its decision to label the Nation itself as a security threat was based on the subjective sense of the decision-makers - whomever they were - that the group as a whole was a gang. However, it is clear that DOCS knows little about the Nation's seemingly legitimate existence outside prison, n28 and DOCS failed to present any evidence concerning how it came to the conclusion that the Nation of Gods and Earths is not a religion in spite of the fact that several inmates have sought religious accommodations for their beliefs as members of the Nation. See Footnote 10 supra. It is also worth noting that DOCS' previous litigation position claiming that the Nation's literature contained violent messages indicates that it was misinformed about at least that aspect of the Nation at the time it made its classification and suggests that its treatment of the Nation exclusively as a gang may be based on either exaggerated fears or speculation.

Lacking a record for its decision, DOCS has attempted to justify its absolute ban post hoc by arguing that the evidence it has compiled in preparation for this litigation demonstrates that "the Five Percenters" are indeed a security threat group, and hence that the mere presence of the Nation's materials in the prison setting or any other forms of "recognition" pose a security threat by legitimating the group and facilitating its recruiting efforts. Several DOCS corrections officers and officials who testified at trial professed a general understanding from their training and experience that Five Percenters in prison were associated with violence and disruption, but had personal knowledge of only a few incidents involving inmates identified as Five Percenters despite their decades of combined experience. n29 See Def. Findings PP 66-68, 70-71, 74. Ron Holvey, a corrections official from the New Jersey Department of Corrections with expertise in gangs and related security issues, testified that the New Jersey prison system considers the Five Percenters to be its largest security threat group and that, after reviewing the materials and statements DOCS compiled for this litigation, he would support New York's ban on the Nation's literature as a security threat. See Trial Tr. at 710:1-2, 722:17-21. Mr. Holvey, however, admitted that he had never spoken with a member of the Nation of Gods and Earths in New York or set foot inside a DOCS prison. See Trial Tr. at 729:24-730:5. Moreover, he went on to testify that his perception of the Nation outside prison is that it is not a religion because "they don't have temples or mosques or churches. They don't have a minister that comes in. There is nothing formal about their organization. They don't have priests. They don't have rabbis. They don't have imams. They don't -- they worship -- they consider themselves to be God." See Trial Tr. at 741:10-14. Additional DOCS evidence concerning alleged Five Percenter gang activity came from two inmate-witnesses who claimed to have experienced violence and threats at the hands of Five Percenters. Their testimony, however, lacked consistency and credibility, leaving us with little reliable evidence beyond the fact that these two inmates regarded the Five Percenters as a gang. n30

DOCS' principal form of "hard evidence" concerning the nature of the Five Percenters consisted of compilations of facility reports concerning unusual incidents, inmate transfer requests, and inmate separation requests that contain gang-like references to Five Percenters and sometimes report violent acts attributed to individuals or groups identified as Five Percenters. See Trial Tr. at 363:23-364:10, 472:9-10, 502:5-8; Def. Trial Exhibit A (inmate transfer requests not received into evidence); Def. Trial Ex. B (sample separatee reports not received into evidence); Def. Trial Exhibit C (unusual incident reports not received into evidence); Def. Trial Exhibit D (protective custody reports received into evidence); Def. Trial Ex. M (summary of separatee report "hits" for "Five Percenters" and other groups from 1990 to 1999 not received into evidence). Although there is no evidence to suggest that DOCS' decision-makers ever reviewed these reports, DOCS argues that they constitute the kind of evidence that its decision-makers would have known about when determining that the Five Percenters were a security threat group and provide an objective basis for its decision to treat the Nation exclusively as a gang. See Def. Findings PP 77-78, 82. The transfer reports were excluded at trial because they contained hearsay within hearsay and did not otherwise exhibit indicia of reliability. n31 See Trial Tr. at 434:11-453:3; Fed. R. Evid. 802; Parsons v. Honeywell, Inc., 929 F.2d 901, 907 (2d Cir. 1991) (quoting with approval the Ninth Circuit's opinion in United States v. Pazsint, 703 F.2d 420, 424 (9th Cir. 1983) stating that "it is well established that entries in a police report which result from the officer's own observations and knowledge may be admitted but that statements made by third persons under no business duty to report may not." (emphasis added by Second Circuit)); Giles v. Rhodes, 2000 U.S. Dist. Lexis 13980, No. 94 Civ. 6835, 2000 WL 1425046, at *8-*9 (S.D.N.Y. Sept. 27, 2000) (ruling that prison unusual incident reports are inadmissible hearsay not subject to the Business Record Exception under Fed. R. Evid. 803(6)).

There are, in fact, several additional reasons to doubt their reliability, as well as the reliability of the reports underlying DOCS' summary chart of separatee "hits" for the term "Five Percenters," which was similarly excluded due to DOCS' failure to comply with the Federal Rules of Evidence by providing plaintiff with the underlying documents. n32 See Trial Tr. at 468:17-480:25; Fed. R. Evid. 1006 (stating that voluminous evidence "may be presented in the form of a chart, summary or calculation," but that the underlying documents "shall be made available for examination or copying, or both, by other parties"). Among the unusual incident reports - which document occurrences of violence or other serious disturbances - the number of relevant "hits" for references to Five Percenters was only 67 out of approximately 102,000 incidents over the ten year period from 1990 to 1999. See Trial Tr. at 241:13-24.

Thus, DOCS' post hoc justifications for its ban are inadequate to establish that it has a principled basis for labeling the Nation a security threat group. Finding DOCS' absolute ban to be justified based on the episodic accounts of its witnesses and unreliable facility reports would require us to make a speculative leap concerning the nature of an entire group based on spotty evidence about some of its supposed members that would be in tension with what we have learned about the group's legitimate existence outside prison. We stress that we are not saying that there are not prisoners who would describe themselves as Five Percenters who have committed crimes or otherwise violated prison regulations. However, the limitations of this "fact" should be obvious. Cf. Breland v. Goord, 1997 U.S. Dist. Lexis 3527, No. 94 Civ. 3696, 1997 WL 139533, at *5 (S.D.N.Y. March 27, 1997) ("The mere fact that inmates identified as Five Percenters have been involved in altercations with other inmates and guards does not establish that the literature at issue here caused those incidents."). There are prisoners who would describe themselves as Catholics, Protestants, Jews, Muslims, NOI, etc. who likewise violate prison regulations, and it is easy to imagine a situation where the common ethnic or religious bond shared by members of a group could serve as the impetus for some to band together and at times act cohesively, but no one would suggest that such facts preclude the classification of these recognized groups as religions deserving of First Amendment protection. n33

A hypothetical dealing with a more mainstream group further illustrates the point: imagine, for example, that one or several gangs of inmates were to form within the New York State Correctional system each of whose membership is united by a common religious/ethnic identity - Judaism. The gangs could either be formal disruptive organizations or simply the result of an agreement among some Jewish inmates to "get each other's back" in a pinch. Imagine further that the members of the Jewish gang(s) identify themselves by displaying the Star of David, utilize Hebrew letters (which also stand for numbers) as a "code" similar to Five Percenters' alleged use of the Supreme Alphabet and Mathematics, and sometimes recruit new members by using the Bible and other traditional Jewish texts. DOCS' records would soon be replete with reports containing statements that "the Jews" were involved in violent and disruptive activities and such groups would clearly pose a security threat to prison staff and inmates. But would this transform Judaism from a religion into a security threat group? Would DOCS, in such a situation, ban anyone who identified themselves as a Jew from possessing a Hebrew Bible and Alphabet or from displaying a Star of David? The trial testimony of DOCS officials convinces us that it would not, or that it would at least exhaust other avenues of redress before subjecting the "sincere believers" of a mainstream group to the type of blanket treatment that Nation members currently receive. n34

While we do not question the sincerity of the witnesses who testified as to their belief that there is a Five Percenters gang, their convictions alone are not sufficient. There must be admissible evidence to justify DOCS' policies, and no such evidence was introduced. Particularly lacking was evidence concerning the structure of the alleged Five Percenters gang. We are also troubled by the "Catch-22" aspect of its policies concerning the Nation, whereby the group's "unauthorized" classification leads DOCS to train its employees to recognize Five Percenters exclusively as gang members and otherwise innocuous literature and activities as threatening. n35 As such, we find the anecdotal evidence that DOCS has presented insufficient to justify after the fact its decision to treat the Nation solely as a gang under RLUIPA. Moreover, the trial testimony and submissions throughout this case suggest that, while DOCS now formally concedes that the Nation's literature does not contain violent or disruptive content, its officials' perception of the threat posed by the Nation and its literature was and potentially still is affected by their belief that it espouses an objectionable racist ideology. n36 Cf. Marria v. Broaddus, 200 F. Supp.2d 280, 295 (S.D.N.Y. 2002) (""DOCS' argument that it bans Nation literature because of what it represents and not what it says seems disingenuous given DOCS' prior position in past litigation from the same time period that the literature itself encourages violence."). Whether or not these lingering objections are justified as a matter of principle, they raise questions about whether DOCS' absolute ban on Nation literature is unrelated to the literature's content. See generally Turner, 482 U.S. at 90 ("We have found it important to inquire whether prison regulations restricting inmates' First Amendment rights operated in a neutral fashion, without regard to the content of the expression."); Church of the Lukumi Babalu Aye, Inc. v. City of Hialeah, 508 U.S. 520, 547, 124 L. Ed. 2d 472, 113 S. Ct. 2217 (1993) ("The Free Exercise Clause commits government itself to religious tolerance, and upon even slight suspicion that proposals for state intervention stem from animosity to religion or distrust of its practices, all officials must pause to remember their own high duty to the Constitution and to the rights it secures. Those in office must ... ensure that the sole reasons for imposing the burdens of law and regulation are secular.").

As a result of the foregoing, we cannot find, based on the trial record, that DOCS' classification of the Nation as a security threat group and absolute ban on Nation literature further a compelling security interest and is the least restrictive means of doing so. n37

D. Relief

This case, like others in which prison inmates have asserted their First Amendment right to practice non-mainstream religions while incarcerated, "underscores the complex nature and difficulty of accommodating various religious belief systems and tenets within a prison system, wherein violence is a real and daily threat." Campos v. Coughlin, 854 F. Supp. 194, 197 (S.D.N.Y. 1994). We have found that plaintiff is a sincere adherent to a religious belief system that qualifies for First Amendment protection, but are also prepared to accept for the purposes of this decision DOCS' claims that prison inmates identified as "Five

Percenters" have been associated with instances of violence and disruption. This raises the possibility that "the Five Percenters" may somewhat uniquely connote both a religion and a gang in the New York State prison system (though the sincere religious adherents and gang members may not be the same inmates).

It is apparent, however, that in pursuing its non-recognition policy DOCS has never fully considered the possibility or the policy consequences of the Nation qualifying for First Amendment protections, and did not do so at any time during the pendency of this case. Based on our review of the evidence and applying RLUIPA's compelling interest and least restrictive means tests in light of our determination that plaintiff is entitled to free exercise protection, we hav0e concluded that plaintiff has clearly established his right to some of the relief requested. With respect to other of plaintiff's requests, given the tradition of judicial deference to the considered judgment of correction officials and the indications that there are some nominal Five Percenter inmates who violate prison rules, we remand them to DOCS in order for DOCS to reevaluate its policies in light of our free exercise ruling and to determine the appropriate accommodations that can be made consistent with security needs. n38 Our conclusions are set forth below.

i. 120 Degrees

In our summary judgment opinion we noted that DOCS' position concerning the 120 Degrees, "namely, that one religious group may possess the same materials that if possessed by another contribute to gang formation" was "a challenging one to sustain." See Marria v. Broaddus, 200 F. Supp.2d 280, 295 (S.D.N.Y. 2002) . Based on the trial evidence, DOCS cannot properly prevent plaintiff from receiving and possessing the 120 Degrees consistently with the Free Exercise clause and RLUIPA. As the book serves as the central text in plaintiff's religious belief system, he is clearly substantially burdened if he is denied access to it. In any event, its content is identical to the texts DOCS currently permits NOI to use and possess. Thus, because the 120 Degrees is associated with more than one group, including a currently "authorized" religious group, DOCS cannot tenably argue that its mere presence in prison legitimizes gang activity. Therefore, we order DOCS to permit plaintiff to possess a copy of the 120 Degrees in accordance with his beliefs as a member of the Nation of Gods and Earths, and that his access cannot be conditioned upon his joining the Nation of Islam. n39

ii. Supreme Alphabet and Mathematics

We similarly grant plaintiffs' request to be allowed to possess a copy of the Supreme Alphabet and Mathematics. As we noted earlier, these numerological devices are central aspects of the Nation's beliefs and practices, have remained unchanged since the 1960's, and are widely available to law enforcement on the Internet and elsewhere. DOCS admits that the alleged "code" is a simple one that can be learned by inmates orally even under its current ban, but maintains that the Supreme Alphabet and Mathematics are sometimes used by Five Percenter inmates to send coded messages to one another in furtherance of gang activities and would require the expenditure of significant resources to train officers to recognize and decode if they were disseminated among the inmate population (DOCS has also argued that the Five Percenter newspaper poses a security threat because it contains "code"). See Def. Findings PP 60-63, 103-104; Trial Tr. 407:13-15; Trial Tr. 665:14-19; Trial Tr. 692:9-693:8. While the Supreme Alphabet and Mathematics may indeed be susceptible to being used as a code, DOCS' arguments are unpersuasive. Toni Bair, a professor of criminal justice, former Warden of Virginia's Mecklenberg Correctional Center "Supermax" facility, and former assistant commissioner of the New York City Department of Corrections who testified as plaintiff's expert on prison security, succinctly refuted DOCS' claims that the Supreme Alphabet and Mathematics threaten prison security:

It's published. The code is published. It is on the Internet. It is in the newspapers. It's everywhere. In order for a code to be effective and used, you know, covertly to be subversive or create problems in the institution, the code must be unbreakable and must not be, you know, common knowledge ... To ban the Mathematics and Alphabet because it is a code, you know, would be ludicrous. If we do that, why don't we ban Spanish, for example, because I would daresay that there is not a tremendous number of correctional officers in DOCS that are bilingual and yet we allow Spanish not only to be spoken but documents inside institutions that are Spanish ... and they are much more difficult to translate than this code would be.

Trial Tr. at 246:17-247:12.

We are persuaded that the Supreme Alphabet's and Mathematics' primary purpose is a religious one, and that, to they extent inmates might attempt to use them as a code, messages could be translated with minimal effort and training. Furthermore, the ability of inmates to communicate with each other by using the Supreme Alphabet and Mathematics in covert fashion would appear to be more challenging and limited than conversations in a foreign language not spoken by guards. Hence, we see no connection between DOCS' current ban on possessing the Supreme Alphabet and Mathematics and a compelling security interest, and order that plaintiff be permitted to possess them. n40

iii. Other Materials and Symbols, Gatherings, and Fasts

We remand the remainder of plaintiff's claims to DOCS to reevaluate its policies concerning the Nation and determine what materials and religious practices it can accommodate in light of our ruling that plaintiff's beliefs as a member of the Nation are entitled to free exercise and RLUIPA protection. It is incumbent upon DOCS to make a determination about the feasibility of allowing sincere adherents like plaintiff to possess literature and to engage in religious practices in light of its security concerns.

In particular, DOCS must reevaluate how, if at all, it can accommodate plaintiff's request to receive The Five Percenter. In this regard, plaintiff has proposed two suggestions addressing DOCS' concerns about permitting security threat group members to use innocuous literature to recruit, control, and intimidate as less restrictive alternatives to a complete ban on the Nation's literature. First, plaintiff suggests that DOCS utilize the existing media review committee process to redact symbols that it views as posing a security threat. Alternatively, plaintiff proposes that DOCS maintain a copy of The Five Percenter in the prison library that plaintiff can presumably sign for and read individually during normal library time without removing the copies from the library. At trial, DOCS' efforts to address the library suggestion were particularly unconvincing. n41 On remand, because plaintiff has established that his religious beliefs are substantially burdened by DOCS' current ban on The Five Percenter, DOCS bears the burden of demonstrating why his proposals are infeasible on remand.

On the issue of congregative gatherings, such as parliaments, rallies, and civilization classes, DOCS has thus far dismissed the possibility of allowing such activities on the assumption that any sanctioned congregation of members of an unauthorized group would elevate that group's status and permit the group's members to conspire to engage in violent activities. Here again, DOCS' position suffers from the incorrect assumption that all Five Percenters are gang members. DOCS has also pinned its objections in part on the assumption that the gatherings would be unsupervised. See Def's. Findings at P 122 ("Permitting plaintiff to participate in unsupervised inmate led parliaments would create a security risk in the prison by allow [sic] Five Percenters to organize recruit additional members and serve as a forum for criminal conspiracy.") (emphasis added); Trial Tr. at 461:3-11 (Dale Artus stating that his understanding of a parliament is "an unsupervised meeting place for the individuals who wish to be involved in this type of activity to be allowed to meet and learn" that he would view as "detrimental to the safety and security of the facility and the department"). Plaintiff's counsel, however, has made it clear that he is not requesting unsupervised parliaments, and we note that Born Justice Allah from the Allah Youth Center testified at trial that he and other Nation members from outside prison would volunteer to assist DOCS in accommodating rallies and parliaments through advice and supervision. See Trial Tr. at 316:20-317:9. We recognize, however, that DOCS must consider security concerns, as well as considerations of limited time, space, and resources, in evaluating whether and how accommodations can be made for such gatherings.

Finally, DOCS must determine what can be done consistent with security concerns with respect to plaintiff's requests to receive late meals and gather with other inmates when he fasts in observance of Holy Days.

CONCLUSION

Based on the foregoing, it is ordered that DOCS conform its policies concerning the group known as the Nation of Gods and Earths with this ruling, and further that DOCS report the results of that policy reevaluation to the Court in sixty days. n42

IT IS SO ORDERED.

DATED: July 31, 2003

NAOMI REICE BUCHWALD

UNITED STATES DISTRICT JUDGE

FOOTNOTES:

n1 Plaintiff legally changed his name in December 2001. See Trial Transcript ("Trial Tr.") at 38:14-18. Apparently, he had also sought to do so approximately two years earlier, but without success. See id. at 38::7.

n2 It should be clear that in protecting plaintiff's constitutional rights to practice his adopted religion, we are fulfilling our sworn duty and in no way endorsing or heralding the Nation's tenets, several of which we find repugnant to the principles of tolerance and equality that are fundamental to our Constitution and the ethos of our country. See Thomas v. Review Board of Indiana Employment Security Division, 450 U.S. 707, 714, 67 L. Ed. 2d 624, 101 S. Ct. 1425 (1981) ("religious beliefs need not be acceptable, logical, consistent, or comprehensible to others in order to merit First Amendment protection").

n3 While the NOI and the Nation differ in their interpretation of the 120 Degrees, referred to as the "Book of Supreme Wisdom" or "Lost-Found Muslim Lessons" by the NOI, both groups study them. See April 12, 2001 Decl. of A. Blocker ("Blocker Decl.") PP 8-11. DOCS permits the Book of Supreme Wisdom to be issued to any inmate who is a registered member of NOI, but Nation members who have not registered as members of the NOI are not permitted to view these materials. See id.

n4 Holy days observed by the Nation include the anniversaries of the birth and death of Clarence 13X Smith and the birthdays of Elijah Muhammad and Fard Muhammad. See Trial Tr. at 62:6-8, 18. The Nation, however, does not participate in Ramadan, Jumma, and some other traditional Islamic customs practiced by NOI members. See Pl. Trial Ex. 180.

n5 For example, in the nomenclature of the Supreme Alphabet, the letter "A" stands for "Allah," "B" stands for "Be," and "C" stands for "See" or "Cee." In the Supreme Mathematics, the number "1" represents "Knowledge," the number "2" represents "Wisdom," and the number "3" represents "Understanding." See id. One example of how Nation members apply this numerological system to their lives, according to plaintiff, is that "1" ("Knowledge") and "2" ("Wisdom") must precede "3" ("Understanding"). See Trial Tr. at 98:8-24 (plaintiff explaining how he uses the Supreme Alphabet and Mathematics to understand the world).

n6 One such article instructs inmates: "'Don't serve time, but make time serve you.' is the principle that you should adopt internally in order to return back to your family and community as an asset and not a continued liability ... When you serve time negatively, you waste precious moments of your life." See Pl. Trial Ex. 3 at

Bates No. 240 (article entitled "Belly of the Beast" from the October 1995 issue of The Five Percenter). The article further instructs inmates to "participate to the best of your ability within the rules of your respective prison and reap what you sow in this righteousness." See id.

n7 In doing so, DOCS does not distinguish between "Five Percenters" and members of the Nation of Gods and Earths. See e.g., Def. Proposed Findings of Fact and Conclusions of Law ("Def. Findings") P 36 ("Plaintiff is able to participate in DOCS' educational and rehabilitative programs in spite of the fact that he is a member of the Five Percenters."). As previously noted, however, DOCS and plaintiff do not necessarily use the term "Five Percenter" to identify the same individuals.

n8 According to plaintiff and a supporting affidavit submitted for summary judgment purposes by an inmate NOI minister, members of the Nation are also unable to obtain the 120 Degrees in bound format from NOI members, as only inmates registered with an NOI temple outside of prison are permitted to have those lessons. See Trial Tr. at 57:8-15; Blocker Decl. PP 10-11.

n9 DOCS Directive 4670, which deals with inmate organizations, makes it clear that religious groups seeking to meet regularly for worship or prayer services cannot apply for inmate organization status. See Def. Trial Ex. F2 (Directive 4670) at P II(C)(2). Trial testimony reflected some confusion concerning exactly how a group claiming to be religious in nature like the

Nation can become "authorized." Compare Trial Tr. at 390:18-25 (DOCS official Richard Roy testifying that he did not know the answer to plaintiff's counsel's question about whether there was a way for a group claiming religious status to become authorized by DOCS short of litigation) with Trial Tr. 416:9-22 (Richard Roy testifying that, though he was not familiar with the details, there is a procedure by which religious groups can become recognized within DOCS through the Division of Ministerial and Family Services) and Trial Tr. at 525:25-528:7 (former DOCS Director of Ministerial and Family Services John LoConte discussing generally how he handled requests for religious accommodation within DOCS, but stating that he did not make the final decision about accommodating religious requests and that "our recognition I don't believe is that important."). The evidence introduced at trial also indicates that at least two other Black Muslim groups, the Nation of Islam and Moorish Science Temple, resorted to litigation similar to this one before DOCS ceased treating them as "unauthorized groups" and began classifying them as religious groups. Both cases were settled without court rulings on the plaintiffs' claims for injunctive relief from DOCS' non-recognition of the groups in question. See Trial Tr. 389:6-20; 533:8-535:25; see also Muhammad v. Coughlin, 1998 U.S. Dist. Lexis 10134, No. 91 Civ. 6333 (S.D.N.Y July 8, 1998) (Nation of Islam); Gilmore-Bey v. Coughlin, 929 F. Supp. 146, No. 93 Civ. 6592 (S.D.N.Y. June 5, 1996) (Moorish Science Temple).

n10 See e.g., Breland v. Goord, 1997 U.S. Dist. Lexis 3527, No. 94 Civ. 3696, 1997 WL 139533 (S.D.N.Y. March 27, 1997); Graham v. Cochran, No. 96 Civ. 6166, 2000 U.S. Dist. Lexis 1477, (S.D.N.Y. February 14,

2000) (Ellis, M.J.); Lord Natural-Self Allah v. Annucci, 1999 U.S. Dist. Lexis 7171, No. 97 Civ. 607, 1999 WL 299310 (W.D.N.Y. March 25, 1999) (Heckman, M.J.); Pl. Trial Exhibit 182 (October 29, 1996 letter from DOCS Deputy Commissioner for Program Services Raymond Broaddus to an inmate regarding a request for religious accommodations stating "I have been informed that the Five Percent Nation is not a religion. Therefore, there is no religious faith to practice."); Pl. Trial Ex. 81 (October 19, 1998 letter from defendant Warith Deen Umar, DOCS coordinator for Islamic Affairs, to plaintiff stating that "there are no directives or rules and regulations regarding the Five Percenters. The reason for this is the courts have ruled the Five Percenters are not a legitimate religious group").

n11 According to DOCS, "joining a gang such as the Five Percenters is about money, power and respect," Def. Findings P 87, and "the Five Percenter newspaper is used as a tool by inmates to recruit other gang members and sometimes inmates are recruited into joining the Five Percenters without realizing that they may be asked to participate in violent or illegal activities." See id. P 91.

n12 In previous litigation arising from the same time period as this one, DOCS claimed that Five Percenter literature incited violence against white people with messages like "kill the White devils and their families" and asserted that a statement urging Nation members to "struggle to get out of prison houses" through education was an incitement to escape (in full, the statement read: "we've experienced the trials and tribulations of his prison house and we must now struggle to get out of his prison houses and remove the veil that has been placed over our people's minds. This can only be done through education, i.e., proper education."). See Breland v. Goord, 1997 U.S. Dist. Lexis 3527, No. 94 Civ. 3696, 1997 WL 139533, at *2 (S.D.N.Y. March 27, 1997). DOCS' content-based justification for banning the Nation's literature was rejected by Judge Baer of this Court, who found that the Nation's literature contained no such incitements to violence and that DOCS had "unfairly characterized the material at issue" and "unfortunately focused on the non-traditional nature of plaintiff's religion." See id. at *17, [WL] *2, *6.

n13 At the summary judgment stage of this case, plaintiff submitted the declarations of numerous Nation members, living both within and outside the DOCS system, asserting that the Nation is not a gang and does not promote violence or retaliate against members who leave. See June 26, 2001 Decl. of Cee Aaquil Allah Barnes (detailing the activities of the Allah Youth Center and asserting that the Five Percenters are not a gang); April 12, 2001 Decl. of Wendell Williams (asserting that Five Percenters are not a gang and do not engage in gang like activities); April 13, 2001 Decl. of Terayus Jones (same); April 25, 2001 Decl. of Rahiem Buford (same); April 18, 2001 Decl. of Gabriel Clausen (same); October 6, 200 Decl. of H. Khalif Khalifah

n14 We note that, according to DOCS witness Superintendent Joseph Smith, serving on the Inmate Liaison Committee is the kind of "positive" activity through which a charismatic inmate can become a "stabilizing influence" within a prison facility. Ironically, Smith sought to contrast this kind of positive activity with his negative perception of Five Percenter inmates. See Trial Tr. at 652:25-653:7.

n15 Mr. Barnes is the Center's Chairman and Mr. Justice Allah serves as an elder and administrator.

n16 DOCS does argue that "Five Percenters outside of prison have engaged in criminal activity." See Def. Findings P 80. However, this argument - relying solely on Shawangunk Superintendent Joseph Smith's recollections of supervising several Five Percenters as a probation officer in the 1970's, Investigator Ron Holvey's experiences with alleged Five Percenter gangs in New Jersey, and an inmate's testimony that he participated in Five Percenter gang activities outside prison after joining the group in a boys home - does not really address or challenge the Nation representatives' testimony to the effect that the Nation is a legitimate organization engaged in constructive and lawful activities outside prison.

n17 According to DOCS' former Director of Ministerial and Family Services John LoConte, the existence of an established, legitimate religious community outside of prison would have been an important factor is his determination of whether a prisoner deserved religious accommodations during his tenure as DOCS Director of the Division of Ministerial and Family Services. See Trial Tr. at 536:23-538:8, 538:17-840:2; see also Trial Tr. 543:4-13 (LoConte testifying that DOCS recognizes Wiccans as a religion because of their "visible presence," complete with articulated doctrine, dogma, traditions, and rituals, outside prison).

n18 Plaintiff's expert on prison administration, former federal prison warden Toni Bair, reached a similar conclusion upon examination of the photocopy during his testimony. See Trial Tr. at 220:18-221:15.

n19 In a similar vein, we reject DOCS' argument that plaintiff's insincerity is evidenced by his failure to formally request parliaments and other gatherings until 2000, see Def. Findings P 22, since DOCS' complete ban on the Nation's materials and previous denials of plaintiff's requests to receive them made it fairly clear that such a request would not have been granted and plaintiff has represented that he did so merely to ensure that he had exhausted his administrative remedies.

n20 In response to his inquiries concerning confiscated copies of the Five Percenter newspaper, DOCS Coordinator for Islamic Affairs, Warith Deen Umar responded as follows:

Dear brother:

This responds to your letter of September 22, 1998. There are no directives or rules and regulations regarding Five Percenters. The reason for this is because the courts have ruled that Five Percenters are not a legitimate religious group. The New York State

Department of Correctional Services does not acknowledge the claims of inmates who designate themselves as Five Percenters. You may want to explore some of the teaching of the Muslims and the Nation of Islam in your facility.

Your brother in Islam, Imam Warith Deen Umar Ministerial Program Coordinator Ministerial and Family Services

Pl. Trial Ex. 81 (emphasis added). We note that, to the Court's knowledge, no case law existed to substantiate Imam Umar's assertion that "the courts have ruled that Five Percenters are not a legitimate religious group."

n21 Despite markedly different conceptions of "the divine" from most Americans, heterodox groups like Rastifarians, Wiccans, and Hare Krishnas have all been afforded free exercise protection. Here, the Nation's doctrine is predicated on a an essentially monotheistic belief in God, its central and secondary texts - including the 120 Degrees, Bible, and Koran - are largely identical to those of other accepted religions, the Supreme Mathematics and Supreme Alphabet are reminiscent of other religions' use of numerology devices to understand the world, and the nature of its observances is far from uncommon. Moreover, the Nation appears to be a close relative of an officially recognized religion, the Nation of Islam.

n22 The constitutional controversy surrounding RFRA and the subsequent congressional enactment of RLUIPA have been discussed extensively elsewhere, see e.g., Madison v. Riter, 240 F. Supp.2d 566, 568-70 (W.D.Va. 2003), and familiarity with RLUIPA's history is assumed.

n23 According to John LoConte, DOCS' former Director of Ministerial and Family Services, such informal gatherings "wouldn't be enough" to allow Catholic inmates to practice their religion while in prison. See Trial Tr. at 532:11-17. Moreover, DOCS admitted the importance of formal gatherings in plaintiff's belief system at an earlier stage of this litigation when, in attempting to show that plaintiff is not a sincere believer in the Nation's tenets because he has never attended a parliament (despite having banned him from doing so), DOCS asserted that parliaments are "a fundamental ritual" for Nation members that, if consistently skipped, would be equivalent to "a Catholic never going to Mass." Defs.' Summ. J. Reply Mem. at 9

n24 DOCS' argument is tantamount to arguing that a Christian's or Muslim's beliefs would not be substantially burdened if he or she were permitted to possess the Jewish Bible, but not the New Testament or the Koran. The courts have recognized, however, that it is the free exercise of a plaintiff's religion, not someone else's, that the First Amendment and RLUIPA protect. See Breland v. Goord, 1997 U.S. Dist. Lexis 3527, No. 94 Civ. 3696, 1997 WL 139533, at *5 (S.D.N.Y. March 27, 1997) (citing Thornburgh v. Abbott, 490 U.S. 401, 418, 104 L. Ed. 2d 459, 109 S. Ct. 1874 (1989) and

O'Lone v. Estate of Shabazz, 482 U.S. 342, 352, 96 L. Ed. 2d 282, 107 S. Ct. 2400 (1987)). But cf. Fraise v. Terhune, 283 F.3d 506, 519-20, (3d Cir. 2002) (accepting such an argument in ruling that alternatives means existed for inmates to practice their beliefs under New Jersey's treatment of Five Percenters exclusively as a security threat group).

n25 In making its argument that plaintiff can gain access to the 120 Degrees from NOI members, DOCS apparently relies on plaintiff's testimony that NOI conducts introductory classes for non-members, similar to the Nation's civilization classes, at which the lessons are sometimes discussed. See Trial Tr. at 60:20-61:14; Def. Findings P 19. However, plaintiff's immediately following testimony makes it clear that he is not able to obtain the 120 Degrees, or even consistent study of them, merely by attending such classes. See Trial Tr. at 61;15-24.

n26 DOCS places undue reliance on the Second Circuit's decision in Giano v Senkowski, 54 F.3d 1050 (2d Cir. 1995), which held that it was unnecessary for DOCS to establish an explicit link between such "emotionally charged" materials as nude photographs of inmates' wives and girlfriends and violence in order to justify its ban on such materials. See Giano, 54 F.3d at 1055; Def. Findings at 20-21. Here, unlike instances in which common sense would indicate that prohibited materials may pose a threat to security, DOCS predicates its policy banning any and all religious expressions associated with the Nation on the group's allegedly violent nature, which is not simply a matter of common sense.

n27 Although DOCS claims that its classification of the Five Percenters as a gang is based on a history of violence and disruptive activities associated with the group, as well as its employees' day-to-day reporting of such activities, Def. Findings P 53; Trial Tr. at 378:7-15, DOCS official Richard Roy testified that there was probably no stack of materials that was reviewed by DOCS' decision-makers at the time they classified the Nation as unauthorized. See Trial Tr. at 408:2-18.

n28 DOCS official Richard Roy, for example, testified that he did not believe that there was a connection between the members of DOCS' alleged "Five Percenters" prison gang and an outside organization called the Nation of Gods and Earths, see Trial Tr. at 346:16-19, while another official, Dale Artus, testified that "the term "Nation of Gods and Earths" is not in my vocabulary. It is nothing I've been - it is just - it doesn't come about in the course of my private life or in my professional life other than this litigation." See Trial Tr. at 481:8-10.

n29 The most credible of these accounts in light of the evidence concerning the Nation's legitimate existence outside prison was that of Deputy Superintendent for Security Services at Collins Correctional Facility Sibato Khahaifa, who testified that, as an Orthodox Muslim who grew up in Brooklyn, he understood the Nation to be a religious group that had split from the NOI prior to joining DOCS. See Trial Tr. at 756:3-9. In recounting his experiences as a corrections officer in several DOCS facilities, Khahaifa also drew a distinction between some Five Percenter inmates who he perceived as sincere adherents of the Nation and others who appeared to be behaving in a gang-like fashion. See Trial Tr. at 757:11-758:5. 766:11-18.

n30 One, who claimed to be a former member and participant in illegal activities on behalf of the Five Percenters, also admitted to having participated in numerous stabbings and other acts of violence, including altercations with members of the Latin Kings gang and inmates he identified as "the Muslims," even after the period he was allegedly a Five Percenter. See Trial Tr. at 814:9-816:7, 818:3-820:12, 823:8-824:8, 826:5-20. Yet, he claimed that his safety is at risk because Five Percenters were seeking to retaliate against him for "going against" the gang in a fight and thereafter leaving the group. See Trial Tr. at 799:22-800:2; Trial Tr. at 805:18-806:11. The other, a former Latin Kings gang "captain," admitted to having "snitched" on four other Latin Kings members after they had killed a fellow prisoner who was a Five Percenter, making it difficult for us to gauge his claims that he feared for his safety because of the potential for retaliation from Five Percenters in addition to the Latin Kings. See Trial Tr. at 846:10-20, 851:20-852:1, 853:7-854:1.

n31 We note that, according to plaintiff's prison security and administration expert Toni Bair, such reports are "one of the most unreliable sources of information we have in prisons" because they are obtained from individuals ("snitches") who are often desperate to get themselves out of some kind of trouble and view it as beneficial to name groups rather than individuals in order to insure that they be placed in protective custody. Trial Tr. at 244:10-245:14.

n32 First, there are a substantial number of duplicates among the transfer requests that DOCS submitted as trial exhibits, see e.g., Def. Trial Ex. A at Bates Nos. 018 & 023, 019 & 024, 010 & 026, 012 & 027, 013 & 028, and it is possible that such duplicates could be affecting the number of "hits" contained in DOCS' separatee chart as well. Second, some of the transfer requests and unusual incident reports were of questionable relevance to the Five Percenter gang activities that were alleged, raising similar concerns about the relevance of the separatee reports underlying DOCS' summary chart of relevant "hits." See e.g., Def. Trial Ex. A at Bates Nos. 032, 109, 116 (transfer requests); Def. Trial Ex. C. at Bates Nos. 006, 043 (unusual incidents). Third, DOCS has defined the Five Percenters as a security threat group for some time and apparently trains its employees to recognize them as such, which undoubtedly affects the reports. See Trial Tr. at 488:12-19 (Dale Artus explaining that DOCS' crisis intervention unit devotes a four-hour portion of its two week basic training specifically to unauthorized groups); Trial Tr. at 632:19-23 (Superintendent Joseph Smith testifying that his understanding of the Five Percenters as a gang came in part "from training"). Fourth, because DOCS treats any organizing activity associated with an unauthorized group as a threat to prison safety and security, its classification of the Five Percenters as "unauthorized" is in some sense self-fulfilling. Activities that would be permissible were they conducted by a religious group, such as recruiting, gathering, passing on literature, are deemed threatening and fuel both the group's and individuals' negative reputations reflected in the various reports. See e.g., Trial Tr. 521:20-24 (John LoConte explaining that, at the time he first learned about the Nation, he was hearing that "both the Nation of Islam, the Nation of Gods and Earths ... they were attempting to infiltrate the Muslim community in order to establish a congregation the opportunity to the [sic] meet together. They were problematic."); Def. Trial Ex. D at Bates No. 014 (stating - with a negative connotation -that the Five Percenters were going to "take some action to establish themselves in the facility"); Def. Findings PP 89-90 (treating as negative the notion that plaintiff's alleged religious beliefs would require him to teach civilization to others).

n33 For example, one of the inmates who testified on DOCS' behalf in this case referred repeatedly to altercations between himself and "Muslims" and replied "Yes sir" when he was asked whether there were any Muslim gangs. See Trial Tr at 814·9-10 We also note that a number of the unusual incident reports containing the term "Five Percenter" proffered by DOCS also contain the term "Muslim." See Trial Tr. 243:16-21. Clearly, however, none of this would lead us to conclude either that Islam is not a religion or that Muslims would properly be classified by DOCS as a security threat group.

Additionally, at least one Second Circuit decision appears to document a street gang whose teenage founders were apparently Five Percenters, but nonetheless existed separately from the Nation of Gods and Earths. See United States v. Miller, 116 F.3d 641 (2d Cir. 1997) (discussing the formation of the "Supreme Team" gang by a group of teenage Five Percenters in the mid-1980's).

n34 The Court posed a similar hypothetical to Shawangunk Superintendent Joseph Smith, see Trial Tr. at 646:2-21, who replied: "[are we going to say that we are no longer going to permit religious services or participation in religious holidays, I would say, no, that would be very unlikely, because I am going to go on a limb and say that this group that you have described would be limited to a few, and that once we were able to take proper action we should be able to go on as business as usual." Trial Tr. at 646:22-647:3. Superintendent Smith added, with regard to the Five Percenters: "Well, I can only answer that as we deal with them today. They are not an authorized religion at this point within our system." Trial Tr. at 647:25-648:2. Similarly, plaintiff's counsel posed hypothetical questions concerning violence by members of the NAACP to Dale Artus, the former director of DOCS' crisis intervention unit, who testified that he would recommend that the violent individuals "be held individually accountable for their acts" and "would not recommend that the overall program be disbanded" because he viewed the overall NAACP program as positive and it was, unlike the Five Percenters, an authorized organization. See Trial Tr. at 491:13-493:13. The DOCS officials' testimony stands in sharp contrast to that of Ron Holvey, who DOCS called as an expert on gangs and gang management, as well as the status Five Percenters in the New Jersey State Correctional system (which segregates those identified as "core members" from the rest of its prison population). When asked whether he would declare the Catholic Church to be a security threat group if numerous prisoners identified as Catholics were being written up for violent acts, he responded: "Within the prison, we would have to, yeah, oh yeah, and I'm sure I would be sitting in another courtroom for that one." Trial Tr. at 748:23-749:4.

n35 For example, in addition to testifying that his perception of the Five Percenters as a gang came in part "from training," see Trial Tr. 632:19-23, Shawangunk Superintendent Joseph Smith agreed that the Nation's unauthorized status makes it "easy" for him to treat the whole group as a gang when he would otherwise seek to distinguish sincere believers from disruptive members of a mainstream religious group. Trial Tr. at 647:25-648:6. Similarly, in response to plaintiff's counsel's questioning about DOCS' basis for treating the Nation as a gang in comparison to other authorized groups, DOCS official Richard Roy responded: "I would go the other way; they were not an authorized organization, so therefore they could not participate as an organization." Trial Tr. at 390:10-12.

n36 DOCS official Richard Roy, for example, testified that he found an article in The Five Percenter expressing the opinion that the death penalty was a form of legalized genocide and that the white man has always used his laws to justify "devilishment" potentially dangerous to prison security because it was hateful toward members of another race, and moreover that he and other DOCS employees reviewed the content of The Five Percenter when DOCS was making the decision to ban the Nation's materials. See Trial Tr. 419:15-412:14. Joseph Smith also agreed that he believes that the Five Percenter materials are dangerous. See Trial Tr. 673:16-18. Ron Holvey - though not a DOCS official - testified that he found the racist aspects of the Nation lessons a threat to prison security and that he objected to the Nation's beliefs because "the overall nature of the group promotes violence," but that these views had nothing to do with his characterization of the Nation as a security threat group. See Trial Tr. at 737:7-738:19.

n37 We acknowledge that there is some case law in tension with our decision in this case. See Fraise v. Terhune, 283 F.3d 506 (3d Cir. 2002) (finding the New Jersey Department of Corrections' treatment of Five Percenters as a security threat group justified for summary judgment purposes under a Turner v. Safley analysis); Mickle v. Moore (In re Long Term Administrative Segregation of Inmates Designated as Five Percenters), 174 F.3d 464 (4th Cir. 1999) (same with regard to the South Carolina Department of Corrections); Lord Natural-Self Allah v. Annucci, 1999 U.S. Dist. Lexis 7171, No. 97 Civ. 607, 1999 WL 299310 (W.D.N.Y. March 25, 1999) (Heckman, M.J.) (finding for preliminary injunctive purposes that DOCS' ban on Five Percenter materials was justified under Turner); Buford v. Goord, 258 A.D.2d 761, 686 N.Y.S.2d 121 (3d Dep't. 1999) (dismissing, in an Article 78 proceeding, a pro se litigant's claim that DOCS' policies banning his receipt of Five Percenter materials violated his first amendment rights). Each of these cases, however, applied a more deferential standard of review than the RLUIPA analysis we apply in this decision, and the three federal case involving free exercise claims all assumed that Five Percenter beliefs would receive free exercise protection, which accords with our ruling in this case. Morevoer, these other courts do not appear to have had an equally well-developed evidentiary record concerning the Nation's legitimate existence outside prison as we did in this case. Finally, we simply disagree with some of the findings and conclusions reached by those courts, most fundamentally the notion that prison policies classifying and treating an entire group as a gang can be upheld despite the fact that they are predicated on a faulty assumption that the group has no legitimate existence as a religion.

n38 Such a remand, which was requested by DOCS at trial, see Def. Findings at 26, is consistent with both the federal courts' tradition of deference and the Supreme Court's guidance concerning their appropriate supervisory role in prisoner litigation: "We have said that 'the strong considerations of comity that require giving a state court system that has convicted a defendant the first opportunity to correct its own errors ... also require giving the States the first opportunity to correct the errors made in the internal administration of their prisons.'" Preiser v. Rodriguez, 411 U.S. 475, 492, 36 L. Ed. 2d 439, 93 S. Ct. 1827 (1973).

n39 In accordance with our remand of plaintiff's requests to possess Nation symbols and other materials, we make no ruling at this time concerning what symbols, if any, DOCS must permit plaintiff to receive and display along with the 120 Degrees.

n40 Again, in accordance with our remand of the remainder of plaintiff's claims to DOCS, we make no ruling at this time about whether plaintiff can possess or display Five Percenter symbols in conjunction with his possession of the Supreme Alphabet and Mathematics.

n41 DOCS' claims that maintaining a library copy of The Five Percenter would be infeasible because it would entail "separating plaintiff from other inmates" and "designating a separate room for plaintiff, and a separate secure space to secure the newspapers, assigning one or more staff members to supervise his movement to and from the room and assigning one or more members to issue him the Newspaper [sic] and to retrieve it," as well as elevating the group's statute through such special treatment. See Def. Findings PP 106-108. This "parade of horribles" seems rather exaggerated.

n42 We would also be remiss if we failed to express the Court's gratitude to pro bono counsel for their excellent effort and professionalism throughout this case and to Sullivan & Cromwell for its sponsorship of their pro bono positions.

Result #1: Public Laws of the United States - Public Law 106-274 of 2000, 106th Congress

Thursday, December 27, 2012
1:31 PM

Public Laws of the United States

Document Manager
Open Document Manager
Email
Download
Send to Printer
Print/Export

Public Law 106-274 of 2000, 106th Congress

An Act

To protect religious liberty, and for other purposes.

Be it enacted by the Senate and House of Representatives of the United States of America in Congress assembled,

SECTION 1. SHORT TITLE.
This Act may be cited as the `Religious Land Use and Institutionalized Persons Act of 2000'.

SEC. 2. PROTECTION OF LAND USE AS RELIGIOUS EXERCISE.
(a) SUBSTANTIAL BURDENS —
(1) GENERAL RULE — No government shall impose or implement a land use regulation in a manner that imposes

a substantial burden on the religious exercise of a person, including a religious assembly or institution, unless the government demonstrates that imposition of the burden on that person, assembly, or institution —
(A) is in furtherance of a compelling governmental interest; and
(B) is the least restrictive means of furthering that compelling governmental interest.
(2) SCOPE OF APPLICATION — This subsection applies in any case in which —
(A) the substantial burden is imposed in a program or activity that receives Federal financial assistance, even if the burden results from a rule of general applicability;
(B) the substantial burden affects, or removal of that substantial
burden would affect, commerce with foreign nations, among the several States, or with Indian tribes, even if the burden results from a rule of general applicability; or
(C) the substantial burden is imposed in the implementation of a land use regulation or system of land use regulations, under which a government makes, or has in place formal or informal procedures or practices that permit the government to make, individualized assessments
of the proposed uses for the property involved.
(b) DISCRIMINATION AND EXCLUSION —
(1) EQUAL TERMS — No government shall impose or implement a land use regulation in a manner that treats a religious assembly or institution on less than equal terms with a nonreligious assembly or institution.
(2) NONDISCRIMINATION — No government shall impose or implement a land use regulation that discriminates against any assembly or institution on the basis of religion or religious denomination.

(3) EXCLUSIONS AND LIMITS — No government shall impose or implement a land use regulation that —
(A) totally excludes religious assemblies from a jurisdiction; or
(B) unreasonably limits religious assemblies, institutions, or structures within a jurisdiction.

SEC. 3. PROTECTION OF RELIGIOUS EXERCISE OF INSTITUTIONALIZED PERSONS.

(a) GENERAL RULE — No government shall impose a substantial burden on the religious exercise of a person residing in or confined to an institution, as defined in section 2 of the Civil Rights of Institutionalized Persons Act (42 U.S.C. § 1997), even if the burden results from a rule of general applicability, unless the government demonstrates that imposition of the burden on that person —
(1) is in furtherance of a compelling governmental interest; and
(2) is the least restrictive means of furthering that compelling governmental interest.
(b) SCOPE OF APPLICATION — This section applies in any case in which —
(1) the substantial burden is imposed in a program or activity that receives Federal financial assistance; or
(2) the substantial burden affects, or removal of that substantial burden would affect, commerce with foreign nations, among the several States, or with Indian tribes.

SEC. 4. JUDICIAL RELIEF.

(a) CAUSE OF ACTION — A person may assert a violation of this Act as a claim or defense in a judicial proceeding and obtain appropriate relief against a government. Standing to assert a claim or defense under this section shall be governed by the general rules of standing under article III of the Constitution.

(b) BURDEN OF PERSUASION — If a plaintiff produces prima facie evidence to support a claim alleging a violation of the Free Exercise Clause or a violation of section 2, the government shall bear the burden of persuasion on any element of the claim, except that the plaintiff shall bear the burden of persuasion on whether the law (including a regulation) or government practice that is challenged by the claim substantially burdens the plaintiff's exercise of religion.

(c) FULL FAITH AND CREDIT — Adjudication of a claim of a violation of section 2 in a non-Federal forum shall not be entitled to full faith and credit in a Federal court unless the claimant had a full and fair adjudication of that claim in the non-Federal forum.

(d) ATTORNEYS' FEES — Section 722(b) of the Revised Statutes (42 U.S.C. § 1988(b)) is amended — (1) by inserting `the Religious Land Use and Institutionalized Persons Act of 2000,' after `Religious Freedom Restoration Act of 1993,'; and (2) by striking the comma that follows a comma.

(e) PRISONERS — Nothing in this Act shall be construed to amend or repeal the Prison Litigation Reform Act of 1995 (including provisions of law amended by that Act).

(f) AUTHORITY OF UNITED STATES TO ENFORCE THIS ACT — The United States may bring an action for injunctive or declaratory relief to enforce compliance with this Act. Nothing in this subsection shall be construed to deny, impair, or otherwise affect any right or authority of the Attorney General, the United States, or any agency, officer, or employee of the United States, acting under any law other than this subsection, to institute or intervene in any proceeding.

(g) LIMITATION — If the only jurisdictional basis for applying a provision of this Act is a claim that a substantial burden by a government on religious exercise affects, or that removal of that substantial burden would affect, commerce with foreign nations, among the several States, or
with Indian tribes, the provision shall not apply if the government demonstrates that all substantial burdens on, or the removal of all substantial burdens from, similar religious exercise throughout the Nation would not lead in the aggregate to a substantial effect on commerce with foreign nations, among the several States, or with Indian tribes.

SEC. 5. RULES OF CONSTRUCTION.
(a) RELIGIOUS BELIEF UNAFFECTED — Nothing in this Act shall be construed to authorize any government to burden any religious belief.
(b) RELIGIOUS EXERCISE NOT REGULATED — Nothing in this Act shall create any basis for restricting or burdening religious exercise or for claims against a religious organization including any religiously affiliated school or university, not acting under color of law.
(c) CLAIMS TO FUNDING UNAFFECTED — Nothing in this Act shall create or preclude a right of any religious organization to receive funding or other assistance from a government, or of any person to receive government funding for a religious activity, but this Act may require a government to incur expenses in its own operations to avoid imposing a substantial burden on religious exercise.
(d) OTHER AUTHORITY TO IMPOSE CONDITIONS ON FUNDING UNAFFECTED — Nothing in this Act shall —
(1) authorize a government to regulate or affect, directly or indirectly, the activities or policies of a person other

than a government as a condition of receiving funding or other assistance; or

(2) restrict any authority that may exist under other law to so regulate or affect, except as provided in this Act.

(e) GOVERNMENTAL DISCRETION IN ALLEVIATING BURDENS ON RELIGIOUS EXERCISE — A government may avoid the preemptive force of any provision of this Act by changing the policy or practice that results in a substantial burden on religious exercise, by retaining the policy or practice and exempting the substantially burdened religious exercise, by providing exemptions from the policy or practice for applications that substantially burden religious exercise, or by any other means that eliminates the substantial burden.

(f) EFFECT ON OTHER LAW — With respect to a claim brought under this Act, proof that a substantial burden on a person's religious exercise affects, or removal of that burden would affect, commerce with foreign nations, among the several States, or with Indian tribes, shall not establish any inference or presumption that Congress intends that any religious exercise is, or is not, subject to any law other than this Act.

(g) BROAD CONSTRUCTION — This Act shall be construed in favor of a broad protection of religious exercise, to the maximum extent permitted by the terms of this Act and the Constitution.

(h) NO PREEMPTION OR REPEAL — Nothing in this Act shall be construed to preempt State law, or repeal Federal law, that is equally as protective of religious exercise as, or more protective of religious exercise than, this Act.

(i) SEVERABILITY — If any provision of this Act or of an amendment made by this Act, or any application of such provision to any person or circumstance, is held to be unconstitutional, the remainder of this Act, the amendments made by this Act, and the application of the provision to any other person or circumstance shall not be affected.

SEC. 6. ESTABLISHMENT CLAUSE UNAFFECTED.

Nothing in this Act shall be construed to affect, interpret, or in any way address that portion of the first amendment to the Constitution prohibiting laws respecting an establishment of religion (referred to in this section as the `Establishment Clause'). Granting government funding, benefits, or exemptions, to the extent permissible under the Establishment Clause, shall not constitute a violation of this Act. In this section, the term `granting', used with respect to government funding, benefits, or exemptions, does not include the denial of government funding, benefits, or exemptions.

SEC. 7. AMENDMENTS TO RELIGIOUS FREEDOM RESTORATION ACT.

(a) DEFINITIONS — Section 5 of the Religious Freedom Restoration Act of 1993 (42 U.S.C. § 2000bb-2) is amended —

(1) in paragraph (1), by striking `a State, or a subdivision of a State' and inserting `or of a covered entity';

(2) in paragraph (2), by striking `term' and all that follows through `includes' and inserting `term `covered entity' means'; and

(3) in paragraph (4), by striking all after `means' and inserting `religious exercise, as defined in section 8 of the Religious Land Use and Institutionalized Persons Act of 2000.'.

(b) CONFORMING AMENDMENT — Section 6(a) of the Religious Freedom Restoration Act of 1993 (42 U.S.C. § 2000bb-3(a)) is amended by striking `and State'.

SEC. 8. DEFINITIONS.

In this Act:

(1) CLAIMANT — The term `claimant' means a person raising a claim or defense under this Act.

(2) DEMONSTRATES — The term `demonstrates' means meets the burdens of going forward with the evidence and of persuasion.

(3) FREE EXERCISE CLAUSE — The term `Free Exercise Clause' means that portion of the first amendment to the Constitution that proscribes laws prohibiting the free exercise of religion.

(4) GOVERNMENT — The term `government' —

(A) means —

(i) a State, county, municipality, or other governmental entity created under the authority of a State;

(ii) any branch, department, agency, instrumentality, or official of an entity listed in clause (i); and

(iii) any other person acting under color of State law; and

(B) for the purposes of sections 4(b) and 5, includes the United States, a branch, department, agency, instrumentality, or official of the United States, and any other person acting under color of Federal law.

(5) LAND USE REGULATION — The term `land use regulation' means a zoning or landmarking law, or the application of such a law, that limits or restricts a claimant's use or development of land (including a structure affixed to land), if the claimant has an ownership, leasehold,

easement, servitude, or other property interest in the regulated land or a contract or option to acquire such an interest.

(6) PROGRAM OR ACTIVITY — The term `program or activity' means all of the operations of any entity as

described in paragraph (1) or (2) of section 606 of the Civil Rights Act of 1964 (42 U.S.C. § 2000d-4a).

(7) RELIGIOUS EXERCISE —

(A) IN GENERAL — The term `religious exercise' includes any exercise of religion, whether or not compelled by, or central to, a system of religious belief.

(B) RULE — The use, building, or conversion of real property for the purpose of religious exercise shall be considered to be religious exercise of the person or entity that uses or intends to use the property for that purpose.

Approved September 22, 2000

NATIONAL CONTACT LISTING

Gods & Earths in your Area

Individual Directory

By City and Rally location

"Root of Civilization"

Allah School In Mecca

http://www.myspace.com/allahyouthcenter inmecca

Allah Youth Center In Mecca

2122 7th Avenue

Mecca (Harlem, NY)

New York, New York 10027

212-865-5294, 212-665-4175 (fax)

Universal Parliament

Harriet Tubman School

250 W 127th St.

Harlem, New York 10027

Fort Green Park during the
Spring/Summer

Brooklyn, New York

Last Sunday of Month or further notice

2:00 p.m.

Allah School In Medina

Akbar's Community Center

318 Liviona Avenue,

Medina (Brooklyn, NY)

Civilization Classes Monday 7 pm

call Lakeim Allah 718 342-2854

The Oasis Rallies (Queens, New York)

Afrikan Poetry Theatre

176-03 Jamaica Avenue

First Sunday of the Month

2-6 pm

Pelan Rallies (Bronx, New York)

Classes at Boltron Billards, 417
E.138th street on Wednesdays at 6 pm

We also have G.C.C. at River Park
Towers at 40 Cadman Plaza for the
babies onTuesdays at the 5 pm

For more info you can call me at the
Allah School, (212) 665-4175

**Rallies, Schools, and Youth Centers
outside of NYC**

**Arranged by State/Territory/Country,
then City**

(Alabama)

Region 5 contact for the state of
Alabama

True Wise Allah

truewise@gmail.com

(California)

Love Allah (Los Angeles)

Visit the website

http://mentoryouthstreetacademy.com/

For Rally information in Southern
California Contact:

Kuahmel Allah:� (323) 292-5630
blacknoise310@aol.com

AIM/YAHOO:� LoveAllah9

�or

Freedom Allah freedom372@gmail.com

AIM/YAHOO: �freedom372"

Oakland Area Rallies

Held every last Sunday of the month

in San Francisco (West Asia)at Bodeca
Park

(Tenderloin District)

Saviors' Temple, See Allah
(Sacramento,CA)

NorthWest (Northern California)

Queen Jadina I Equality Earth

PO Box 293705

Sacramento, CA 95829-3705

email: iequality@citlink.net

AIM: enature5

currently running: afterschool tutor
program & food closet

(Connecticut)

New Heaven

(New Haven, CT.)

We hold Parliaments for the entire
state the first Sunday of each monthat
2pm.

◆During the summer months we hold them
at Edgewood Park in New

Heaven. ◆During the winter months we
hold them in New Life (New London)at
the public librairy in the community

room. ◆Civilization Classes aretaught
each Wed. at 7pm at Career High School
in New Heaven.

For more information call 1-800-699-
2466 ext 246*135*7777

C'BS Allah

newheaven123@aol.com

New Heaven Website

(District of Columbia)

DIVINE CEE (Washington, DC)

myspace. com/divine cee

divine_cee@live.com

Black Asiatic Allah @ 240-375-5863 or blackasiatic7@yahoo.com

Divine Cee Rally

2:00 p m

Dupont Park, Washington DC

Contact: Critique Allah 301-399-0417

repeats every 3rd Sunday

Civilization Classes

5:00p Every Wednesday

Divine Cee Civilization Class

MLK Memorial Library 901 G St. Washington DC

Contact: Divine Culture Allah 202-460-0802

(Florida)

New Judea (Jacksonville, Florida)

RA Scie0ntific Justice Allah 120

6927 Como Rd Jacksonville Fl. 32244-APT 4

904-551-4267

EMAIL: NEW_JUDEA_FLORIDA@YAHOO.COM

Truth Seen(Tallahassee), Father Love Allah (Florida)

Contacts:

ShaPeace B. Allah # (850) 590-8675

Asiatic Allah Master # (813) 713-2900

Parliament Location:

Florida A & M University

"The Set"

Parliament Date/Time:

The 3rd. Sunday of Each Month 2:00/pm

Civilization Class:

Rotating Locations

Civilization Class Date/Time:

Every Wednesday, 8:00/pm

Please contact ShaPeace B. Allah or Asiatic Allah Master for the Civilization Class location

Truth Born(Tampa Bay), Father Love(Fl)

Universal Parliaments being held monthly as well as ciphers being held all-week

For more information contact either:

King Victory Allah (813)270-1223

Righteous Understanding Allah (813)965-8535

(Georgia)

Allah's Garden Rallies (Atlanta, GA)

last Sunday of month

Howell Park: corner of Abernathy S.W. + Peeples over by West End

1 block west of west end mall

Reasun 404 508 3449

Saviour, God Allah (Savannah, GA)

Call Lord Adeeb Shabazz Allah toll free 1-866-570-8050 for information

(Illinois)

Chicago(C-Medina)

Rallies last Sunday of every month,

Civilization Classes 1st. Sunday of every month,

120 Classes 2nd. Sunday of every month,

for location call toll free 1(866)206-9069 ext. 5302#

or email: c-medina@onebox.com

http://www.c-medina.info

(Indiana)

Rallies in Self Born (South Bend)

Ciphers every Sunday @ 1 pm at Solar Supreme God Allah's Kingdom

pager 219-232-7029

email solarsupreme@blackseek.com

Parliaments every last Saturday of the month

10:00 am - 1:00 pm

Barbecues for the BABIES every Friday before

the Parliament, contact Solar Supreme for the location

Babies eat for FREE, nominal cost for adults

Colfax Cultural Center, 9814 Lincolnway West

Earth Civilization Classes starting in July

contact Civlized Born Queen 219 289 1935

email civilizedbornqueen@blackseek.com

(Louisiana)

Region 5 contacts for the State of Louisiana

Knowledge Said Allah

vistorn@aol.com

True Wise Allah

truewise@gmail.com

Grambling, Louisiana

The Gods here in Love Allah (Louisiana) just started their Parliament at Gods Saviour(Grambling State University)and I-God would appreciate it if you would put our info on the Parliaments page.

email Born Allah at smokin_gunz@yahoo.com

or call(318)247-1568

(Maryland)

Region 3 contact region_understanding@yahoo.com

Rallies in Born Mecca (Baltimore, MD)

The parliaments in Born Mecca (Baltimore, Maryland)are being held on the 2nd Sunday of the month @ Druid Hill Park 2pm (on opposite side of the reservoir) from April through October, fall and winter Parliament locations to be announced....

contact True Asiatic Allah-410.678.1414, Supreme

Asiatic Just-Ice Allah-410.262.6720, or Kalif Allah 410.892.1632

Tislam God Allah 410 961 0459

Class is ever Tuesday at the God hour at Master Born Allah's home.

Contact Tislam God Allah 410 961 0459 for more info.

(Massuchusetts)

Mecca Mass(Region 1) (Springfield, MA)

General Civilization Classes will be held every Wednesday at the God hour(7 pm). We will be holding rallies the first Sunday of each month.

The location varies due to weather conditions. For more information call

Wise Teacher Allah @ 413-543-4135.

(Michigan)

D-Mecca (Detroit)

dmeccaschool@gmail.com

120 Class Location:

Allah School In D-Mecca

17338 Lahser, Detroit, MI 48219

Parliament Location:

Artist Village

17340 Lahser

Detroit, MI 48219

Rally Location (Just U Now Equality-
Allah U God)

Belle Isle Park (Across from the Giant
Slide)

East Grand Blvd and Jefferson Ave.

Detroit, MI 48243

Contact Info:

I C Zara Allah

313-471-4883

Universal Understanding Life Allah

universal3@sbcglobal.net

313-516-3797

Lord Za�d Power Allah

builddaily@gmail.com

313-433-6867

Queen Chun�q Earth

810-423-1650 ~ patte283@msu.edu

(Mississippi)

Region 5 contact for the state of Mississippi

True Wise Allah

truewise@gmail.com

(New Jersey)

Universal Square Rallies (Trenton, NJ)

Contact

YAKAMO COMPLETE ALLAH

asiaticworld@blackplanet.com

(609)392-5831

for information about Trenton, NJ parliaments.

The rallies are now held at The Martin House on

E.State St. and Chambers St.

(New York)

Far Rockaway Civilization Classes

365 Beach 58 St., Fridays 7-9 pm & Saturday 1-4 pm

Benjamin Cordoza Junior High School 198

contact Lord Lukwan Allah

718 381 1373

Allah School in Albany (Albany, NY)

34 North Swan Street

Albany, N.Y. 12210

A.S.I.A. Allah School In Atlantis
(Niagara Falls, NY)

is an Online/Offline Community Network
and Research Center.

www.atlantisschool.blogspot.com

quanaah@math.com

I currently operate my programming for
A.S.I.A. at the NACC

(Niagara Arts and Cultural Center) 1201
Pine Avenue, Niagara, NY

through my L.I.F.E. Program

Monday-Thursday 3-7 and Civilization
Classes Saturday 12-4.

Power Kingdom (Poughkeepsie, NY)

Civilization Classes in Poughkeepsie,
NY

Call Lord Adeeb Shabazz Allah toll free
1-866-570-8050 for information

Khemet (Rochester, NY.)

RALLIES IN KHEMET (ROCHESTER)   N.Y.

EVERY SECOND SUNDAY OF THE MONTH

LOCATED AT

The Montgomery Neighborhood Center

10 Cady Street Rochester New York
14608.

STARTING TIME: 2pm-7pm

TOPICS INCLUDE:

- Community Awareness

- Knowledge of Self

- Growth and Development

- Educating our Youth

- Who Are The 5%

For more information and directions,
please contact:

Khemet Growth and Development Committee

Allah Divine 585-284-9582
AllahDivine1014@gmail.com, Islam

Justice Allah 585-309-5860, Ra Born allah 585-267-0052.

(North Carolina)

Parliaments are every last Sunday of the Month at the Wisdom hour

(2 pm) and rotate between Charlotte, God's Boro (Greensboro) Lexington,

Raleigh and High Point.

Contact:Shabazz Born Allah 336 987 1902

Lord Asiatic Allah 704 267 7079

Divine Ruler Equality Allah 336 675 1628

(Ohio)

Cleveland, OH

Contact: Shakim Allah

5400 Denison, Cleveland, Oh 44102

Phone: 216-338-7294

Fax: 216-338-7294

shakimallah@yahoo.com

Cleveland Website

Rallies in Cinninnati, OH

Washington Park on Race & 14th St.

Every Sunday

For information, contact Be God at
(513) 351-8357

Rallies in Columbus, OH

Rallies will be the first Sunday of
each month at the Wisdom hour.

(The next one Jan. 6th)

Contact: Sear-ius Allah; Sear-
ius@blackseek.com or

Sear-ius@blackplanet.com

614-783-8394, for more info

(Pennsylvania)

Power Hill Rallies (Philadelphia,
Penn.)

This is True Ruler Universal Equality
Allah. Issey, there is a rally the
first Sunday of each month in
Philadelphia, Power Allah (PA). At the
rallies, the Gods and Earth Build with
the day's math, the lessons, and so
forth.

The location of the rally is 58th & Kingsessing Streets. We start at the Wisdom Hour (2:00). The next rally is of course scheduled for Sept. 7

Power Born (Pittsburgh, Pa)

Parliaments are held the 2nd Sunday of every month, location changes seasonally, please contact for more information:

❷

Sha-King Cehum Allah

cell# 412 403 3519

email- scehum@yahoo.com

or

Knowledge Build Allah

cell# 412 607 7516

email- knowledgebuild@yahoo.com

I Majestic Allah

email- i_majestic@yahoo.com

imajestic@allahworldmanifest.com

website is Allah World Manifest Online

http://www.awm-online.com

(Tennessee)

Region 5 contact for the state of
Tennessee

True Wise Allah

truewise@gmail.com

(Texas)

Region 5 contacts for the state of
Texas

Truth Known (Texas):

Self Born Mathematics Allah

sbmathematicsallah@gmail.com

Allah School in Sudan (Dallas)

OPEN!!!!

4312 S. Oakland Ave.(Malcom X Avenue)

Suite #202, Dallas, Tx 75215

Ph: 214 565 1588

Ph: (214)555-5555

E-Mail: tazataa@hotmail.com

(Virginia)

Rich Mind (Richmond, VA)

Parliaments in RichMInd, Va. are held every 3rd Sunday of every month.

Start time: 2pm.

Location: Admer Clay Park @300 East Clay, Richmond, Va.

Contact: Tubar Malik Allah # (917) 676-3152

GodlyMath Allah (804)497-0998

The God Cities(7 cities-Virginia Beach, Norfolk, Portsmouth, Chesapeake, Suffolk, Hampton, and Newport news) have our Parliaments on the 2nd Sunday of every month.

The Earth cipher gets together the 4th Sunday of the month. Contact information for the area is Ramel Allah Mathematics 757-567-0242, Born Saviour Allah 757-816-8022, and Beautiful Asiatic Earth 757-831-6250. It starts at the wisdom hour as well for more info on location anyone can call one of the three numbers listed.

(Washington)

Morocco (Seattle)

The Universal Rallies of the Nation of Gods and Earths in this

Geographic are on the Last Sunday of the Month at The Shining Star 1412 24th Aven, Seattle, WA 98122, (206) 328-5819

2:00 p.m. any further information please contact:

True-Father :   206-317-2289(cell)

206-760-1965(mecca)

Victorious:206-769-3530(mecca)

Logic Seven : 206-835-0494 (mecca)

206-271-3279(also for "The Almighty 7"

magazine subscriptions)

(Wisconsin)

The Promise Land (Greenbay, WI)

We have 120 class every Wednesday at 6:00 pm at 1269 Shawno Ave. apt.#4

Contact: Born Logic Allah� (920) 406-0427

pager (920) 440-0275

bornlogic@ameritech.net

P.E.A.C.E.

(Milwaukee, WI)

We are not anti-white, nor pro black, we are pro righteousness.

Cream City (We only teach that the Original man is God)

120 class Monday & Wednesday at the Power hour

Contact: Self Kingdom Allah at (414)339-9761

kingdomself@yahoo.com

Third floor S building

MATC 700 W State Street

More 120 Class info at the link below

http://understandingbuilder.com/id11.html

Street Academy of Cream City

(414) 372-7584

General Meetings are held every
Monday�at 8:30pm

120 Classes are held every
Saturday�7:30pm

Universal Parliaments are held every
second Sunday of the month at 2:00pm at
the Street Academy of Cream City.

2438 N Bremen St. Milwaukee, WI�53212

In the summer months the Universal
Parliaments are held at Kilbourne Park
at the intersection of Garfeild and
North Ave.

**We are not anti-white, nor pro black,
we are pro righteousness.**

(Intercontinental Information)

(Toronto, Canada)

CEE ALLAH NATION

IN TRUTH CIPHER (TORONTO) AND STEEL
CITY

*BORN KING M ALLAH (905) 383 - 9
KNOWLEDGE WISDOM UNDERSTANDING OR (905)
818 1332

EMAIL. ALLAHTHEORIGINALMAN@HOTMAIL.COM
OR FATHER.ALLAH@GMAIL.COM

*ASIATIC SIFU ALLAH (416) 715 8214

Asiatic email asiaticsifu@gmail.com

Do you have any satisfied clients? Did they write and tell you so? Share! Have a photo of client or the work your business did for them, share that too. Nothing sells your services like a photo of a job well done.

THE INCARCERATED 71S ARE CIVILIZING PEOPLE BEHIND THE WALL
ONE MIND AT A TIME !!!

The INCARCERATED 7'S ANTHOLOGY Volume # 1 introduces the world to the moveme
one man in an Ohio prison cell seeking a positive change within himself and his immec
and grew into a cultural revolution that empowered countless people throughout the
Prison System with Knowledge of Self. This information packed collection of poetry, sh
testimonials and philosophical insights gives the reader a peak into the minds of some
creative men and women as they vividly paint pictures with words.

The Incarcerated 7's Anthology is also a resource manual with organization lists and co
Reference book for Legal research and Pro Se litigation. Whether it's used for the abov
study guide and resource for those seeking deeper insight into the Nation of Gods and
Curriculum, this book will definitely be used more than once by veteran Nation of God
members, new or potential members and/or Professional Academics in higher educati
The books appendage section also contains a Nation of Gods and Earths National Cont
connect readers with current Nation of Gods and Earths schools, local contacts and ot
vehicles wherever the reader is when they purchase the book and the book contains t
District Court civil suit filed and won by Intelligent Tareef Allah aka Rashaad Marria (Ra
Raymond Broaddus, et.al) with all of its relevant case law citations intact for any Natic
Earths member that is seeking a blueprint to initiate the process of filing a Civil suit pu
RELIGIOUS LAND USE AND INSTITUTIONALIZED PERSONS ACT OF 2000 while incarcera

www.ingramcontent.com/pod-product-compliance
Lightning Source LLC
LaVergne TN
LVHW051040080426
835508LV00019B/1619